'The essential first guide to understanding the origins of the AUKUS agreement. Deeply researched and finely crafted, this book raises important and serious questions about the failure of the Morrison and Albanese governments to undertake the most basic, essential tests of policy due diligence concerning the risks and the feasibility of Australia's aspiration to acquire nuclear-powered submarines. A must, if sobering, read about deception, policy breakdown, misplaced ambition and an ongoing failure to inform the Australian public about what the agreement signifies and entails.'

James Curran

'Andrew Fowler's one-man Commission of Inquiry is a nuclear-armed torpedo of a book and a major service to the Australian public. There is astonishing detail in every chapter. Fowler unearths the evidence, names the names, and shows how national security, which should be a goal, is used as a cover for something more sinister.'

Clinton Fernandes

Andrew Fowler is an award-winning investigative journalist and a former reporter for the ABC's *Foreign Correspondent* and *Four Corners* programs. Fowler began his journalism career in the early 1970s, covering the IRA bombing campaign for the *London Evening News*. He has been the chief of staff and acting foreign editor of *The Australian* newspaper. He wrote *The Most Dangerous Man in the World*, the story of Julian Assange and WikiLeaks in 2011, which was updated in 2012 and 2020. Fowler first interviewed Assange for *Foreign Correspondent* in 2010, for which the program won the New York Festival Gold Medal. His two other books are *The War on Journalism* (Random House, 2015) and *Shooting the Messenger: Criminalising Journalism* (Routledge, 2017). Fowler is a winner of the United Nations Peace Prize, has lectured on journalism at universities in Australia and the UK, and has contributed to various academic papers.

NUKED

The Submarine Fiasco that Sank Australia's Sovereignty

ANDREW FOWLER

MELBOURNE
UNIVERSITY
PRESS

Melbourne University Publishing acknowledge the traditional owners of the unceded land on which we work, learn and live: the Wurundjeri Woi-wurrung peoples of the Kulin nation. We pay respect to elders past, present and future, and acknowledge the importance of Indigenous knowledge.

MELBOURNE UNIVERSITY PRESS
An imprint of Melbourne University Publishing Limited
Level 1, 715 Swanston Street, Carlton, Victoria 3053, Australia
mup-contact@unimelb.edu.au
www.mup.com.au

First published 2024
Reprinted 2024
Text © Andrew Fowler, 2024
Design and typography © Melbourne University Publishing Limited, 2024

This book is copyright. Apart from any use permitted under the *Copyright Act 1968* and subsequent amendments, no part may be reproduced, stored in a retrieval system or transmitted by any means or process whatsoever without the prior written permission of the publishers.

Every attempt has been made to locate the copyright holders for material quoted in this book. Any person or organisation that may have been overlooked or misattributed may contact the publisher.

Cover design by Philip Campbell Design
Typeset by Megan Ellis Typesetting
Cover image by jacktheflipper/istock
Printed in Australia by McPherson's Printing Group

 A catalogue record for this book is available from the National Library of Australia

9780522880311 (paperback)
9780522880328 (ebook)

For the truth tellers

Contents

Initialisms   ix

1 Introduction   1
2 Murky Depths   11
3 Champagne Days   21
4 What Washington Wants   31
5 France Overboard   46
6 A Secret State   61
7 That Sinking Feeling   77
8 The Media and the Message   92
9 In the Frame   110
10 The Sting   123
11 The Bomb   145
12 No Way Out?   157

Acknowledgements   170
Notes   171
Further Reading   187
Index   188

Initialisms

A2/AD	anti-access/aerial denial
AAEC	Australian Atomic Energy Commission
ADF	Australian Defence Force
ANAO	Australian National Audit Office
ANU	Australian National University
ASC	Australian Submarine Corporation
ASIO	Australian Security Intelligence Organisation
ASPI	Australian Strategic Policy Institute
CSIS	Center for Strategic and International Studies (USA)
HEU	highly enriched uranium
IAEA	International Atomic Energy Agency
LEU	low-enriched uranium
NASA	National Aeronautics and Space Administration (USA)
NPT	Non-Proliferation Treaty (Treaty on the Non-Proliferation of Nuclear Weapons)
NRO	National Reconnaissance Office (USA)
NSC	National Security Committee (USA)
ONI	Office of National Intelligence (Australia)
PM&C	Department of the Prime Minister and Cabinet
RAN	Royal Australian Navy
SMR	small modular reactor
SPA	strategic partnership agreement
SST	Space Surveillance Telescope
USSC	United States Studies Centre (Australia)
USSF	United States Space Force

1

Introduction

The world's most famous boulevard, the Champs-Élysées, stretches from the Arc de Triomphe, which celebrates France's greatest military victories, to the Place de la Concorde, where King Louis XVI was executed. Just off the Champs-Élysées stands the Élysée Palace, home of the president of the Republic.

On 25 April 2016, French president François Hollande received a phone call from the other side of the world. It was early morning in France, but in Australia the sun was slipping towards the horizon. Though the prime minister, Malcolm Turnbull, had been awake since well before dawn for the Anzac Day remembrance ceremony, he clearly relished making the call to his opposite number in France on such an auspicious day.

'Mr President,' Turnbull said, 'I have some good news.'[1]

If the sacrifices of Australian troops in World War I had created a special place in the memories of the people of France, what Turnbull said next would cement even further the relationship between the two countries. He told Hollande that France had just beaten the German and Japanese competition to build twelve state-of-the-art submarines for the Royal Australian Navy (RAN). At AU$50 billion, it was Australia's biggest-ever defence contract. Perhaps more significantly, for a nation with Europe's second-biggest economy, it was the largest single defence contract France had signed in its history. *Le Monde*, the French daily newspaper, described the deal as 'historic'.[2]

Hollande was effusive in his praise. From seemingly nowhere had come a huge boost to French industry. When the news broke in the brasseries and bars in the old town of the northern port city of Cherbourg, near the site of France's huge submarine manufacturing plant, Australian tourists got a warmer welcome than usual. In Adelaide, where Australia's current submarine fleet had been built, the workers could see the possibility of jobs for decades to come.

The French defence minister, Jean-Yves Le Drian, told radio station Europe 1: 'We are married to Australia for fifty years.'[3] It was a poke in the eye for France's old enemy across the English Channel, where the United Kingdom was on the verge of voting to leave the European Union. Britain saw Australia as a natural market for its goods, but it couldn't compete with France to build Australia's new submarines. The British—and the Americans—only made nuclear subs, and Australia wanted conventionally powered boats. If the Australian Government were to change its mind and switch to nuclear power, both Britain and the United States would be in with a chance. No one, however, gave much thought to that as the tricolour flapped proudly atop of the Élysée Palace on that Anzac Day.

It wasn't just the jobs and the boost to industry that so enamoured the French: the deal gave them an even greater stake in a part of the world where they already had a significant presence. French overseas territories straddle vast areas of the Indo-Pacific, from Réunion island in the Indian Ocean to French Polynesia in the Pacific, giving France the second-largest economic zone coverage in the world. Closer to Australia, another French territory, New Caledonia, provides a deep-water anchorage for French submarines and a signals intelligence station that taps into international data and phone traffic, as does its sister station in Réunion.

All up, the Indo-Pacific area is home to 1.8 million French nationals and 7000 French military personnel. Australia's naval and maintenance bases are already run by Thales, a company that is part-owned by the French Government. Now the submarines would be berthing in those French-run ports. It seemed like a perfect fit for a resurgent Global France.

Neither Turnbull nor Hollande could have understood at the time that powerful forces were already working assiduously against them—risking everything, including Australia's national security—to undo the deal from the moment it was signed. There were those in high office, particularly in the intelligence agencies, who were wary of Australia becoming too close to France and shifting away from the countries they saw as Australia's natural philosophical, political and strategic allies: the United Kingdom and the United States.

The French deal, they believed, added fresh complications to Washington's plans to contain China's rise. Instead of the old Australia–US axis, France would now have to be directly played into the mix. It was a perceptible move towards a more independent foreign and defence position for Australia—hardly revolutionary, but disturbing for the hardliners in Washington and Canberra.

A deal with France would certainly unshackle Australia and, as Turnbull argues, allow the nation to maintain its sovereignty. France, after all, had its own nuclear strike force, separate from other members of NATO, and had refused to support the United States in many of that country's foreign policy forays, in particular the disastrous war on Iraq. Australia, it seemed, had the opportunity to head down a similar independent track.

Prime Minister Turnbull had a record for independent thought. He was a founding member and chair of the Australian Republic Movement, an organisation that sought to establish an independent Australia, freed from its links to the British Crown. He was also on the progressive side of an increasingly reactionary Liberal Party.

Turnbull had not made many friends on the right when he appointed career diplomat Brendan Berne to be the Australian ambassador to France. It was a much sought-after position and Berne won it against stiff competition, but that didn't stifle the jealousy, particularly because Berne was seriously smart and, like Turnbull, supported the ideals of a more independent Australia. When he moved into the Australian embassy in Paris, Berne seized the opportunity to capitalise on what he saw as a honeymoon period in France–Australia relations.

As a former Reserve Bank economist, Berne came from the branch of Foreign Affairs that was more concerned with trade and economics than national security. But what he did after just four months in the job had nothing to do with either. In a move that was almost as stunning to the French as pouring billions of dollars into their military manufacturing, within days of marriage equality being achieved in Australia just before Christmas 2017, Berne caused a sensation: he posted a video online of him proposing to his partner, Thomas, on bended knee.

Ambassadors in France, it's safe to say, don't normally do that kind of thing. Suddenly Australia—which many French people identified as rather uncultured, home to kangaroos and koalas, and an extraordinary 24-hour flight from Paris—was emerging not only as a close ally but as a vibrant, interesting and progressive nation. If the submarines had lifted Australia's profile in France, Berne was taking it a step further. In constant demand for TV breakfast talk shows, he extolled the virtues of Australia as an outward-looking, tolerant society, engaging with the world. It was as close as an ambassador could get to diplomatic heaven.

Yet even before Berne did the rounds of the television stations, the groundwork to oppose the submarine deal was being laid. The opposition came from a group closely tied to the former Liberal Party prime minister John Howard, whose election in 1996 had swung the party from the middle ground of politics to the right. The group included one of Howard's greatest supporters, Tony Abbott, whom Turnbull had replaced as prime minister, and a vehemently pro-American China hawk, Andrew Shearer, a national security adviser to both Howard and Abbott. Shearer would later be appointed as the director-general of national intelligence and play a key role in negotiating a secret deal that would see Australia abandon the French and switch to nuclear-powered submarines from the United States and United Kingdom.

It was a clear victory for Washington, which had been concerned for some time that France had a different view on how to deal with the rise of China. The fact that the French were about to be duped would not have surprised them if they had focused more on the fickle politics of

Australia and less on trying to build a submarine and form a stronger strategic relationship.

For the past nearly two decades Australia had wrestled with how to replace its six Collins-class subs, which had been in service since 1996 and desperately needed to be retired. The decision-making process at times operated in a moral and logical vacuum, consumed by politics and cynical opportunism. The government of Scott Morrison, in particular, immersed itself in a covert deal whose primary purpose was to save its own political skin, not to protect the population from military adversaries. Public servants were hijacked to serve the government, forsaking their main purpose, which is to protect the people from an overly zealous, authoritarian executive arm of government.

It would be wrong to believe that the decision to 'go nuclear' was exclusively a response to the rising power of China. The move was but one more step down the road by successive Liberal governments that had constantly pushed for Australia to become a nuclear nation. They had begun flirting with obtaining atomic weapons in the 1960s and 1970s and promoted the construction of nuclear power stations—which left the door open to build the bomb with the plutonium by-product.

The nuclear pact that came to be known as AUKUS (a portmanteau of 'Australia', 'UK' and 'US') was a perfect fit: it continued the Liberal Party's nuclear ambitions and at the same time bound the United States even closer, allaying the Liberal Party's near-neurotic fear that Washington would abandon Australia if Australia didn't stay close and help with the containment of China.

In the aftermath of John Howard's decision to provide troops for America's catastrophic war with Iraq in 2003, US president George W Bush exploited Australia's anxiety that it might have to defend itself alone, describing the Australian prime minister as his 'deputy sheriff'[4] after a journalist wrote that 'the Howard Doctrine—the PM himself embraces the term—sees Australia acting in a sort of "deputy" peacekeeping capacity in our region to the global policeman role of the US'.[5] Bush clearly saw the epithet as a badge of honour. But there are other interpretations. Australian military analyst Professor Clinton Fernandes, a former intelligence officer who lectures at the Australian Defence Force (ADF) Academy campus of the University of

New South Wales, coined a perhaps more fitting description: Australia wasn't so much a deputy sheriff as a 'sub-imperial power' of the United States.[6]

It's a measure of his desire to please the United States that before he was removed as prime minister, Tony Abbott made a special trip to Japan in 2014. Abbott believed he could achieve what America had tried to do for decades: persuade Japan to loosen its pacifist constitution, which restricts arms sales. Abbott wanted to buy Japan's conventionally powered submarines off the shelf, which meant there would be no employment opportunities for Australian workers. Separating Australia's defence procurement process from the country's industrial policy might have been logical, but it hid the true intent of Abbott's actions: buying a Japanese boat from a strong US ally wedded to the containment of China would impress Washington and show that Australia was in lock step with that policy.

Yet even when Turnbull replaced Abbott in a messy fight over the number of Australian jobs the submarine manufacturing process might produce, Abbott did not give up the battle. Just as significantly, neither did his former national security adviser, Shearer, who continued to argue that the Japanese submarines were the best on offer. They certainly weren't the best, though anything was better than France, whose ideals of sovereignty were ingrained in its military and national identity.

But the great dreams of emulating France were dashed on more mundane matters. Amid plunging opinion poll ratings, the Liberal Party removed Turnbull and replaced him with someone of a very different character: Scott Morrison, a right-wing operator with a knack for marketing. At the Élysée, too, there was a changing of the guard, with Emmanuel Macron replacing Hollande as president of France. One of Macron's more thoughtful international advisers, who greatly understood the sometimes thin-skinned nature of Australian politicians, had managed to land a plum job as France's ambassador to the United States. His replacement was a French bureaucrat who, according to those who know him, could not have been more different from Morrison's 'Aussie mate' style of bravado. Morrison grated on the French, and the French did not handle it well.

The thinking at the Élysée changed from nurturing an important business and strategic venture to believing the deal with Australia had been signed, sealed and delivered and needed no further attention. Appointments with the French Government were difficult to get even for the head of the Australian Department of Foreign Affairs, and sometimes they were delayed or only agreed to at the last moment. At one point Berne became so frustrated with the French as he tried to arrange a phone call between Morrison and Macron that he ordered the entire embassy staff to cancel all meetings and cut off all communications with the Élysée until the French agreed to take the call.

Back in Australia, in the Prime Minister's Office, there was open criticism of what was happening in France, with Morrison's staff noting that, in contrast, 'We can get Trump on the phone in less than a day!'[7] The treatment of Morrison by the French provided a perfect opening for the heavily pro-US Shearer and Abbott. In the months before the decision to terminate the French submarine deal, Shearer, in a co-authored essay, warned that the US military wanted Australia to go with the Japanese because of the 'long-term strategic benefits of the United States'.[8] He also pointedly stated that despite what he called 'government spin', Australia had 'limited strategic interest with France'.[9]

The Morrison government was playing a double game. In March 2021, with the French believing the submarine deal was still on track, the Australian chief of navy, Vice Admiral Michael Noonan, headed for London for a top-level meeting. Noonan was riding high at that time. He even used his position to allow his civilian girlfriend to board a Collins-class submarine, where he proposed to her. In one of the great ironies of the AUKUS affair the Liberal Party Coalition described Noonan's action as an 'abuse of power.'[10]

All that was to come, though, as he met with the head of the British Navy, Sir Tony Radakin, at Australia House, the grand classical-style building that stands at a critical point in the centre of London next to the High Court, not far from the old press hub of Fleet Street and down the road from parliament. It was a sensible first stop for learning how to prise nuclear secrets from the United States, which had last shared what are known as the 'crown jewels' with Britain in 1958.

Less than four weeks later, on 23 April 2021, Shearer walked into the Eisenhower Building in Washington, DC, next door to the White House, to meet with President Joe Biden's deputy national security adviser, Anne Neuberger.[11] Neuberger is a former chief in the National Security Agency (NSA), which co-runs the United States' worldwide spy network—including Pine Gap, an integral part of the US global interception and targeting system, in Australia. One week later, Shearer met with Kurt Campbell, the coordinator for the Indo-Pacific on the US National Security Council. Later, Campbell would say that Morrison and the Australians had said 'the French submarine project was a train wreck. It was running way behind time and had blown the budget.'[12]

It was true that there had been delays and cost problems, but they were in the process of being resolved. Compared to other defence acquisitions with massive cost blowouts and delays, the French submarine project appeared to be an outstanding example of how to buy military hardware and get taxpayers value for money. The French vessels would provide similar range to nuclear-powered submarines without the extraordinary cost. As Fernandes points out, 'We wanted conventional boats with nuclear range. No other country asks for this.'[13]

But that was of little account to Morrison. In June 2021 he met UK prime minister Boris Johnson and President Biden to put the final touches to AUKUS. On his way back to Australia, he stopped in Paris to visit the French president and left Macron with the understanding that all was on track.

Three and a half months later, in September, just days before AUKUS was announced, Shearer was back in the White House again,[14] this time to check out how the decision to go with nuclear submarines would be viewed by China. In the Eisenhower Building he met Peter Dien, who had made his mark as an economic adviser in the US embassy in Beijing. His work 'focused on cyber-security' and 'advanced technology'.[15] Shearer was getting himself well briefed by the US administration.

With an election looming, in early 2022 Morrison began firming up the idea of broadening the submarine replacement plan to involve a near-total integration of the US and Australian military. He had kept the notion secret from the Australian Labor Party (ALP), though he told the United States he was consulting them, and he kept it from the French.

Entangling the United States in a web of deception, lying to the French and blindsiding his political opponents was of no account. Morrison, famous as head of Tourism Australia at the time of the controversial commercial 'So Where the Bloody Hell Are Ya?', which saw him accused of deceptive practice,[16] managed in one act to offend the White House and badly damage Australia's relationship with France. He whipped up a frenzy of fear in the public that the drums of war were beating and China posed a major threat to Australia's future security. Screaming headlines echoed his message. Now he produced the answer: AUKUS, with its staggering AU$368 billion price tag. There was barely a murmur of opposition from the media. Morrison had pulled off a major achievement of what US public intellectual Noam Chomsky describes as the political art of 'manufacturing consent'.[17] It was Karl Marx, extending a thought by German philosopher Friedrich Hegel, who said that history repeats itself first as tragedy, then as farce. In the case of AUKUS, there was an element of both right from the start.

How did it happen that the bulk of the analysis and criticism of the submarine deal came from two former prime ministers, Paul Keating and Malcolm Turnbull, who, though on opposing sides of politics, were united in warning that the submarine deal stripped away Australia's sovereignty? Journalists were mainly silent on the fact that there were those in government who, for ideological reasons, had wanted to sabotage the French submarine deal right from the start, ignoring the warnings from former Liberal prime minister Malcolm Fraser that a close relationship with the United States was dangerous and might not be in Australia's national interest. It was even left to an American newspaper, the *Washington Post*, to reveal the huge number of former senior US naval staff employed by the Australian Government in the submarine selection process.[18] Once Australia switched to the nuclear option, the US military personnel hired by the Defence Department provided Shearer and Australia's other China hawks with a ready-made bridge to Washington.

An increasing body of evidence suggests that the move to nuclear was inevitable once the French were selected. As outrageous as it might appear,

Berne believes that in championing the creation of AUKUS, Shearer—pushing to abandon the French—had 'flattered Morrison' that this was his big chance to defeat his detractors who thought he was nothing more than a salesman.[19] Ironically, it would be his marketing skills that Morrison used so successfully to 'frame' the submarine deal as part of a grander plan for Australia. Boris Johnson claims to have had a similar idea. It should not be a surprise that two of the greatest fabricators leading major countries in the Western world both asserted the branding rights of such a debacle.

Despite promises by Morrison to the United States that the Labor Opposition would agree with the decision, in researching this book it became apparent to me that the United States understood that Morrison had set out to wedge Labor as weak on national security if it did not support AUKUS. There is also evidence that the United States played a direct role in blindsiding Labor and sinking the French deal. President Biden had opposed Australia buying the French submarines because they were a bad fit with the US Navy.

Even the date when discussions between Canberra and Washington first began remains classified 'secret' by the Australian Government. The first approach appears to have been near the end of the Trump administration in 2020, but a senior diplomat who spoke on the basis that they would not be identified told me that the issue of exactly when the submarine deal was first raised with the US administration was a matter of national security, and they feared going to prison if they revealed that information.[20]

This ultra-secrecy protected the United States and bound Labor to a deal sprung on it just twenty-four hours before Morrison publicly launched AUKUS with Biden and Johnson. Though Labor won the subsequent election, in 2022, at least one new Cabinet minister wondered if it was possible to stop AUKUS. But the suggestion went no further. The incoming government was left with a booby-trapped minefield of national security issues involving not just nuclear-powered submarines but US B-52 nuclear-capable bombers, to be stationed in the nation's north.

Yet it need not have been such a disaster. Australia came close to pulling off a truly remarkable achievement by buying the French submarines, which would have given it greater independence and a more influential position in the world.

2

Murky Depths

Just before Christmas 2015, Prime Minister Malcolm Turnbull boarded his official aircraft at Sydney Airport, bound for Tokyo and an important meeting with the Japanese prime minister, Shinzo Abe. As he settled in for the ten-hour flight, Turnbull knew it was an important trip. Tony Abbott, his predecessor, had developed a strong relationship with Abe; they shared similar politics that hewed towards right-wing nationalism and unwavering support for the United States.

But what Turnbull didn't know was that Abe had been led to believe by Abbott that Japan was the leading contender to build Australia's next fleet of submarines. When Turnbull talked to Abe about the competitive evaluation process, Abe appeared unfazed by the discussions. According to one observer, it appeared Abe thought the discussion was just for show, that Japan had already won the submarine deal. 'In all my dealings with Abe it was very straightforward,' Turnbull said. 'He inquired about the subs and commended the Japanese bid, I said it was subject to a rigorous and objective process. In other words played a straight bat—utterly unaware he had been previously led to believe Japan was in the box seat.'[1]

As Turnbull trod the rocky path left by Abbott, he also had to deal with another highly sensitive matter for the Japanese. The International Court of Justice had just ordered Japan to stop its whaling activities. Australia and New Zealand had won their case at the court, pointing out that Japan's argument that it was only catching whales for 'scientific purposes' was a fraud.[2] The court accepted that the whale meat now being sold in Japanese vending machines was a commercial operation and had more to do with the country's right-wing government's wish to appease its nationalist support base than any scientific work. As Turnbull toured Japan, there was no reporting in Australia that Tokyo was in breach of the 'rules-based order' with its 'scientific' whaling operations. That kind of language was saved almost exclusively for China.

Standing together and smiling for the formal photo, the two leaders went through the normal formalities, issuing a statement promising 'deeper and broader defence co-operation'.[3] An insight into what happened behind the scenes came in another Japanese Government statement that said it hoped to set aside one-and-a-half hours of 'special time' so that Abe and Turnbull could form a 'personal relationship' that would cement a stronger relationship between Australia and Japan.[4]

But that's not what happened. When Abe was finally told that Japan's bid was unsuccessful he had every reason to feel betrayed. 'They weren't easy conversations—it was the closest to anger that I ever saw in senior Japanese officials,' according to one observer familiar with the situation. The Japanese had been so convinced they had won the deal they had not even put in their best bid.[5] The Japanese prime minister had every reason to feel misled. Japan had rolled out the red carpet for Abbott's defence minister, David Johnston, when he became the first foreign official to be allowed on board a Soryu submarine during a visit to Japan in 2014. Johnston had been greatly impressed, particularly because the vessels could be produced quickly. It's reported that he was so convinced Japan had won that the Abbott government ordered a press release to be drawn up announcing the decision.[6]

No fan of ASC (formerly the Australian Submarine Corporation), which built the Collins-class submarines in Adelaide, Johnston said he 'wouldn't trust [them] to build a canoe'.[7] Like his prime minister, he wanted Australia's submarines built in Japan. It's what the United States and Shearer wanted, too—a quick fix so Australia, and Japan, could join the United States in facing down a more assertive China, which was challenging Western control of the South China Sea.

The militarists on the right wing of the Liberal party, such as Peter Dutton, backed by John Howard and Shearer, were always looking for an opportunity, should Turnbull stumble. They were opposed to his moderate, liberal politics and concerned about his desire for Australia to be more independent in its foreign policy. He had, after all, revealed a streak of the unconventional as the brilliant lawyer who defeated the British establishment in the *Spycatcher* case in the 1980s and delivered another blow by helping create the Australian Republic Movement.

Johnston's insult inflamed an already-tense political situation with Liberal Party politicians who thought their state of South Australia should benefit from any new submarine contract. If there were any jobs, they should be in South Australia, not Japan. Under pressure to back out of the Japan offer and in a last-gasp attempt to save his faltering leadership, in June 2015 Abbott instructed his defence minister, Kevin Andrews, to set up an expert advisory panel to oversee what he called a 'competitive evaluation process' for the navy's future submarine fleet. Japan's boat would be in the mix with the rest. There were no guarantees, although Japan later softened its position on where the boats would be built, to accommodate a workforce in Adelaide.

So who exactly did the Abbott government appoint to its Naval Shipbuilding Advisory Board to select the best options for a non-nuclear submarine? Whichever names and countries spring to mind, the answer will almost certainly not be the ones they chose. The four-member team included former US secretary of the navy under George W Bush, Donald Winter, and a former chair of the Australian Nuclear Science and Technology Organisation. Deciding exactly which submarines would be examined in the competitive evaluation process became the job of David Gould, a former UK under-secretary for defence who also worked in the UK Cabinet Office, where he had responsibility for counterterrorism, defence equipment, and civil and military nuclear policy. In 2012 Gould had been headhunted by the Australian Labor government as a consultant to work on a replacement for the Collins class.

When Gould spoke to me for this book at the Army and Navy Club in London's Pall Mall, he'd never before talked publicly about what he discovered when he arrived at Australia's Defence headquarters in Canberra's Russell Hill.

'When I got there, they had four options,' he said. The first was 'off the shelf', the second was 'off the shelf modified', which Gould said was 'a contradiction in terms', the third involved a 'redesigned Collins', and the fourth involved Australia designing its own submarine.[8]

Gould said he was asked: 'What do you think of these? Which option do you prefer?' He said, 'None of them are any good, because there is no such thing as an off-the-shelf submarine.' He said it wasn't like a shop where you could walk in and say, 'I'll have one of those.' This was especially true for Australia because of the extended distances the submarine would need to travel and the salinity and other conditions of Australia's northern waters that affect the boats' performance.

Along with a design team, Gould set about drawing up the precise specifications needed for the boat to replace the Collins-class submarines. He says he remembers sitting around the table in 2015 with Defence Secretary Dennis Richardson and the Australian chief of defence. He told them he had a plan he and his team had been working on for the past two years: 'We will select three potential suppliers of submarines. We will give them the design that we've done, and we will tell them: "Now you give us your solution"'. Defence could then 'pick the one of you that gives us the best exam answer'. He says they were delighted with his solution and told him to draw up a list of the submarine's requirements.

As we sat talking, Gould revealed for the first time what has long been suspected: one of the submarine's most important requirements would be to work with the Americans in the South China Sea. He explained that the submarine would need 'to get through the archipelago to the north of Australia and into the South China Sea and operate in the South China Sea for a reasonable period of time and then come back again, without docking, or refuelling or anything. That's what it needs to do.' In the South China Sea, a huge area from Borneo to the coast of China, it would work alongside the United States and Japan in what he called an 'integrated system', which had become 'even more pertinent with China'. This statement undermines any argument that the new submarines—whether nuclear or not—would be used primarily to defend Australia or to protect the nation's shipping lanes. The focus was to contain China and threaten its trade routes and food and energy supplies in a crisis.

In 2015 Gould, who had been employed as a consultant, left the Defence Department. The person who replaced him was a former US rear admiral, Stephen E Johnson. Johnson would shed his role as a consultant and take on an extraordinarily powerful role in the Australian Government: a full-time position as deputy secretary of defence.

Shortly after Turnbull moved into the Lodge in Canberra after he defeated Abbott in a party-room vote to become Australia's twenty-ninth prime minister, Winter came to him with a list of the three submarines that had made the final cut. They were from France, Germany and Japan. The fact that Japan's Soryu subs were still in the running raised immediate questions about the selection process. The Japanese submarine 'captain's pick' by Abbott had been rejected in the first place because it had failed to qualify in one of the most important categories: being built in Australia. According to Gould, the Japanese would have designed and built the submarines very well but 'we wouldn't have known what it was until we got it'. The kind of collaborative work necessary for the venture would not have been easily forthcoming. He said he believed the Japanese companies Kawasaki and Mitsubishi were quite keen to do the work, but the Japanese ministry involved in arms manufacturing did not want to share what he called its 'hard-earned intellectual property' with the Australians. They didn't want to do that, and they also didn't want to build part of the submarine in Adelaide.

But there were more problems with the Japanese option than where the submarines would be built. Gould was highly critical of Abbott's desire for the Soryu-class submarine. It might be a good submarine for Japanese purposes—'It could sail from its port, it could dive deep, it could be very quiet, it could operate surveillance and attack roles,' he said—but importantly, it could 'only travel for relatively short distances'.

Many in the Australian submariner community also remained sceptical of the Soryu-class submarines. They pointed out that on average Japanese subs are constructed to last for around nineteen years, whereas the Australian Government expected at least a thirty-year active-service life span. The Japanese boats also had cramped accommodation for the crew, an important consideration for long weeks at sea.

Like the Japanese, the Germans believed they were favoured. Exactly why was not apparent, but several senior officials from the ThyssenKrupp Marine Systems manufacturing giant booked flights to Australia, convinced they were the winners. The company had 'scaled up' a version of its 2000-ton diesel-electric submarine, increasing the size by extending the forward section and adding more space inside. The Germans have a fine track record of producing high-quality submarines and have sold them around the world. Yet though the German boat impressed Winter's selection committee, the Defence Department was not so sure. It complained that the German boat was too noisy and would thus be easy to detect.

All submarines make noise, some of it created by the rotation of the propeller, which causes bubbles in the water known as cavitation. There's also direct noise from the turbines, the propellers and water flowing over the hull when the boat is travelling faster than 10 knots (18.5 kilometres per hour). In a bad case, the sub rattles like a spoon banging inside an empty baked-bean tin. No one is suggesting it went that far, but even a quiet sub will vibrate, sending out low-frequency sounds that create what is known as the submarine's signature—a unique identifier. The United States has a massive library of these acoustic sounds, a highly classified system that allows most adversaries to be immediately identified. Out on patrol in the depths of the Indian and Pacific oceans, US naval acoustic engineers sit alongside Australian submariners in Collins-class submarines as they work together identifying and logging all the maritime traffic in the area, though it is not clear how much of this detailed knowledge of the 'submarine signature catalogue' is shared by the United States with its Australian counterparts.

When the German manufacturers asked the Australian Defence Department to be more specific about the noise problem, they were met with a blank refusal. Defence cited issues of national security: revealing the frequency of the sound might disclose an insight into the type of monitoring systems and equipment being used by Australia.

It is certainly true that one of the most significant criteria for a successful submarine operation is silence. During the 1999 East Timor crisis, when Australia was belatedly sent in to curtail the Indonesian military's brutal attempts to maintain control, a Collins-class submarine maintained watch off the coast. The boat was so quiet that the Indonesian military were blithely unaware they were being watched as they manoeuvred their naval forces close to the island. Only when Australia told Jakarta that it was aware of the exact location of the Indonesian submarines did they back off.[9]

Conventionally powered boats such as the Collins are far quieter than those powered by nuclear energy. While the Collins can shut down its engines and remain silent for long periods of time operating on battery power, nuclear boats powered by a pressurised water reactor don't have that luxury. They need to keep a number of pumps circulating coolant running all the time to stop the onboard nuclear reactor from overheating. These pumps discharge hot water into the ocean, which is why they can be detected. It's one of nuclear-powered boats' biggest disadvantages.

Despite the Hollywood depiction of submarines lurking in the depths waiting to unleash nuclear weapons against an unsuspecting foe, submarines mainly have a more mundane role. Australia's are no different: they are mainly used for spying on the nation's neighbours, dropping SAS and commando troops over the side near deserted beaches, and doing what satellites can't—get close enough to pick up faint signals from small mobile radio communications used by the local military, or hack into telecommunications networks through mobile phone towers.

Gathering information using submarines is a highly technical and dangerous business. If a submarine is discovered, it can put the lives of the crew at risk, not to mention the diplomatic fallout from a 'friendly' neighbouring country. It's fair to say that the Defence Department had reasonable grounds not to reveal the exact frequency of the sound that was causing the problem. But who was the department hiding this information from? Surely not the Germans whose submarines were creating the noise—they would have had a reasonable idea where the problem existed, and its frequency. These facts were apparently not addressed by the Defence Department. It was not the first, nor would it be the last, time that the black curtain of national security would be drawn across the submarine selection program, where not just good governance but the very security of the country was at risk.

Even as the French boat soared way above its competition from Germany and particularly Japan, it still faced strong opposition. In the final weeks of the competitive evaluation process, the government brought David Gould back in to act as an independent judge to cast a final fresh set of eyes over its conclusions. Gould suggested a few 'tweaks' before its report was shared with a Defence Committee, chaired by Defence Department Secretary Greg Moriarty and including the head of navy and other top-level defence officials.[10] As a final step, the recommendation was then formally presented by the defence minister, Christopher Pyne, to the National Security Committee of Cabinet.

Gould said that the decision to go with ship- and submarine-building giant Naval Group was very easy in the end. If there was any single decisive factor, it was the perception that there was less risk involved in the French proposal because of Naval Group's experience in building submarines of the required size, while the Germans faced the daunting task of building a vessel that was much larger than anything they had built before.

The Japanese were a distant third place. What intrigued Gould was the support the German submarine had in Defence during the selection process. The Germans had agreed to include giving Australia the design rights for the submarine, whereas the French had not. This meant that if it won, the German company would hand over all the material required to make the boat, including highly classified details. Gould argued with the Defence Department that the reason the Germans were prepared to give away all the information about the submarine was that they had 'nothing to hide … they've got nothing that's very good'.[11] On the other hand, the French submarine contained highly valuable intellectual property: 'The French are saying, "You can have our crown jewels but you've got to look after them, because they're valuable." The French would give you all the information and the technology, but only for your own use.'

Gould believed that the Defence Department had a hidden motive for wanting full ownership of the French intellectual property. He suspected the department wanted to be able to 'suddenly say to the French, "Right, we've had enough of you, now bugger off"' and carry on manufacturing the boat by itself'. He says that in one heated exchange he confronted a Defence official, telling him, 'Look, this is crazy—you've only got one decent vehicle. Don't fuck about.' Gould said he thought he made himself 'a bit unpopular, actually, at the time, because I was only consulting'.

A source said that claims of the Germans being so much cheaper were largely exaggerated, because there was still uncertainty at that stage about costs; more importantly, it was no good being cheaper than the French if there was not as much confidence that you would deliver what was required.[12]

The difference that opened up during the assessment process was the ability the three finalists were each able to demonstrate regarding the technical superiority of their offer. The technical evaluation was very deep, and only when that level of work was completed was it possible to make a detailed assessment of the various bidders and their capacity.

The German technical proposal was hampered by their lack of experience at building submarines of that size. Gould said the French boat was a clear winner: 'France had done the best job. They had come up with an absolutely comprehensive solution to the problem. [They had] answered the exam question.' He said the French would let Australia have the most sensitive information about their submarine technology and they had made 'a strategic decision that they would treat the Australian Navy like the French Navy'. They would provide a totally integrated system.

One of the biggest selling points of the French submarine was its quietness. Unlike the Japanese and German submarines, the French boats were powered by a pressurised propulsion system that forced water out the back of the vessel with what they called a 'swirl propellor', giving the boat great speed and manoeuvrability, but most of all stealth.[13] Such is the secrecy surrounding the French stealth technology that Gould was reticent to talk about pump-jet propulsion. He said it was 'sensitive technology' and added: 'I'm not saying (it was) pumped jet—I'm saying it might have been' one of the closely guarded secrets the French were going to share with Australia.

A classified document produced in 2015 by Naval Group marked for release only to the governments of Australia, France, Great Britain and the United States explained that the swirl propellor had indeed been offered to Australia.[14] It was a derivative of the system used by French nuclear submarines, which are famous for their quietness, efficiency and speed. The technology is closely guarded by France for a very important reason: it gives their nuclear-powered submarines a significant advantage in underwater warfare.

'It wasn't the reason for the choice, but accepting the French submarine bid, as opposed to the Japanese or German bids, at least gives us a potential option to move to a nuclear design in the years ahead,' Turnbull wrote in his 2020 autobiography. He added a statement which in retrospect shows unwitting prescience: 'The United States would almost certainly welcome our having nuclear submarines—it would make us a more useful and capable ally.'[15]

Whatever opposition there might have been to the French boat now appeared to be unsustainable. The French submarine was the clear winner. After such a torturous process a decision had been reached. Turnbull would now relish the sweet taste of success on the world stage—or so he thought.

3

Champagne Days

As Malcom Turnbull and his wife, Lucy, settled in to dinner at the Élysée Palace with the new French president, Emmanuel Macron, on a balmy Parisian evening in July 2017, there was much to look forward to. Turnbull had formed a strong bond with Macron who, as president of the European Union, would be a useful ally as Australia continued its negotiations for a free trade agreement.

As the two leaders discussed world affairs in the garden of the Élysée, they both understood the political and strategic significance of the submarine deal. It just might shift the view of the other countries of the 27-member European Union that Australia would always have a closer relationship, both commercially and politically, with the United States than with Europe. Turnbull understood how important it was to prove to the French that they could have a strong ally in the South Pacific.

The following day, he headed off to Cherbourg to put the public seal on a project that had done so much to invigorate the relationship between the two countries. Cherbourg is home to Naval Group. When Turnbull arrived, the construction workers were still celebrating their victory at winning the Australian contract. Under an industrial agreement, they have shares in the company; many believe this has helped make Naval Group one of the most successful submarine manufacturers in the world, with an order book bulging to €15 billion in 2019.

The Australian contract was just the latest in a series of wins for the company, but at the same time it produced a novel challenge for Naval Group. The French were going to take their Barracuda-class nuclear-powered submarine, remove the reactor that powered it, and insert a diesel-electric engine. It was a job that required great attention to detail as the design team—with the French training the first of dozens of Australians—set out to totally remake the submarine to Australian requirements. Another 130 key staff would also need training, and French workers were getting ready to fly to Adelaide where the boats would be built. It was going to be a difficult job, but there was no doubt the French had the technical capabilities to do it.

France had won the contract by a country mile, easily defeating the German ThyssenKrupp submarine; the Japanese with their Soryu-class were a distant third. The Japanese boats had been so woeful that when Australian engineers gave them the once-over, they were surprised to find out how limited they were in both range and capability.

On that summer's afternoon in Cherbourg on the north coast of France, there was nothing to disturb the formal opening of Naval Group's project office at the huge industrial site. Yet if Turnbull had had the time, he might have read the news from back home in Australia. Thirteen days earlier Tony Abbott had been on Sydney radio station 2GB casting doubt on the entire project; he said that given the submarine acquisition process was long and involved, it was important that Australia had a 'plan B'.[1] There was worse to come. The following day Abbott called for Australia to change course and consider buying submarines powered by nuclear reactors.

If Abbott's comments had rankled Turnbull, this apparently didn't show. Turnbull knew the non-nuclear subs could always be reverted to nuclear submarines if necessary. He'd deliberately written into the contract that Australia could switch after two, three or four non-nuclear subs, without a penalty. With a 500-strong highly educated and flexible workforce, the changes would not be that hard to achieve. There was another advantage: France was the only country in the world that made both nuclear and non-nuclear submarines.

And it had a strong pedigree in submarine manufacturing. Naval Group had grown massively from its beginnings as DCNS (Directions des Constructions Navales Services). While it had industrial offshoots throughout France, it had put down its roots in Cherbourg. An ideally situated deep-water port on the Normandy coast, Cherbourg's harbour was designed by the French naval architect Vauban as a defensive fortress against the British. Facing the greatest sea power in the world across a thin strip of water sharpened French naval shipbuilding capabilities. The shipyards at Cherbourg built the world's first mechanically powered submarine in 1863 and from there created a formidable industrial base, becoming a major exporter of submarines and ships.

These overseas sales created a capability for Naval Group to work more easily with foreign governments and their non-French-speaking workforces. Accommodating often big cultural differences, Naval Group sold submarines and ships around the world, transferring highly sensitive technology that allowed local industry to flourish. In recent years Brazil and India had joined the long list of countries that had chosen Naval Group submarines, while Egypt's shipyards were assembling the first of four French corvettes (small and highly mobile attack ships). Like many other governments, Australia wanted to use the French submarines as a form of job creation and a way to develop and sustain an industrial base.

For the French, the Australian deal should have been business as usual. Though the size of the undertaking and the complexity of changing a nuclear submarine to diesel-electric would always be challenging, in the end it was simply a matter of planning and process. To prepare for the arrival of the Australian workforce in Cherbourg, housing had been set aside, kindergartens with bilingual teachers established. There were courses for Australians to learn French, and for the local workforce to learn English.

For all the effort that had gone into winning the contract against stiff competition, it did not go unremarked, even in the higher echelons of Naval Group, that there were 'cultural' problems that should have been addressed earlier. France might have won the deal just a year ago, but Naval Group had spent years in Canberra, Paris and Cherbourg talking to its Australian counterparts. Despite the many lunches, working breakfasts and after-hours drinks, the French had not fully grasped what was a mounting cultural problem that would make them vulnerable to being undermined by those who were aggrieved about their win in the first place and wanted Australia to team up with a more friendly US ally instead.

According to Naval Group, in all the years it had been doing business, working with Australians was the first time the company had been asked to reconsider its cultural approach to working with a foreign customer. In an interview in 2019, Jean-Michel Billig, the Naval Group program director for the Barracuda submarine, gave a candid assessment of the problem: 'Not everyone thinks like the French.'[2] He pointed out that the French would discuss every process and every problem in great detail before deciding what to do. The Australian workforce had a different attitude: decisions would be made quickly and then if they were wrong or needed adjusting, that would be done at a later date. Billig might easily have added less diplomatically that from the French point of view, no one thinks like the Australians.

There is no doubt that despite their differences of approach, with such a huge contract in the offing the French were prepared to go far to straighten out the cultural differences. But this approach required flexibility from both sides. The company told its workforce there was a necessity to understand and know each other's qualities and faults, not to use them as a weapon but to find agreement so the French and Australians could work together. Naval Group even went so far as to begin translating French not just into English but into what they described as 'Australian English'.[3]

There was one word that did not translate well. In English it is punctuality. The French word *ponctualité* appears to be very similar and supposedly has the same meaning, but looks can be deceiving. The Australians insisted on starting and ending a meeting on time. A meeting scheduled for an hour meant just that, not an extra fifteen minutes. So when Australians got up and left a meeting whether an agreement had been reached or not, the French were startled. Naval Group pointed out that in France there was the concept of a 'diplomatic 15 minutes',[4] indicating that being a quarter of an hour late was not regarded as late.

As the management at Naval Group tried to navigate the choppy oceans of difference, they pointed out that there was a reciprocal need for Australians to understand the French. It should not have come as a surprise to anyone that food would be an important point of difference. Perhaps too bluntly, Naval Group pointed out the sanctity of the lunch break. It wasn't just a sandwich eaten in front of the computer screen, but a more leisurely affair to be savoured. The French regard lunch as a kind of afternoon *siesta* without the sleep.

Ironically, it was one of the most iconic of Australian icons that drew the two sides together. Weekend barbecues organised by Naval Group bridged the cultural gap and helped sort out many of the differences that emerged— but one decision made by Naval Group stopped the barbecues in their tracks.

The company would use French rather than Australian steel to build at least part of the hull of the submarines. Even the British used French steel to construct the replacement for its Trident nuclear-armed submarines. That caused as much alarm and consternation in the United Kingdom as Naval Group's decision did among the Australians. Yet, once again, the decision to use French steel was not what it seemed. The steel would be made in Australia by an Australian company, but instead of using a traditional system, the steel would be manufactured using ingredients and processes which the French had never before shared with another country.

The closely guarded French recipe produces what is universally recognised as the best steel for armour plating. As Bisalloy, the Australian steel company that won the contract boasted: 'This grade of steel has never been manufactured outside of France before.'[5]

The secrets of its steel making was just one part of the intellectual property that France shared with Australia 'in handfuls'.[6] It inspired confidence that France was genuinely committed to sharing its submarine technology, but at the same time it posed grave dangers for the French if the deal did not proceed. An Australian company now had access to one of the French Government's most prized manufacturing secrets. What they had learned from the French, not just the 'know how but the know why' could not be unlearned.

It became apparent to even the slowest learners that it wasn't just the culture that was different: the French had different work practices. Even how they cut the steel was different. Many countries use lasers; the French use water.

It might not have been the best way to start a multibillion-dollar joint venture, but the French believed that by being open, identifying the problems and working early to solve them, they had cleared the air. The program began moving ahead, guaranteeing that the first Australian-built French submarine would be launched from the Adelaide slipway in early 2030. Though that event was more than a decade away, President Macron was in a hurry to push France in capitalising on the Naval Group win and reinforcing France's place in Asia and the Indo-Pacific.

At the Australian embassy in Paris, the lights burned late into the night as Ambassador Brendan Berne and his team worked on a plan to secure the best possible outcome for the newfound relevance of Australia in France. Berne had plenty of experience in dealing with awkward situations. While he was in the Department of Foreign Affairs, despite his protests he'd been posted to work in a political position as a Liberal Party minister's chief of staff. Berne, who speaks impeccable French, also had superb contacts and friends at the Élysée, including Macron's chief diplomatic adviser, Philippe Étienne. Macron so valued the advice of Étienne that he appointed him to one of France's most important diplomatic posts, ambassador to the United States. But before he left Paris, Étienne was persuaded to work on another project that, if it came off, would further enhance his reputation as one of France's most gifted diplomats. Only one French president, François Hollande, had visited Australia before, and only then because he was on his way to a G20 meeting in Asia. What Berne and Étienne wanted was what's known as a 'standalone visit' by Emmanuel Macron: a French president travelling to Australia with the single purpose of recognising the importance of Australia's relationship with France. As Étienne told me, the submarine deal was at the core of a new strategic partnership between Australia and France and 'changed the view we had in France of Australia'. It shifted from that of a country not necessarily considered as a 'priority connecting with us' to a really essential partner. It was, he said, 'a sea change'.[7]

Not far from the Élysée, as we sat in a cafe at Saint-Germain-des-Prés, Berne explained the game plan to me.[8] There were rare moments in diplomacy, he said, and mainly they were negatives, where it was possible to feel a relationship physically shift. Berne believed that the submarine contract had produced a once-in-a-lifetime positive movement, and he set about capitalising on the attention Australia had gained in the Élysée.

There were significant historical waypoints that augured well for quickening the pace of the relationship between France and Australia. It was 100 years since the hugely significant battle of Villers-Bretonneux in north-eastern France, where Australia had lost 1200 young soldiers as they fought to recapture the village and stop the German advance in World War I. So thankful were the people of Villers-Bretonneux that the local council had named roads after towns and cities in Australia and at the local school the sign says boldly in English, 'Never Forget Australia'. Not only did so many Australian soldiers give their lives for the town, but the bomb-damaged school was rebuilt in part with contributions from children in Victoria.

As Berne put it, 'There were a series of high points of great significance that we set about turning into something substantial.' By the end of 2018, on the back of the submarine deal, the embassy had established a number of economic and environmental defence programs under the banner AFiniti (Australia–France Initiative)—a word that works in both French and English.

Importantly, Berne said, Australia used this step up in the relationship to 'clean up some long-standing problems'. France had been the last country in Europe to launch negotiations for a free trade agreement with Australia—the holy grail of Australian trade policy. Farmers had for decades lamented the fact that Europe sold more agricultural product to Australia, a country of 25 million people, than Australia sold to the European Union, with a population of 450 million. European subsidies and tariffs had been a long-standing irritant to Australian farmers.

After the hours of meetings at the Élysée and the shaping and reshaping of agendas, Berne, with the help of Étienne, persuaded Macron that it was in the best interests of France for him to travel to Australia, not just because France had signed on to the biggest single defence project in its history, but because the Indo-Pacific was developing into a hugely important economic powerhouse and a potential flashpoint in the great rivalry between the United States and China. France had a large territorial stake in the region, and the more friends it had there, the better.

Macron would have been encouraged that the Australian Government provided the deck of the helicopter and troop carrier HMAS *Canberra* for him to deliver his speech when he arrived. The *Canberra* was the first ship the RAN acquired that was capable of landing troops on foreign shores in large numbers—a signal that Australia was ready to project its force into the Pacific and beyond, where France had so many of its citizens.

Macron, who arrived in Sydney on 1 May 2018, could not have asked for a more appropriate location. The *Canberra* was at anchor in Sydney Harbour, off Garden Island, the east-coast base of the RAN, where Thales, a major arms manufacturer part-owned by the French state, provides munitions and command, communications and control systems. Macron must have felt he was on home turf.

Flanked by Turnbull, he laid out a vision of creating an independent grouping of countries in the Indo-Pacific involving France, Australia and India. Significantly, Washington wasn't given a high profile, though Macron did mention later that the Americans were invaluable allies. He talked of the Indo-Pacific axis not as a slogan or motto but a geostrategic new order—the Paris–Canberra–Delhi axis—signalling a more independent group in the Indo-Pacific.

For France, the reach was beyond diplomatic. Paris was also competing with the United States for armaments sales. The French military aircraft manufacturer Dassault had just landed a large order with India to match the Naval Group submarine deal, and India had also placed an order for submarines with the French group. The emergence of this more independent thinking involving Australia, which until then had been a large purchaser of US military hardware, caused consternation in Washington, where then-president Donald Trump was busy launching a trade war against Beijing, accusing it of stealing American jobs.

Macron's vision was a direct affront to American power in the Indo-Pacific. He told the politicians and military leadership who had gathered to hear him speak that France shared the strategic view of the Turnbull government about how to cope with the expanded power of China in the region. He spoke of what he called China's commitment to 'become a global power',[9] but warned that existing rules had to be preserved (notably, Macron did not use the US cliché 'rules-based order', meaning the international system of the United Nations, the World Bank and the International Monetary Fund and their rules and ways of operating) and that multilateralism—not control dictated by any one nation—was a precondition of Chinese development in the region. China was fully aware of the difference between supremacy, stability and hegemony, he said.

Macron also confronted the China hawks who oppose Beijing's famed Belt and Road Initiative, a new 'silk road' building industrial and commercial links between Beijing, Europe, Africa and Asia. He gave veiled encouragement to Australia to be brave in the face of opposition from the United States. For Macron, the question was not 'to oppose this initiative, but, much more significatively, to build a dialogue with our allies'. In other words, France was not going to slavishly follow the United States in suppressing the rise of China as an economic power. This was not the kind of view that went down well in Washington, where China was to be not only contained but prevented from becoming a global power. Finally, Macron directly addressed Turnbull, reminding him of the importance of 'sovereignty'—a term Turnbull had used in Paris the previous year. If, as was the case, it was important to France, it would become increasingly important to Australia in the future.

The team at the Australian embassy considered Macron's visit to be a big personal win. According to Berne, Macron even picked up the language the Australians had been advocating to the Élysée that Australia was now focused on the 'Indo-Pacific'. That description had been used in Australia as a way of not having to choose between talking about either the Pacific or the Indian ocean when discussing foreign policy. They were now a single entity in the Australian Government's view. With France's territorial interests spanning both oceans, it was further evidence that Australia and France had a common strategic outlook.

So enamoured was Macron with France's new relationship with Australia that he broke with his normal protocol and wrote the speech he delivered in Sydney himself. His personal investment in the role France would play in this geopolitical realignment helps explain why he felt so betrayed when it all fell apart three years later.

But that was still to come, and at the embassy in Paris in May 2018 the team led by Berne were celebrating what they saw as a magnificent diplomatic win. France, which had previously viewed its foreign relations with Australia through a civilisational lens—meaning it saw Canberra as a colonial offshoot of a once great rival power, the United Kingdom—had been persuaded to change its mind. Suddenly Australia had been elevated in French thinking to a critical partner.

Australia now had a significant counterweight to the United States in its foreign relations and defence strategy. Though France and the United States are members of the Group of Seven industrialised nations (G7) and permanent members of the UN Security Council, they do not always vote the same way on major issues of global importance. Australia would now be less beholden to the United States. The French connection would provide Canberra with a greater degree of sovereign choice in both defence and foreign policy.

4

What Washington Wants

The Americans were already pouring troops and aircraft into northern Australia as part of their 'Pivot to Asia' to contain the rise of China. Concerned about being boxed in by the United States, Beijing had broken an earlier promise and begun militarising disputed islands in the South China Sea, warning, too, that it would take back Taiwan. It was also running heated battles with Philippine fishing vessels over disputed areas of the ocean.

The right of the Liberal Party reacted furiously. Under attack, Malcolm Turnbull appointed right-winger Peter Dutton to head up a new Home Affairs Department—a super-ministry controlling immigration, border protection and domestic security agencies, including the Australian Security Intelligence Organisation (ASIO) and the Federal Police. But giving the right more power only emboldened them—and their supporters. Amid a number of leaks from the security services, the media reported in feverish detail that China was spying on Australian industries and targeting politicians. The Turnbull government reacted by passing a 'foreign interference law' aimed squarely at China, and banned the Chinese telecommunications company Huawei from operating in Australia.

The Trump administration was also whipping up a frenzy against China. There was little doubt what would happen if Andrew Shearer, who had moved out when Abbott lost the PM job, ever returned to government to give strategic advice. Now back with the Center for Strategic and International Studies (CSIS), a highly partisan right-wing think tank in Washington fixated on confronting China and warning a war was inevitable, Shearer co-authored an article that mirrored the Americans' anxieties and called for a 'rotational presence' of US warships at the HMAS *Stirling* naval base in Western Australia, and the possibility of 'investing in the nuclear support infrastructure necessary for basing of attack submarines'.[1]

It was the first sign of what was to come, but Turnbull probably felt he had no choice: within weeks he brought Shearer back into the government as deputy director-general of national intelligence. A few weeks later Turnbull toughened up his defence credentials again by ordering the military to 'formally consider the potential for nuclear-powered submarines in Australia'. Technologies were changing, he said, and the risk environment was worsening.[2]

It seemed the French had got lucky: they are the only country in the world to make both nuclear and non-nuclear boats. It was time to examine the possibility of taking up France's offer and leaving the reactor in the boat. Though the French were at pains to point out that the Australian version, known as the Shortfin Barracuda, was a new design, there was no doubt its pedigree was nuclear. It was based on a new nuclear-powered Barracuda-class submarine that included features such as improved communication capabilities and increased accuracy of the cruise missiles it carried.

One month before Turnbull announced the French win, the Naval Group chief executive, Hervé Guillou, speaking in Cherbourg, alluded to what might lie ahead. He said France was offering Australia twelve non-nuclear submarines with the capability for Australia to create its own submarine, 'whether nuclear or conventionally powered', in the future.[3] Turnbull says he deliberately left that option available to the Australian Government if the domestic opposition to nuclear power faded, or if it was felt that nuclear submarines were important for a changed security environment for Australia.[4] Naval Group agreed, breaking the contract into sections that allowed the government to end the non-nuclear build at any time and then restart it as a nuclear option without any penalty or extra payment.

Kim Gillis, an Australian who had run Boeing Australia's lucrative Australian defence business and had been drafted in by Naval Group to help with the submarine negotiations, said there was what he called an 'unsolicited proposal' from the French to the Australian Government to deliver nuclear-powered submarines.⁵ Australia could have eight submarines for only 10 per cent more than the cost of the twelve non-nuclear ones.

Apart from being an easy change to nuclear power, the French boat had another benefit. Unlike their UK and US counterparts, the French submarine reactors use low-enriched uranium (LEU). Fuel rods—long corrosion-resistant tubes containing sealed uranium dioxide fuel pellets—are inserted into the front-end deck of the submarine through a special hatch, bundled together and mounted inside the reactor's heavy steel pressure vessel. They comprise the reactor core. While they are kept apart there is no danger of a critical reaction taking place, but once inside the reactor they can be moved close together, starting the fission process that produces intense but controlled heat. It's that heat that boils water, which produces the power to run the propulsion system: despite the exotic image of nuclear energy, the nature of the power it produces hasn't changed much since the first steam engine.

There is no doubt nuclear submarines have the reputation of being the Rolls-Royce of underwater travel; they can race to a depth where they can hide and then run at top speed (approximately 50 kilometres per hour) over a long distance.⁶ They are also the submariners' platform of choice for firing Tomahawk missiles, the kind the United States launched in the early days of the Iraq War in 2003 to devastate central Baghdad, and similar to the missiles that will be fitted to Australia's new nuclear-powered submarines. Though cruising several hundred metres below the surface a submarine might be invisible to the enemy, once it launches a missile a huge trail of white exhaust smoke gives away its location. It's here their speed comes in handy again: they can make a fast getaway before the enemy can target the submarine and strike back.

Former Australian senator Rex Patrick has been on board plenty of nuclear subs and knows them first hand. He is the only ex-submariner to have served in the Australian Parliament. The picture he paints strips back nuclear submarines' sexy PR gloss. They may look like a Ferrari, he told me, but the internal workings are no different from an old Holden.⁷ Submariners themselves refer to the onboard nuclear reactor as the kettle, because it simply heats water to produce steam that drives a turbine. The propellor that moves the ship is connected to the turbine by a number of huge gears, which produce a large amount of noise as the metal parts mesh together. It is impossible to make them completely quiet. In fact the boat is never quiet, even when it's not moving. Unlike conventionally powered submarines, a nuclear-powered sub's cooling pumps need to keep running day and night to cool the reactor. The pumps discharge hot water into the ocean, making their heat signature detectable.

The biggest selling point for nuclear submarines, apart from their speed, is the ability to remain underwater for lengthy periods—up to three months—without having to surface. But even that advantage is being whittled away. Though conventional submarines have to surface to draw in oxygen to run diesel turbines that charge the subs' batteries, the latest air-independent propulsion submarines operate on a fuel cell that holds its charge for much longer. Patrick has been to sea on Greek and South Korean submarines that have hydrogen fuel cells and can stay underwater for a couple of weeks without the need to snorkel. He says they are also better at operating in shallow-water areas. Unlike their more bulky nuclear cousins, conventionally powered submarines can get in closer to shore to eavesdrop, and can remain totally silent. They have the capability to shut down their engines and air-conditioning and cooling systems altogether, producing no noise except perhaps the sound of the crew breathing.

The US and British navies use highly enriched uranium (HEU) in their submarines. Natural uranium found in the ground is mostly uranium-238 mixed with very small amounts (0.7 per cent) of uranium-235. Enriching it involves increasing the proportion of U-235, making it suitable for use as fuel in nuclear reactors. The United States' and Britain's submarines operate reactors that use 93.5 per cent–enriched uranium as fuel, while the French Suffren-class submarine runs on fuel enriched below 6 per cent.

France has long been a leader in LEU. The fuel that runs its submarines is also used in the power stations that generate 70 per cent of the nation's electricity. Not only is it easier to handle, it's less expensive to make—and safer. It's a straightforward equation: the less HEU there is in the world, the less likely it is that it will be stolen by a terrorist group or diverted to make a bomb. Yet not even LEU is completely safe. Three-hundred kilos can contribute to the building of what is described as a 'mediocre bomb'—a fraction the size of the Hiroshima weapon, but still effective.[8]

For a number of years, the US Navy has been investigating using LEU in one of its aircraft carriers and the possibility of its future submarine projects burning LEU. But by 2024, it had yet to be convinced and was still strongly wedded to HEU. Change was a long way off.[9]

Just why the United States and the United Kingdom have refused to switch to LEU is not clear, but one reason given is that HEU provides more power even though it is potentially more lethal. One advantage of HEU is that a reactor using it doesn't need to be refuelled for the life of the submarine, known as LOS—an estimated thirty-five years. At least, that is the theory. In 2023 there were still fifteen years to go for the earliest-produced Virginia-class submarines before anyone would know whether that was right or not.

Dr George Moore, an expert in nuclear reactor operations, carried out a detailed investigation into whether the US Navy might have cut corners in its attempt to save money for its nuclear submarines. Moore, a former International Atomic Energy Agency (IAEA) special fellow, posed the question apparently no one can answer: Is it safe to lock up a nuclear reactor for thirty-five years without examining its internal workings? There is little transparency, even for those involved in academic research, to understand exactly what testing has been carried out by the US Navy to ensure the reactor will operate safely for more than three decades. The navy's response to questioning is that it uses what is known as 'accelerated testing', where the tests attempt to simulate over a short period the effects of running the reactor for the life of the submarine.

But Moore is not persuaded that the set-and-forget position of the US Navy is tenable. He points to the problems detected with commercial nuclear power plants, writing in 2017:

> The experience with commercial nuclear power reactors indicates that refuelling outages have sometimes detected problems in both the fuel and

pressure vessel. The risks of being wrong in choosing the LOS concept are significant. At the low end there would be increased economic cost and loss of operational capability if the LOS fuel does not perform as anticipated, and at the high end there would be a serious reactor accident with economic and potential life-threatening consequences were a pressure vessel to fail.[10]

There are few places this is better understood than at the Ivy League university of Princeton. The day after the bombing of Nagasaki on 9 August 1945, the local newspaper's front-page story boasted: 'Princeton aids with atomic bomb'.[11] Perhaps understandably, the university is now home to some of the strongest opposition to the spread of nuclear arms, and consequently to the use of HEU for power generation. It's where Professor Frank N von Hippel, a leading theoretical physicist who was part of a US team who advised former Soviet leader Mikhail Gorbachev on how to end the arms race, was the founding co-director of the university's Program on Science and Global Security. Professor von Hippel told me that 'one of the biggest risks of nuclear proliferation stems from the use of HEU as a reactor fuel because it is so easy to use it to make a nuclear bomb'. He expressed the concern that 'AUKUS legitimizes non-nuclear-armed states producing or acquiring HEU for nuclear-powered ships or submarines, which would allow them to secretly build bombs as well.'[12]

For decades the United States led the world in attempting to stop the flow of weapons-grade uranium, enforcing a strict regime at home that determines that its research reactors use only LEU. With the world increasingly anxious about the spread of nuclear weapons, in 1968 five of the nuclear-armed states—the United States, the United Kingdom, France, China and the Soviet Union—agreed to the establishment of the Treaty on the Non-Proliferation of Nuclear Weapons, commonly known as the Non-Proliferation Treaty (NPT). Under the NPT, the nuclear powers promised to share their nuclear energy expertise with non-nuclear countries. But to qualify for assistance, non-nuclear countries had to sign up to the NPT and promise not to develop nuclear weapons. They also had to throw open the doors of their nuclear research establishments to show they weren't cheating on the deal. Though it wasn't perfect (despite the curbs, India, South Africa, Pakistan and Israel all developed the bomb), the NPT managed to slow the spread of nuclear weapons.

However, there is one very large loophole in the treaty, big enough to drive a nuclear submarine through. Though the IAEA's NPT inspectors have the right to visit any nuclear site in a signatory state, they are forbidden from entering military areas. The IAEA supervises only 'peaceful' nuclear activities, so its inspection agreements explicitly exclude, for example, military submarine programs, stating, 'While the nuclear material is in such an activity, the safeguards provided for in the Agreement will not be applied.'[13]

As a softener to persuade non-nuclear states to sign the NPT, this loophole might have seemed prudent at the time, but it has had far-reaching consequences. HEU submarines provide the perfect cover for a nuclear weapons program to be developed far from the prying eyes of NPT inspectors. Iran already has a nuclear industry. There have been reports that the country is keen on acquiring HEU-powered submarines,[14] raising the potential of a nuclear arms race in the Middle East. Israel already has the bomb, according to the former Knesset speaker Avraham Burg.[15] If Australia breaks the mould and becomes the first country without nuclear weapons—or a nuclear industry at all—to get nuclear-powered submarines, why wouldn't others do the same?

It's a vexed question that is exercising the best legal and technical minds at the IAEA, the organisation responsible for policing the NPT. The IAEA director general, Rafael Grossi, expressed his concern shortly after the AUKUS deal was announced: 'It is a technically very tricky question and it will be the first time that a country that does not have nuclear weapons has a nuclear sub ... What this means is that we, with Australia, with the United States and with the United Kingdom, we have to enter into a very complex, technical negotiation to see to it that as a result of this there is no weakening of the nuclear non-proliferation regime.'[16]

The figures for Australia's nuclear submarines are startling. Each boat's reactor will contain about 500 kilograms of HEU, meaning Australia's nuclear-powered fleet will receive in the region of 4 tonnes of HEU, sufficient for about 70 nuclear bombs.[17] They would be a simple but deadly form of atomic weapon. A 'critical mass' would be formed simply by slamming two pieces of uranium together. As US physicist Luis Alvarez, who helped make the atomic bomb dropped on Hiroshima in 1945, later wrote, 'Terrorists, if they had such materials, would have a good chance of setting off a high-yield explosion, simply by dropping one-half of the material on the other half.'[18]

At a meeting of the IAEA board in June 2023, Grossi, whose team of inspectors had visited the *Stirling* naval base that would host the Australian nuclear submarines, sounded a note of caution: 'This process will take some time and the Agency will undertake it with its technical, impartial and objective approach.'[19]

Even if Iran volunteered for inspections during its vessels' occasional return to port, it would be impossible to avoid long gaps of months or even years when the HEU would be out of sight of IAEA inspectors. And that greatly worries the IAEA, which says that fresh HEU fuel can be converted to nuclear-weapon components in just one to three weeks.

It's a problem that weighed heavily on the mind of Dr Alan J Kuperman, who teaches courses in military strategy at the University of Texas. A recognised world authority on the perils of atomic energy and the author of the 2013 book *Nuclear Terrorism and Global Security: The Challenge of Phasing out Highly Enriched Uranium*, he has written extensively for the Federation of American Scientists, an organisation established after World War II by those who had worked on the Manhattan Project and who wanted to stop the future use of nuclear weapons.

Kuperman was sceptical that the US submarine's nuclear reactor could operate for thirty-five years nonstop. It would be like running a car without ever looking under the hood. What also concerned him was the secrecy surrounding the HEU-powered submarines. How could the US Navy be so sure they would never need to have their reactors serviced? It was impossible to say, with only publicly available data to go on, whether the systems the navy used to stress-test and replicate how the reactors might withstand three decades at sea were reliable.

After the AUKUS announcement, Kuperman was so concerned about HEU being used by Australia that he arranged to talk to the French Government. Shortly after he arrived in Paris, he began a relentless tour of meetings with government and industry officials to discuss the technical and political feasibility of France selling LEU-fuelled nuclear attack submarines to Australia. Technically, it appeared that not only could France provide Australia with LEU submarines, but Kuperman believed they could do so faster than the United States or United Kingdom could supply HEU versions. France had a single production line for nuclear submarines that was dedicated to producing the country's entire nuclear-powered—but not nuclear-armed—Barracuda class by 2032. After that, it planned to convert the production line to produce its next generation of ballistic-missile submarines, which were already in the final design phase.

Writing for the Australian think tank the Lowy Institute,[20] Kuperman argued that if Australia and France reached agreement, the non-nuclear-armed production line could be kept up and running to produce submarines for Australia, with the first arriving around 2035, up to a decade ahead of a UK option that would see submarines built in the 2040s in Barrow-in-Furness on the UK west coast, and in Adelaide. Under a contract with France, Australia could share in the construction. French nuclear submarines are produced in modules that are then welded together. This, Kuperman argued, would help satisfy Australian political concerns about support for local industry, and the simultaneous manufacture of separate modules in each country would expedite production. France, he wrote, had extensive experience with the joint manufacturing of submarines—working together to produce conventional models for Brazil, Chile, India and Malaysia—whereas the United States had never attempted joint manufacturing.

To the critics, the biggest drawback of France's LEU submarines is that they require refuelling every decade, unlike US submarines, which contain enough HEU fuel for the full 35-year life of the boat. But the French have sped up the refuelling pit stops by creating special hatches so the time needed to remove used fuel and insert fresh LEU rods is about a week. Preparatory work, including removing the reactor's steam generator, lengthens the process to as long as four months. Australia's submarines would also need to transit from the Pacific to France and back, adding another two months. Thus, refuelling would require the Australian submarines to be out of service for about six months every ten years. That downtime is relatively minimal compared to the midlife maintenance that all US nuclear-powered submarines undergo—including the Virginia class that Australia wants to buy—which takes them out of the water for at least two years. The US subs also have to return to the United States for this midlife service.

Of course, a prospective French deal would need to overcome some political, bureaucratic, legal and financial hurdles, Kuperman observed. The French Government had never exported, or even permitted formal negotiations to export, the nuclear submarine technology it considers the most significant part of its military capabilities.

It seems that someone in the French Government was listening to Kuperman. For a while it was reported that the French had offered four conventionally powered submarines from their own fleet to fill the capability gap caused by the AUKUS decision. But what has not been revealed until now is that France also offered to share its nuclear technology with Australia. The deal was drawn up before Australian prime minister Anthony Albanese visited Paris in August 2022 after his election win. It seems that in public, at least, the restitution of $850 million that Albanese offered Macron to make amends for Scott Morrison's clumsy dumping of the French project was more than enough to soothe Naval Group's wounded pride.

Even as the two leaders posed for the cameras on the steps of the Élysée, there were plans in Naval Group to rescue the deal. According to Gillis, the French offer involved a number of different options. The first submarines could be built in France to speed up delivery. Later construction would be shared between France and Australia, with the back half of the submarine containing the nuclear reactor being built in France and the other half built in Adelaide. The two halves would then be joined together in Australia. 'You could get the first nuclear submarine built in 2032,' Gillis said.[21] There would be one delivered every two years after that. The plan could also involve a transition from non-nuclear to nuclear over a period of time, if the nuclear option involving a build in France was problematic. Gillis said, 'I have seen the proposal with those options on it and I can't guarantee that it was shown [to the Australian government], but I've seen what was drafted up within Naval Group that said, "Here's how you would do it".'

The question remained: Why had Australia suddenly decided to spend up to $368 billion on nuclear-powered subs? Patrick's fear is that the answer lies in their underwater speed: 'It is the ability for a submarine to go from Perth into the South China Sea in a relatively short period of time. That is the driving factor behind Australia's decision to go nuclear.'[22] As Gould pointed out, the decision had little to do with the defence of Australia.

On the morning of 19 September 2019, a light drizzle began falling on Parliament House in Canberra as members of the Senate instructed a committee to begin investigating Australia's submarine acquisition program. Its final report was scheduled to be handed down in less than a year, but it would be delayed time and time again. It was symbolic that part of the reason for the delay involved the emergence of a virus in China that would kill millions and change the way we all lived for the next two years. The disruption to the normal processes of government would give cover for an administration that had already set course to hide its true intentions from public view.

As the committee began its deliberations, a clique of ministers and defence and intelligence officials were operating in secret to overturn all the processes that might challenge their ultimate goal. A hint of what they were planning could be seen in the government's strategic blueprint, the 2016 Defence White Paper.

Every decade or so, the government commissions an assessment that lays out the broad principles of how the Department of Defence sees the world and Australia's place in it for the next twenty years. By identifying the issues involved in protecting Australia and its interests, the White Paper also gives an insight into details contained in a secret document closely held by

Defence known as the force posture review, which identifies military threats and how Australia might deal with them. The highest-level policy document is the Defence Planning Guidance, which is also classified; it explains how the department will implement the government's directions, guides the ADF's expected missions and contains Australia's military strategy.

The 2016 White Paper predicted, without producing any supporting evidence, that the United States would remain the pre-eminent global military power, presumably for the next twenty years. Australia would 'seek to broaden and deepen our alliance with the United States, including supporting its critical role in underpinning security in our region through the continued rebalance of United States military forces'.[23] In other words, the United States would remain the leader of a unipolar world and Australia would do all it could to make sure it remained a close ally.

As the Senate Committee began its work seeking submissions and holding public hearings, on the other side of Canberra's Lake Burley Griffin at Defence headquarters a secret group headed up by Defence Secretary Greg Moriarty and answerable to the defence minister and the prime minister were working on a plan that would challenge the huge effort that had gone into selecting the best submarine for the defence of Australia. The Naval Shipbuilding Advisory Board, headed by Donald Winter, had already alluded to what was going on.

While the French submarine team was busy dealing with time-consuming work on what was called the Strategic Partnership Agreement (SPA), which dealt with not just the delivery of the submarines but French technology transfer to Australian industry and the building of special facilities in Adelaide, what Winter's team told the government had nothing to do with the French submarine's capability. They warned that even if the SPA negotiations that the government was ironing out with the French were successful, Defence should 'consider if proceeding is in the national interest'.[24] The advice from Winter, an Abbott appointee, was blunt: no matter what the French did, the government should consider dumping them 'in the national interest'.

It might be a catch-all phrase that covered a multiplicity of issues, but it had an eerie resonance with the sentiments of Shearer, who had attacked the French submarine from the moment it won the tender. 'Strategically, the decision amounts to a major missed opportunity,' he had said, and in a swipe at Turnbull he had added: 'Australia shares limited strategic interests with France.'[25] He was echoing the advice he had been given by the US military. In his co-authored 2016 article he wrote that 'although the US has been careful not to take sides ... senior US officials and military officers are in no doubt both as to the superior capability of the Japanese Soryu class [submarine] and to the long-term strategic benefits to the United States and the region of an interoperable fleet of Australian and Japanese conventional submarines equipped with US combat systems'.[26]

Shearer certainly understood that France had huge strategic interests in both the Indian and Pacific oceans, but those interests did not mesh with what he saw as the strategic benefits for Australia of a closer relationship with the United States. What he did not add to his article but would have been more truthful was that France had a different, and possibly more reasonable, view about how best to deal with the rise of China. The fact that in April 2023 Macron, returning to Paris from Beijing after meeting President Xi Jinping, declared that Europe should not blindly follow the United States only underlined Shearer's view. It could also be seen as a warning to the United States not to provoke China into war. What the French president said highlighted the widening rift between an independent Australian foreign policy and one closely allied to the United States.

It was about to get much narrower. In August 2018, when Dutton unsuccessfully challenged Turnbull for the leadership, he opened the door for the 'compromise candidate', Scott Morrison, to be elected Liberal Party leader and then to become Australia's thirtieth prime minister. Within weeks Morrison moved Shearer from deputy head of the Office of National Intelligence (ONI) to an even more powerful position: Cabinet secretary. The Cabinet secretary controls much of the business of Cabinet and is a close confidant of the prime minister. Washington now had someone they greatly admired at the heart of the Australian Government. As one ex-intelligence officer told me, 'The regard in which [Shearer] is held in DC is something else.'[27]

Shearer became very close to President Biden's national security adviser, Jake Sullivan, and to Kurt Campbell, Biden's Indo-Pacific coordinator.

According to the source, Shearer was very concerned that Australia 'no longer punched above its weight'. The United States was disappointed, the source told me, that Shearer had not been appointed Australia's ambassador to Washington. According to this person, the ambassadorial role 'was Andrew's dream job'. He had been the minister-counsellor (Political) in the embassy and had impressed officials in the Republican administration, in particular Richard Armitage, who had held high-ranking security posts during the Ronald Reagan presidency.

Between 2001 and 2005, Armitage was deputy secretary of state for George W Bush. Even back in those days he had a firm view about Australia's role should the United States go to war over Taiwan. In 1999 Armitage had been the star attraction at the Australian American Leadership Dialogue, a meeting of political movers and shakers hosted by Melbourne businessman Phil Scanlan. One of the guests, Hugh White, at the time a deputy secretary in the Australian Defence Department, was writing the 2000 Defence White Paper for the Howard government. According to journalist Hamish McDonald, White recalls giving the meeting a rundown of Australia's defence planning, foreshadowing the White Paper, and this following exchange.

> 'That's all very well, Hugh,' Armitage cut in. 'But I really don't see the force structure you are developing giving you a lot of options to support us when the balloon goes up over Taiwan.'
>
> 'Well, Rich,' White says he replied, 'you've got to understand that Australian defence policy is not based on the idea that we support the United States in those scenarios.'
>
> 'Well, they ought to be,' Armitage declared. 'What do you think this alliance is about?'
>
> ... He recalled that Armitage 'in his inimitable way literally, not just metaphorically, thumped the table and said that in the event of a US-China conflict over Taiwan we'd expect Australia to be there'.
>
> 'And there was a lot of ambivalence in the room amongst the Australians as to whether we would or not,' White said. 'That ambivalence included Coalition ministers.'[28]

Armitage is probably best known for his role in leaking the name of Valerie Plame's identity as a serving CIA officer to the press, an action observed by many as payback for her ambassador husband's public revelation that the White House assertion that Iraq was trying to acquire uranium from Nigeria to build an atomic weapon was a hoax.

Armitage had a special relationship with Australia that he built up during the early 1980s when he was deputy assistant secretary of defense for East Asia and Pacific affairs. As well as the dirty tricks he played on those who questioned the legitimacy of the Iraq War, he heavily courted politicians, and any foreigners believed to be rising stars whose politics supported the United States, be they journalists or diplomats. He was reported as saying of Shearer, 'We look after our own.'[29] Exactly what he meant by that is not known, but according to the former intelligence officer, shortly after failing to get the ambassadorial call, it was 'around [that] time that Shearer went to DC to work at the CSIS'.[30]

From the moment Shearer re-entered government, the tempo of the argument about which submarine to buy shifted from the best for defending Australia to the best for attacking China. In December 2018, the Morrison government announced that the first new submarine would be named HMAS *Attack*.[31] Before that, the submarines had been known by their generic term, 'the future submarine project'. It was a subtle but significant shift that would not have been missed by diplomats, who weigh every word in their attempts to understand a nation's mood or political direction.

The name change might also have been Morrison the marketing executive putting his brand on a huge item of important defence expenditure, a signal that a new macho leader was in charge of the Liberal Party. His government was softening up the Australian public for a change of role for its submarine acquisition—and much more than that.

5

France Overboard

From the day he was elected leader of the Liberal Party on 24 August 2018, removing Malcolm Turnbull, Scott Morrison began shifting Australia's military closer to the United States, virtually intertwining the two nations' armed forces. Few in the Australian military will forget the day he turned up at Canberra Airport to announce that Virgin Airlines would be giving US-style priority boarding to veterans, with a pre-take-off announcement thanking them for their service to Australia. The idea was dead within a week as Australian military personnel opposed what they saw as a cheap political stunt and a rejection of their egalitarian values.[1]

One month after being sworn in, Morrison made a more substantial shift towards Washington. Entrenching the US military in the Australian Defence Department at the highest level, he formally sanctioned Stephen E Johnson, a former commander of the US Navy's Undersea Warfare Center, as a deputy secretary of defence. This powerful and highly influential position gave Johnson access to the fine-grain details of Australia's security and strategic secrets. Was it considered at the time that Johnson, a citizen of the United States, might have a conflict of interest as he wrestled with what was in the best interests of Australia? It would have been worth remembering US General Douglas MacArthur's blunt assessment to Australian prime minister John Curtin in 1942 that 'the United States had no sovereign interest in the integrity of Australia. Its interest in Australia was from the strategical aspect of the utility of Australia as a base from which to attack and defeat the [enemy].'[2]

There is no doubt that the US Navy has an incredible understanding of underwater warfare, but its most outstanding expertise is in nuclear weapons systems and nuclear power. It was odd, to say the least, for Australia to turn for advice to a country with no expertise in conventionally powered submarines. Spain, Italy, Israel and Sweden all use diesel-electric submarines, but no one from those countries was asked for advice. The Liberal–National coalition could see no difference between what was best for Australia's security and what was best for the United States.

The luxury Hay-Adams Hotel in Washington, DC isn't the most expensive place in town but it has two large advantages: sweeping views to the White House, and it's within easy walking distance. On the morning of 30 April 2021, Andrew Shearer sat down for breakfast with his long-time friend Kurt Campbell.

Afterwards, the two men walked through Lafayette Square to Campbell's office at the Eisenhower Executive Office Building adjoining the White House. It would not have been lost on Shearer that Lafayette Square is named in honour of the French general who helped liberate America from the British in the War of Independence. The United States owed much to the French, but Australia's top spy was about to embark on a course of action that would not only entangle the Americans in an act of deception against their old ally, but also cause a massive loss of trust between Australia and France.

Exactly what transpired that morning in Campbell's office is not known, but according to several sources it's here that Shearer, operating on behalf of Prime Minister Scott Morrison, asked if the United States would share its nuclear submarine technology with Australia. Australia's was in trouble and needed America's help. What has been reported so far is that Shearer cut a lone figure pleading Australia's case to the Americans—he was a spy running a covert mission to save the nation.[3]

But nothing could be further from the truth.

The White House log, which reports the names of visitors, shows that at 8.29 a.m. on 30 April—at the time Shearer passed through security—he was accompanied by the Australian ambassador, Arthur Sinodinos, the former chief of staff of John Howard and Cabinet secretary under Malcolm Turnbull.

Sinodinos is probably better known as the Liberal Party treasurer who had an extraordinary capability for receiving party donations from a company of which he was chairman and yet have no knowledge of it. He was investigated by the Independent Commission Against Corruption in New South Wales, but it determined he had done nothing wrong.[4]

With that kind of magical capability, it's quite reasonable to believe that Shearer, with Sinodinos by his side, could have persuaded Campbell during their half-hour meeting that the French submarine project was way over price and behind schedule. It was true there was debate over the multibillion-dollar price tag, but the submarines were as 'on time' as it was possible to be with such a huge venture.

Campbell, who had urged a US 'pivot' to Asia during his time in the Obama administration, was impressed by Shearer's argument and brought the Australian request to Jake Sullivan, Biden's national security adviser. The pitch greatly appealed to the White House, where Biden had emphasised the need to work more closely with allies.

According to several reports, the first approaches had been made to the United States around the time Morrison was a guest of honour at the Trump White House the previous year. Unlike many world leaders, Morrison had not been critical of Trump and openly boasted of his relationship with Mike Pompeo, Trump's secretary of state and a former CIA director. Pompeo and Morrison were in regular contact, either by email or phone. Morrison said his relationship with the Trump administration was 'deeply rooted' in his relationship with Vice President Mike Pence and Pompeo. He attributed their closeness to the fact that 'we're evangelical Christians'.[5]

Morrison also had a close relationship with Shearer, though it was an odd choice to send the head of a nation's intelligence agencies on such a tricky mission for government. Normally this is the work of the diplomatic service or the prime minister. For Morrison it was particularly unusual. He was a prime minister who was such a controlling force in government that he secretly took on the jobs of five other ministers, sometimes without telling them. Now, he had outsourced to an intelligence officer detailed discussions about the biggest shift in Australia's strategic relationship since World War II. There was, however, one big advantage of not being personally involved in such a delicate matter: it would allow Morrison plausible deniability about what the Americans were being told. Later, Biden was forced to apologise to Emmanuel Macron in public at a G20 meeting in Rome, saying the United States had believed that Australia had kept the French fully informed. As Turnbull said, 'You can imagine how much he [Biden] enjoyed that.'[6]

Morrison had simply manufactured an argument and used it as a ruse to get the Americans and the United Kingdom on side. Kim Gillis from Naval Group believes that misleading the United States was key to getting it into the nuclear agreement: 'The only way that Morrison could ever have got the Americans to go in and desert the French in this contract was to tell them how badly the French program was going, which was the exact opposite of what the Australian defence program manager was advising the Morrison government at the time.'[7]

What we now know is that the French submarine budget had not blown out. A draft Cabinet document I acquired under FOI shows that the boats would cost $46.4 billion in 2016 'constant dollars' (these are the estimated costs, without allowing for inflation). Their delivery was also on time. The first submarines would be in the water in 2032. Just sixteen days before the AUKUS announcement, on 31 August 2021, Greg Sammut from the Australian Defence Department, who was heading the French submarine project, received an email from Defence Secretary Greg Moriarty. Moriarty congratulated Naval Group for presenting an affordable and acceptable offer to proceed with the next phase of the work. In the close-knit world of the Australian Defence Department it must have been difficult for Moriarty to issue such effusive praise to his colleagues knowing he was secretly working on a plan to ditch the French.

The attack on the French had a long genesis, stretching back to when Turnbull decided against going with the Japanese submarine. According to Gillis, Australia's former deputy defence secretary who was deeply involved in the submarine negotiations, whenever there was a problem with the project, the US admirals and retired public servants blamed the French: 'The anti-French sentiment was palpable … it was like, oh, the bloody French.

It was like they just assumed the French were bad.'[8] Gillis says that much of the anti-French mood could be traced back to the 2003 Iraq War, when France had refused to join the Americans because it rightly doubted the evidence that Saddam Hussein possessed weapons of mass destruction.

In May 2020, one year before Shearer met Campbell in Washington, Morrison had ordered a feasibility study to examine how Australia could acquire nuclear submarines without having an Australian nuclear industry to support them. It was an important issue and revealed either a total lack of understanding of strategic thinking or a wilful disregard for the consequences of such action. No other nation operated nuclear submarines without the capability to maintain and repair them, with very good reason: without that resource, a nation would be in danger of handing over its sovereignty to the nation that provided the nuclear support systems. Morrison could not have been unaware of this immutable truth. Both the United States and the United Kingdom jealously guard their highly trained nuclear workforce to avoid being reliant on another country.

Nobody knows that more than David Gould, who gave evidence to the UK Parliament when it was discussing whether or not to renew its Trident nuclear deterrent. The point was repeatedly made that maintaining a strong industrial base to support its nuclear-armed and -powered Vanguard submarines was of paramount importance. Without it, the United Kingdom would lose sovereign control of its most vital strategic asset.

Gould told me that while he was in Australia between 2012 and 2015 there had been discussion about switching to nuclear-powered submarines, but the idea had been rejected because Australia did not have the 'capability' to run a nuclear industry. If it wanted nuclear submarines it should wait until the next round of submarine acquisitions, he said.[9] It was difficult enough to recruit crews for the Collins-class subs, which were staffed by fifty or sixty submariners. The Virginia-class submarines—the kind Australia wanted from the United States—are much bigger, needing more than double the number of crew. But that's only part of the staffing problem: nuclear-powered submarines like the Virginia also need approximately eight highly qualified submariners known as nuclear watchkeepers to operate the reactor on each boat. Gould estimates it takes five or six years to train an already highly educated submariner to the level required—not exactly to the level of a physicist, but close to it. On top of that, Gould points out, while the submariners are studying physics they are not doing the training necessary for the basic level of seamanship. And those training to be nuclear watchkeepers have to be trained by someone even more qualified, adding more years. That was why the submarines would by necessity have 'mixed crews' of US and UK watchkeepers for an extended period. None of the boats would be truly Australian and independent for years to come, if ever, no matter which flag they flew from the mast.

Yet that appeared to be of little importance to Morrison, who was secretly laying the groundwork for what the right wing in the Liberal Party had long wanted: the introduction of nuclear power into Australia and a closer relationship with the United States. The question of Australian sovereignty seemed to be of little or no account. So the huge shift in Australia's foreign policy alignment was hatched by a Christian fundamentalist former tourism marketing manager with no training in strategic or foreign affairs but a great gift for secrecy and deception.

What the auditor-general's office, which had been tracking the submarine project since 2017, published in early 2020 should have been a grave warning to Naval Group. The Naval Shipbuilding Advisory Board was quoted as questioning whether the French deal should continue: 'Defence should assess whether program risks outweigh the benefits of proceeding.'[10]

There had been slight delays and other problems, particularly cultural, between the French and the Australians, but those issues were well on the way to being sorted out. By the standard of many other Australian defence acquisitions, this was plain sailing. The French were spending a great deal of time sorting out potential issues in designing the submarine before being ready to move ahead, but there was no suggestion that the twelve diesel-powered submarines would be late or more expensive than expected.

That, however, seemed beside the point. With Turnbull gone, the French had lost a major supporter. In his place was an awkward man with grand ideas to shape the country in his image. Much as Howard had said in the 1990s that the times would suit him, Morrison believed that, too. Surrounded by Howard-era advisers such as Shearer and with friends in the Trump administration such as Pompeo and Pence, Morrison believed he was on a divine mission. In that environment there emerged an opportunity for those who had been opposed to the French deal in the first place and wanted an even closer relationship with the United States.

The shift in Australia's security alignment might have started during World War II, but the nation became increasingly linked to Washington under the leadership of Howard. From the moment he won government in 1996 he began moving Australia's foreign policy away from engagement with Asia to protection from Asia by America. Both he and then foreign minister Alexander Downer repeatedly implored successive US administrations to increase their military presence in Australia. As historian James Curran revealed in his Lowy Institute paper 'Fighting with America', '[The] first thing he [Howard] and Downer did was to instruct our Ambassador in Washington to offer the Americans training facilities for their marines in Northern Australia. They declined. He was instructed to ask again, they said no again.'[11]

In 2001, after the Twin Towers attack, Howard invoked the US–Australia security agreement, ANZUS, as a symbol of Australia's unwavering support for the United States. Two years later, Australia followed the Americans into Iraq despite warnings that the intelligence was either cooked up or faulty. Howard also signed up to the controversial US F-35 program to replace Australia's ageing F/A-18 fighter bombers. The F-35, a 'captain's call' by Howard, has been beset with faults, criticised repeatedly by the US Government Accountability Office for being both late and hugely over budget. But unlike the French submarine deal, which at the time it was scrapped was neither over budget nor late, no one in the Australian Defence Department ever considered axing the F-35. Australia had tied itself to the United States whatever the cost. From Howard's first government onwards, there was no looking back for the Liberal Party: it was wedded to Washington. Even after being out of office for nearly twenty years Howard was still extremely influential—a deeply conservative monarchist from whom Abbott, Dutton and Morrison regularly sought advice.

There is no more significant and symbolic representation of Washington's power and strategic influence in Australia than its spy base at Pine Gap, near Alice Springs in the Northern Territory. In 1974, eight years after it opened, no one in government knew exactly what it did. When the Labor government of Gough Whitlam raised questions about its activities, Henry Kissinger, President Richard Nixon's national security adviser, suggested the possibility of shifting Pine Gap out of Australia to another country 'because of Canberra's shift to the left'.[12] Significantly, the CIA cut back its intelligence sharing with Australia. This attempt to assert sovereign independence cost Labor dearly. The Liberal Party cast Whitlam as weak on national security, and within a year he was out of office.

The fear of what happened to the Whitlam government still haunts Australian Labor. Though the ALP has at times stood up to the United States, as former leaders Bill Hayden and Simon Crean did, the Pine Gap history looms large, mainly because US intelligence agencies see progressive political parties as potentially a threat to US interests.

What was hidden from both the Whitlam government and the Australian people for nearly a decade was Pine Gap's real role. Described as a deep space research station, it was in fact staffed by the CIA and the NSA and was more concerned with what was happening on earth than in space. Ground control for a global network of eavesdropping satellites in geostationary low earth orbits, Pine Gap acted like a vacuum cleaner, sucking up details of phone calls and electronic transmissions in areas as far apart as Western Europe and the east coast of Russia. Even in the 1980s, the 'national communications and cypher room', where US officers analysed intelligence gathered by Pine Gap before encrypting it and sending it to Washington, remained out of bounds to Australian personnel.[13]

Over the decades successive governments have tried to assure the public that the US presence in Australia poses no threat to the nation's sovereignty. On a regular basis, Australian defence ministers have made announcements to parliament known as 'full knowledge and concurrence'—statements to reassure Australians that the United States' capabilities are known and agreed to by the Australian Government. However, as then Labor defence minister Stephen Smith told parliament in 2013, 'Concurrence does not mean that

Australia approves of every tasking undertaken.'[14] This open-ended agreement left plenty of room for manoeuvres by the Americans provided their actions were in keeping with the 'mutually agreed goals' of the United States and Australia.[15]

In 2024 it appears that the communications and cypher room at Pine Gap is now open to Australians. Australian intelligence analysts sit alongside their US counterparts and have access to all the raw data gathered by Pine Gap and the satellites it controls. But this new accessibility, designed to deal with questions of Australia's sovereignty, poses new problems. Australian governments have long abandoned the narrative that Pine Gap is solely used to ensure that strategic arms agreements are enforced, but they have been silent on what its role is now. In fact, it provides real-time battlefield information to American troops throughout the world and gives target information for the CIA's assassination programs. As the late Professor Des Ball, the head of strategic studies at the Australian National University (ANU) in Canberra and avowed expert on Pine Gap, who briefed both Labor and Liberal–National governments on its activities, said, '[Pine Gap] is about finding individuals and targeting them for killing by drone and air strikes, in battle zones and in places that are not designated war zones.'[16] Ball, who supported Pine Gap's operations throughout the Cold War because of its important role in strategic arms limitation verification, changed his mind when it turned into a battlefield station for America's military. He said that Australia's participation in US activities 'should be governed by rules, principles and procedures. Capture, arrests, warrants, evidence. We should leave the killings to the CIA' and what Ball described as the 'cowboys' of the US Joint Special Operations Command at Pine Gap's sister station, Menwith Hill, in the United Kingdom.[17]

It might have been wiser advice than many realised, particularly for Australians working at Pine Gap who under the AUKUS agreement will become even more immersed in US operations. This wasn't just an argument about morality or Australia's sovereignty: there were legal implications, too. For while the United States is not a signatory to the International Criminal Court (ICC), and its military is explicitly protected by US law from criminal prosecution overseas, there is no protection for Australian citizens. Australia signed the UN Rome Statute in 1998 that established the ICC, and ratified it in 2002. The involvement of an Australian in any assassination or extrajudicial killing could well render them vulnerable to prosecution. For Australia and its much-vaunted support of the United States and its rules-based order, which it so often uses to chide China, this is an uncomfortable issue that has never been publicly dealt with.

Though the focus on US activities in Australia has justifiably remained on Pine Gap, another US base, 800 kilometres north of Perth near Exmouth Gulf, has largely escaped detailed inquiry. North West Cape's operations have been explained in vague language. Like defence ministers before him, in his 2013 statement to parliament Smith said that it simply provided communications facilities for US and Australian submarines.

But in February 2019 there was a major change in the way the role of North West Cape was explained. It coincided with a move to ban the world's biggest telecommunications equipment maker, the Chinese company Huawei, from providing 5G equipment to Australia because of a risk it would give Beijing the ability to shut down power networks and other critical infrastructure. Under pressure from the United States, the decision marked the start of a Cold War between Australia and China and retaliatory Chinese trade sanctions. Australian farmers and wine producers fared the worst, with an 85 per cent tariff on barley, a 206 per cent tariff on wine and 40 per cent on cotton, plus the blacklisting of four abattoirs by China.

It was against this backdrop that Defence Minister Christopher Pyne in 2019 ripped back the veil of secrecy surrounding North West Cape, revealing its exact role to parliament. There was no more skirting around what it did, suggesting that it acted as a relay station for benign conversations with lonely submarine crews at sea. North West Cape was used, Pyne said, by the United States to communicate with its nuclear-armed submarines in the Indo-Pacific—or, as he put it, to provide 'communications for the submarine-based nuclear deterrence capabilities of the United States in the Indo-Pacific'.[18]

This was a full and frank admission of why the United States sees North West Cape as such a valuable asset. At the depths they operate, submarines are both blind and deaf. Normal radio communication is impossible. But the massive antennas of North West Cape, some of them soaring more than 300 metres into the air, transmit low-frequency signals that penetrate deep into the ocean over a huge distance, possibly hundreds of kilometres. It's from here on the remote Exmouth peninsula overlooking the crystal-blue waters of the Indian Ocean that the United States uses one of its prized assets in its attempt to contain the rise of China. Information gathered by the fixed underwater sonar arrays the Americans have installed across the South China Sea and closer to Australia's shores is relayed to its submarines from North West Cape, allowing them to identify, track and destroy an adversary if necessary. North West Cape gives the United States the advantage of being able to 'see' in what would otherwise be an equal game of blind man's bluff.

There is, however, an even more significant role for North West Cape, which in 1968 was named by the United States as the Naval Communications Station Harold E Holt in honour of the Australian prime minister who went missing while swimming off Portsea, Victoria in 1967. It won't be used just to communicate during a war—it will be used to send a coded signal to US Ohio submarines to launch their Trident II D5 nuclear missiles at targets designated by the Pentagon on instruction from the US president. Each missile carries multiple warheads; every one of them has the destructive power of 476 kilotonnes. It's estimated that a bomb less than a quarter that size, at 100 kilotonnes, dropped on a densely inhabited city would kill more than half a million people.

Despite the need for North West Cape to be used only for 'mutually agreed goals',[19] in a time of crisis it's hard to see how Australia could physically stop the United States from using North West Cape even if it disagreed with its decision to launch a nuclear strike. Whether or not Australia would be given advance warning by the Americans, or even 'consulted' before the launch order, is also questionable.

It's not clear why Pyne decided to break ranks with more benign past statements about North West Cape. It certainly revealed someone who was not afraid to expose the obvious ties that bind the United States and Australia in any nuclear war. Whatever the reason, his comments were a step up in both realpolitik and rhetoric, reminding the public that nuclear-powered and nuclear-armed submarines were already a part of Australia's military mix, and preparing the public for a shift that would draw the two nations even closer together in a nuclear future.

Like the US military officers who now crowded the Australian Defence Department, Pyne was not alone in seeing the possibilities of making money from the heightened concerns of a resurgent China. Less than two months after his statement to parliament, he was discussing a job offer with the international consulting group EY, which was lining itself up for a slice of the billions of extra dollars Australia was about to spend on its military. The talks were clearly fruitful: Pyne decided to abandon a decades-long parliamentary career to take up EY's offer. On 26 June, the company sent out an email boasting it had engaged him to help it in 'ramping up its defence capability ahead of a surge in consolidation activity and the largest expansion of our [Australia's] military capability in our peacetime history—$200 billion over ten years out to 2026'.[20]

EY could see plenty of business with Australia's increasing level of defence spending. Turnbull had brought forward the decision to increase the allocation for defence to 2 per cent of GDP, lifting it by $30 billion to about $260 billion over the following ten years. A large proportion of that money was scheduled for the Adelaide shipyard at Osborne, where the French submarines were due to be constructed. Clearly Pyne, from South Australia, would be of great help to EY's customers, keen to profit from the billions of dollars being poured into the submarine project. EY admitted as much in another email: 'Christopher Pyne is also here to help lead conversations about what South Australia needs to do to meet the challenges and opportunities this huge defence investment will bring.'[21] Pyne texted publicly: 'I'm looking forward to providing strategic advice to EY, as the firm looks to expand its footprint in the Defence Industry.'[22] He clearly would not be carrying out any lobbying for EY, because that would be a clear breach of the ministerial code, which forbids that activity for eighteen months after a minister leaves office.

Politicians on both sides of parliament were outraged at Pyne's actions. Morrison ordered an independent investigation by respected former head of the Department of the Prime Minister and Cabinet (PM&C) Martin Parkinson. The ministerial code of conduct also requires that former ministers undertake that they will 'not take personal advantage of information to which they have had access as a minister, where that information is not generally available to the public'.[23]

Such are the rules on conflict of interest and ministerial conduct that Parkinson found Pyne had done nothing wrong. If anything, Pyne was late getting to the military cash trough. Morrison had been splashing money around like a drunken submariner on shore leave, as had his predecessors. Most of the beneficiaries, however, weren't Australian. They were retired members of the US military's top brass. Donald Winter had been lured to Australia with a handsome remuneration. In 2015, Stephen E Johnson took over as the general manager for submarines. Defence Department records show that in 2018–19 he was paid $336,831 for his services. William Hilarides, a retired US vice admiral, served as chairman of Australia's Naval Shipbuilding Expert Advisory Panel. He commanded the USS *Key West*, a Los Angeles–class nuclear-powered attack submarine, and led the Naval Sea Systems Command, overseeing 80,000 civilian and military personnel who build, buy and maintain ships and submarines.

Though many of the individual payments to former US military leaders are hidden from public view, records from the Australian Defence Department give a glimpse of the cash flow. Hilarides said in his application to work for the Australian Government that he would be paid through Burdeshaw Associates, a consulting firm based in Fairfax City, Virginia.[24] US Navy officials blacked out details of his pay, citing privacy concerns, but records posted online by the Australian Government show that it had signed a contract worth $6.8 million with Burdeshaw to pay Hilarides and several other American consultants from 2015 onwards. They were paid for their 'expert advice on the performance of the naval shipbuilding enterprise. This includes the acquisition of nuclear-powered submarines and other issues relevant to naval acquisition and sustainment.' At about the same time, the Australians recruited another American, Paul E Sullivan, a retired vice admiral who, like Hilarides, had once headed the US Navy's giant Sea Systems Command. Australian Government records show he received contracts worth $414,228 over the next four years.

Not only were the Americans being recruited in large numbers to work for the Australian Defence Department, Johnson—the US admiral who had been appointed deputy secretary of the department—was doing his own recruiting of compatriots. In 2016, he hired retired US admiral Kirkland Donald. A four-star officer, Donald served for eight years in one of the most important uniformed jobs in the navy—director of Naval Nuclear Propulsion, overseeing nuclear-powered submarines and aircraft carriers. He told the US Government that the Australian Defence Department had requested his support to take part in an independent review of the country's naval defence capability. The primary purpose of the study was to highlight areas of strength, identify areas of weakness and determine if there were gaps in capability. The findings would be used to support the Collins-class life extension and the future submarine program, he wrote. In other words, the Defence Department wanted to know if the Collins-class submarines could be extended beyond 2023 in case the French submarines were not delivered on time. In July 2016 the Australian Government awarded Donald a two-year contract worth about $255,000. He later received a second consulting contract, worth about $420,000.

Johnson had appointed Donald in July 2016, shortly after Turnbull announced that France had won the submarine contract. It seemed an odd choice at the time, since Donald's expertise was in nuclear-powered submarines. Though Morrison clearly had plans for Donald that he was only sharing with a selected few in government, Donald seemingly had plans of his own. In January 2017 he joined the board of Huntington Ingalls, the US shipbuilder that makes nuclear-powered Virginia-class submarines; three months later, he took his 'first holding' of Huntington Ingalls shares, and in 2020 he became chairman of the board. By April 2024 he held shares worth

$US1.42 million.[25] He was also on the board of Centrus Energy, a company that supplies uranium for nuclear power plants and that builds, tests, operates and validates 'the world's most advanced uranium enrichment centrifuges to meet both commercial and US national security requirements'.[26]

None of this stood in the way of him advising the Morrison government on which kind of submarine was best for Australia. It was part of the increasing dominance of the United States in the Australian military.

6

A Secret State

The fact that the Australian Defence Department was filled with former US Navy officers and admirals should not have come as a surprise: the Australian and US militaries have been increasingly integrated over the past three decades. After the submarine selection project was launched, the numbers of ex US military at the ADF's headquarters in Canberra increased dramatically—a perfect fit for Scott Morrison, whose view of world affairs so mirrored that of the United States and Donald Trump. Here was a no-nonsense strongman with whom he could do business.

Within four months of Morrison winning the 'unwinnable' election in 2019, Trump obviously felt the same way, throwing open the White House for a state dinner for Morrison. State dinners in the United States are by tradition only granted to heads of state, which in Australia's case is the governor-general. But Trump was not big on protocol, and clearly wanted to make an impression on his new friend. It was also only the second time in his presidency that Trump had granted a foreign leader such an honour, and the first for an Australian prime minister since George W Bush hosted John Howard in 2006. What was in it for Trump is not clear, but he had been extremely vociferous about the need for the United States to cut its overseas military budget and for host countries to pick up some of the bill.

An indication of the political and philosophical underpinning of Trump's relationship with Morrison was on show that warm September day in the White House Rose Garden. If the head of the ADF, General Angus Campbell, had glanced up from the linen-bedecked table as he downed his first sliver of Dover sole with a fennel mousseline, he would have seen a good cross-section of the company Trump kept: his now-discredited lawyer Rudy Giuliani; the late Henry Kissinger, President Richard Nixon's former national security adviser, wanted for war crimes by so many countries that even at the age of ninety-six he had to watch out where he travelled for fear of arrest;[1] Lachlan Murdoch, the News Corp executive more right wing than but not as gifted as his father; and the Australian Greg Norman, who took money from Saudi Arabia to promote a golf tournament boycotted by most players. Norman was so close to Trump that former Australian ambassador to the United States Joe Hockey (who was also at the state dinner) had called him to get Trump's phone number after Trump's shock election win in 2016.

The previous year, in a speech entitled 'War in 2025', at a conference held by the government's favourite think tank, the Australian Strategic Policy Institute (ASPI), Campbell had highlighted the end of the CIA's black ops programs in the 1970s, which were part of Kissinger's policy with Nixon to destroy America's enemies.[2] He had painted a picture of the West weakened by its openness, pliable to the propaganda of totalitarian regimes, and fired the opening shots for what was to come in Australia as the government ramped up its rhetoric against China.

The next day, 20 September, he and Morrison headed out to the Pentagon. It probably didn't cross Campbell's mind that one of the greatest propaganda lies of all time, involving Iraq's weapons of mass destruction, had emanated not from Moscow or Beijing but just down the road at the White House. Inside the Pentagon there was the obligatory photo op with the defense secretary, Mark Esper, but Morrison showed particular interest in what the Pentagon calls the ANZUS Corridor, where a photo of the signing of the 1951 treaty hangs and gives new meaning to 'the corridors of power'. But if Morrison felt Australia had been slighted by the United States, he didn't show it. The Australian prime minister was the perfect guest, posing for photographs in front of the image, staring admiringly at the signatories.

The same day, Morrison had another meeting with Trump. He also met with the chairman of the US Joint Chiefs of Staff, who is the head of the US armed forces and whose power is eclipsed only by the president. The details of what was discussed have not been revealed, but the meeting came at a time when by his own admission Morrison had begun 'turning his mind to submarines'.³ Two journalists from the *Australian* interviewing him for a book wrote that Morrison 'wanted to assure himself there would be no regrets' over the French submarine deal.⁴

Morrison had now met Trump three times since being elected. The first was in Osaka, Japan on 27 June 2019, just after Morrison had won the federal election in March. In what was described as Trump's 'most consequential trip of the year',⁵ with any number of other world leaders to choose from—including the host, Shinzo Abe, Brazil's Jair Bolsonaro, the Saudi leader Prince Mohammad bin Salman, China's Xi Jinping and Russia's Vladimir Putin—straight off the plane Trump chose to spend an hour dining alone with Morrison.

They met again the following August in the coastal town of Biarritz in south-western France, at a meeting of the G7. Australia had been invited by Emmanuel Macron as one of a handful of countries granted observer status at the prestigious meeting. Macron had met Morrison two months earlier in Portsmouth, England at the 75-year celebration of D-day, which marked the beginning of the liberation of France and the end of World War II. But the formality of the G7 was a perfect time for Morrison to fully discuss any ongoing issues surrounding the submarine project.

As the RAAF plane began its slow descent into Biarritz, the Australian ambassador, Brendan Berne, had high expectations of what might be achieved. It was the first time Australia had been granted 'close attendance' at a G7 meeting. Significantly, it was France, not the United Kingdom or the United States, that had issued the invitation. Here was a chance to sort out some of the problems that a multibillion-dollar defence and strategic agreement would inevitably face.

The original invitation had been given by Macron to Malcolm Turnbull, and with the change of prime minister the French were concerned about how Morrison might respond. Turnbull had a strong relationship with Macron, but Morrison was an unknown quantity. Berne had assured the French that the invitation was to Australia and not to any particular individual, an argument they accepted.

As Morrison's team came down the rear stairs of the plane, Berne moved forward to welcome the prime minister. Morrison was accompanied by his wife, Jenny. Berne, as is customary for ambassadors during foreign visits, had rehearsed a short statement on how he planned to frame the activities of the next few days. There was much at stake. Berne explained to Morrison and his staff that it wasn't just the submarine deal and the strategic partnership spanning the Indo-Pacific that could be discussed. Australia was anxious to sign off on a free trade agreement with the European Union that would open the door for Australia's farming exports to more than 450 million people. As France is a nation with a huge agricultural sector, there would be those who would resist the competition from Australia, and the support of Macron was of great importance. As Berne finished his three-minute summing-up he was shocked at Morrison's response: 'He looked at me with utter contempt, basically turned his back to me and said, "Mate, I'm tired. I just want to go to the hotel."' Berne says the comment was intended to humiliate him.[6]

For Berne there was a 'whiff of homophobia' in Morrison's dismissive comments. Yet Jenny Morrison could not have been more different from Scott. Berne's husband, Thomas, who interpreted for her and the other spouses of the G7 leaders, found Jenny 'delightful', according to Berne.

Once again, Morrison was alone in a world of his own creation, complaining that a one-on-one meeting with Macron had not been secured; apparently the Élysée had turned one down because the two had already met in Portsmouth a few weeks earlier. Morrison was almost certainly being disingenuous about wanting another meeting with Macron. In fact, all the signs out of Biarritz were that he was trying to avoid the French president. Those who saw the two men together and knew Morrison said he was 'bristling' when he and Macron crossed paths for what they call in diplomatic language 'pull-asides'—quick conversations on the run.

By being somewhat elusive and not having a second meeting, the French had played into Morrison's grand plan. With the person who had been intimately involved with the submarine deal, Philippe Étienne, having moved to become the French ambassador to the United States, a long-time diplomat, Emmanuel Bonne, now ruled supreme as Macron's chief diplomatic adviser. Whereas Étienne had been an outgoing, modern French diplomat, Bonne was very much of the old school, a bureaucrat of the Gaullist tradition. According to those who know him, he held a regal, colonialist view of France as the great civiliser. The multibillion-dollar submarine deal with all its attendant benefits to France did not interest him as much as the prestige of pulling off a major prize at the G7 meeting, where his expertise and love of Middle East politics could be used to save the failing Iranian nuclear deal that sought to prevent its development of nuclear weapons. Those present say it's where most of his effort was focused as the Iranian foreign minister arrived as an observer. Like Morrison, the Iranian minister had been invited as a guest of Macron, but with Bonne there was only one show in town: Iran. He was going to save the Iranian nuclear deal, an agreement Trump had set out to sabotage almost as soon as he took office.

There was no doubt where Morrison's sympathies lay, and it wasn't with the European attempts to keep the nuclear deal alive. He was more enamoured with the United States under Trump, even picking up manners of speech such as pronouncing the letter 'Z' as 'zee', possibly as a result of his almost-daily conversations with the US administration. Morrison's main aim was to continue the process set in place by his predecessors Howard and Tony Abbott: further integrating Australia's military with the United States, and all that entailed.

Significantly, Morrison had been 'turning his mind' to the submarine issue well before the White House dinner and the Pentagon meeting with the chairman of the Joint Chiefs of Staff. Accompanied to the G7 as he was by his new Cabinet secretary, Andrew Shearer, whom he had recently appointed to his inner circle from the position of ONI deputy director, it is inconceivable that the French submarines were not mentioned either in official talks or later in a social setting. Shearer, the eyes and ears of the prime minister, was part of a tight-knit team Morrison had assembled to shape policy and public opinion.

Morrison had appointed as his private secretary Yaron Finkelstein. Finkelstein was a former chief executive officer of Crosby Textor, the firm of pollsters and political strategists infamous for their controversial tactics. He would be a valuable asset for Morrison as he sought to run one of the most secretive and deceptive governments in Australian history.

Crosby Textor had form. They were leaders in the field of what became a corrosive and polarising form of politics. In 1999 the then Labor Senate leader, John Faulkner, described in the Australian Senate what he called 'the disturbing rise of wedge politics, of which Mark Textor is an unashamed practitioner'. Faulkner said, 'Wedge politics operates on the cynical and shameful political calculation that you can win in politics only when you divide the community. His research methodology is designed to identify, exploit and inflame division for the benefit of his political clientele.'[7]

Lynton Crosby was a perfect partner in the Crosby Textor company. It was he who supported the Howard government's infamous 'children overboard' election win, which portrayed refugees as being so callous and uncaring about their children that they threw them into the sea in an attempt to gain asylum in Australia. It wasn't true, but it helped Howard win a third term in office thanks to a population fearful of a refugee 'invasion'. In another example, Textor had deployed 'push polling', a US tactic of spreading damaging information about opponents under the guise of questions.[8] As a result, in 1995 one Labor candidate received £34,000 in damages after suggestions in a polling question that she supported abortions at nine months.[9]

Perhaps not surprisingly, Morrison the marketing guru was about to run a campaign that drew upon the tactics of guile and deception he had used in his past life. From the moment he gathered his new team around him, the media coverage of the French submarine deal swung violently into negative territory.

It was true that the program was behind schedule. In January 2020 the report from the Australian National Audit Office (ANAO) that the submarine design phase was running nine months late was met with a barrage of negative media. Because it had failed to meet the agreed time frame, Defence was criticised for not having properly spent the nearly $400 million set aside for the submarines' development phase. It was understandable, but little notice was taken of the fact that the submarines would still be delivered on time in 2032.

There were other positives, too. The ANAO found that Defence had established a 'fit-for-purpose strategic partnership framework' with the

French that 'addresses the Government's objectives for the Future Submarine Program'.[10] Its report also noted that 'Defence records indicate that within the Future Submarine Program Office there was an acceptance that delays in the negotiation process were a cost of achieving acceptable terms and conditions in the Agreement'. There would be no cutting corners. For Australia's largest-ever defence acquisition it was better to get it right in the first place than try to play catch-up later. The Future Submarine Program Office records reveal an obsession to do thorough groundwork before moving ahead with building the submarines: 'we need to continue to act with consistency (and integrity), and avoid expediency'. The office warned: 'We will do long-term damage to the Program by trying to avoid any shorter term delays to ensure we secure appropriate terms and conditions.'

The ANAO pointed out that a big risk to the submarine program came not from the French or the Defence Department but from the government itself, demanding that the submarines contain significant Australian content. The decision not to buy off-the-shelf submarines but instead engage a 'strategic partner' to design and deliver them with significant Australian industry input had 'increased the risk of this acquisition'. It would also make them more expensive but, according to the ANAO, Defence had decided not to make an allowance for that when it priced the submarine tenders. This was a matter that would cause headaches for Defence later over the true costs of the French submarines.

The dispute over costing can be traced back to a document tabled during a Senate hearing that showed that the Defence Department had priced the future submarine program at $50 billion in 2015.[11] But this figure was not necessarily for the cost of the French boats, because a decision to go with Paris would not be taken until the following month. On the left side of this $50 billion figure was a tiny symbol resembling an arrowhead, pointing to the right; this symbol is used in accounting to signify a possibly larger number. What was not said but understood at the time was that Defence was talking about the purchase of Japanese Soryu-class submarines, to be built completely in Japan and delivered in the 'early 2040s'. It's important to remember that the Japanese submarines would require no new infrastructure in Australia and no Australian content targets.

Two years later, Rear Admiral Greg Sammut told the Senate that the acquisition cost estimate was $50 billion on a 'constant price basis'.[12] In other words, despite the symbol indicating a possible increase in price, there had been no change in the cost of the submarines. But, it is argued, if you take the original figure of $50 billion from 2015 and adjust it for inflation over the potential life of the program (something that is called 'out-turned'), the figure increases to around $80 billion, a number that caused negative headlines shouting in large print that the price of the subs had jumped from $50 billion to $80 billion. Defence experts and accountants have analysed and argued over these costings, but what can be said for sure is that the price of the submarines did increase the more they were asked to do. For example, in 2016 the government added a demand that the subs be 'regionally superior', yet there was no explanation of what that meant.[13] It was an open door to large increases in price.

Whether or not it was worth spending billions of dollars on twelve state-of-the art submarines partly built in Australia with French technology that Paris had agreed for the first time to share with a foreign country, was still being debated. But the confusion over costings only aided the campaign to axe the program. At the end of 2019, according to a *Sydney Morning Herald* report that appeared to be based on extensive briefings from the government, Morrison had begun laying the groundwork to end the French contract. According to the *Herald*, he told the French about his 'concerns'.[14] But as we shall see, these 'concerns' were a deceptive understatement for his true intentions.

Macron, unaware of the strong campaign to end the program from within Morrison's close circle of advisers, had apparently asked Morrison, 'Keep me informed.' It was a naive request from the French president. Maybe he had not been briefed about Morrison's history of deception and lying. By Morrison's own later admission, the French were not to be told what his government was planning. Macron would not be 'informed' until it was too late.

On 11 February 2020, Greg Moriarty and Angus Campbell wrote to the head of the RAN submarine agency, Vice Admiral Jonathan Mead, instructing him to launch what was called a defence capability enhancement review. There's nothing unusual about reviews being carried out in defence, but this one was different. The government was creating a paper trail—again in secret—of reasons to drop the French submarine program. The three-page letter, marked 'SECRET AUSTEO', a classification that restricts access to Australians, said Australia's strategic circumstances had deteriorated and warned that 'the rapid introduction of more advanced submarines, sensors and weapons will further complicate the subsurface threat environment over the coming decades'.[15] 'Submarines are fundamental to the nation's maritime security,' it said. 'They secure Australia's strategic advantage and underpin Australia's credibility and influence as a modern military power.' Moriarty and Campbell instructed Mead to report back on the 'faster than envisaged' military modernisation in the Indo-Pacific. The letter cited 'intensifying' major-power competition and the undermining of confidence in the 'rules-based order'. The review was 'afforded the highest priority' and Mead was told he was to 'advise us as to the resources you require'. It wasn't exactly a blank cheque for nuclear submarines, but only a fool would not have understood what was required.

Mead reported back that nuclear submarines were an option, but only if they involved the United Kingdom or the United States. By not even considering France as a possible alternative to provide the submarines, Morrison was playing directly to his pro-US base. Always the political opportunist, he had his eye firmly fixed on the next federal election, which would be held at the latest in early 2022. He was working on a plan to wedge Labor. Who better to help him than John Howard's former national security adviser and darling of the Washington Republican Party Andrew Shearer, now head of the ONI? Shearer, whose appointment to lead the ONI had been opposed by Labor because he was politically partisan, had other credentials that ideally suited him for the job: he had been virulently opposed to the French submarine program even before it had started. It did not matter that Naval Group head Pierre-Eric Pommellet had reached agreement with the government enshrining 60 per cent local content in the submarine contract. It had all been a waste of time.

By March 2020, Naval Group Australia head John Davis was writing to his fellow board directors warning of the Australian Government's 'adverse, hard-line commercial behaviour'.[16] By the end of the month the French would have even greater concerns: Morrison had appointed Peter Dutton, a blunt enforcer, as his defence minister—but Dutton's job was to attack, not defend. Morrison had outsourced to a political headkicker the job of creating a Chinese 'Red Scare' and terrifying the population. He would need a compliant media to manufacture the level of consent that was required to carry out his grand plans, and all the help he could get from the right-wing think tanks now scattered across the nation.

For a politician like Morrison, obsessed with secrecy and the use of underhand tactics, COVID-19 was a blessing. In early 2020, with the pandemic sweeping the world, he used Australia's *Biosecurity Act* to seal the nation's borders, preventing not just overseas arrivals from landing in Australia, but Australian citizens from leaving the country without what the government determined was a valid reason. Whether or not it was effective in reducing the impact of the virus is still contentious, but isolating Australia had a profound effect on business, and on the submarine project.

Though many of the discussions about the intricate design changes needed to alter the submarine from nuclear-powered to a conventional system were being carried out electronically, it was also important at times to have person-to-person contact, particularly when dealing with the details of such a complex production. The perils of distance were problematic for both Naval Group and the Australian Department of Defence, but it was the French who suffered most. Their communications with the Australian Government had already not been handled well. The switch from the urbane Turnbull to the 'daggy dad' persona of Morrison, plus changes in the senior ranks at the Élysée, posed grave dangers for the French. They should have been more nurturing of the new government. Instead, they found themselves increasingly friendless in Canberra.

Morrison, for his part, began secretly exerting greater and greater control of his government and its institutions. He had himself covertly appointed to five ministerial positions without the knowledge of the public or his own government. He even kept his coterie of trusted lieutenants in the dark as he took on more and more power.

Ewen Levick, a Lowy Institute contributor to the *Australian Defence Magazine*, later reported that by March 2020, planning to allow Australia access to US nuclear propulsion secrets was underway.[17] What's at issue here isn't whether nuclear propulsion should have been considered. Turnbull himself is not opposed, and there is a logic to Australia using nuclear submarines. The issue is that the proposal should have been openly discussed and put out to tender. The French might not have been happy, but they had a proven nuclear-powered submarine and it would have been relatively easy to switch propulsion systems. After all, the original French design of the Barracuda boat was nuclear. The evidence that Australia was talking to the Americans about nuclear power at the beginning of 2020 and keeping its plans secret from the French reinforces the evidence that welding Australia's military to the United States was always the aim. The submarines became merely a vehicle with which to do that.

According to a Defence Department document I obtained via FOI, in May 2020 Morrison ordered the chief of navy, Vice Admiral Michael Noonan, to set up a 'nuclear submarine feasibility study taskforce'.[18] According to my heavily redacted copy of the document, information would only be shared on a need-to-know basis. What Noonan said he wanted was an open debate to assess information that both supported and contested the capability options presented. He appointed Commodore Timothy Brown to head the task force, which would examine the strategic industrial and international relations implications of nuclear-powered submarines. Brown was an experienced defence veteran who had been commander of a Collins-class submarine and served as the fleet submarine operations officer, responsible for all submarine operations, plans, communications and intelligence support.

Under the headline 'Deliverables and Tasks' the task force was ordered to answer how Australia could obtain access to the relevant technology. From whom could it be obtained, how and when?

The document obtained via FOI contains many redactions authorised on the grounds that, if disclosed, the information might damage Australia's security or international relations. Other parts of the document contain additional redactions under section 47(F) of the *FOI Act* (1982), which deals with the release of 'unreasonable personal information'. It is a strange combination. The material is doubly redacted: on the grounds of national security and also on the basis that names should not be disclosed for confidentiality reasons. Revealing the names would merely disclose whom Defence had been talking to. If the department had been openly canvassing a wide range of nuclear possibilities, there would be little to hide.

The document contains questions that any number of experts could answer:

- Can we obtain access to the [nuclear] technology?
- Who could it be obtained from, and when?
- What would be a good option for implementation)?
- How can Australia operate and sustain [a] nuclear capability?
- [What are] the state and federal legal and policy implications?

These questions raise many questions themselves. Who were the people whose names were hidden because of personal and national security issues? Which countries did they come from? Did they represent any submarine builders?

What we do know is that no one from France or the French nuclear submarine manufacturers was involved. They'd been shut out already.

Was there any conflict of interest for those involved in the nuclear selection process? There was no competitive tendering process, no transparency or accountability, and anyone being asked secretly to build a case for nuclear submarines not involving the French would know what the government was thinking. Whomever the government dealt with in the future would be given all the cards in any negotiations involving nuclear-powered subs. Australia was simply giving away any leverage it might have on price or on accessibility of nuclear technology.

But for Morrison, that did not seem to matter. He was delighted when the task force reported that the nuclear option was feasible but 'only possible with the help of the United States, Britain, or both' because Australia didn't have a civil nuclear industry to provide support and maintenance for the boats.[19]

The secret feasibility study produced more ammunition for the plan to dump the French and switch to the United States. For those in the know, it was certainly a good time to buy shares in US nuclear submarine manufacturers. There is nothing to suggest that any of the former US Navy top brass in the Australian Defence Department had any prior knowledge of Morrison's nuclear plans, but as will become apparent, even when they did, the government was blind to conflict of interest.

Kirkland Donald, the four-star US Navy chief appointed in 2017 to advise on Australia's submarine program, was already on the board of Huntington Ingalls, whose company owned Newport News Shipbuilding (named after a town, not a newspaper), the major nuclear submarine manufacturer in the United States. He was also chair of Centrus Energy, the leading provider of nuclear fuel for US nuclear weapons and naval reactors. It says much about the Morrison government's lack of concern about protecting the national interest, especially when the United States was involved, that Donald remained a government adviser long after the preliminary decision had been taken to buy the US submarines made by his company. Under pressure, he finally resigned in April 2022—a full six months after the AUKUS announcement—citing a possible 'conflict of interest'.[20]

By the middle of 2020, a glimpse of the hidden true intentions of the Morrison government had slowly hoved into view. China might have been building its military for nearly a decade, but suddenly for Morrison there was a new imperative. He made the obvious point that the strategic balance to Australia's north had changed, and announced what he called a Defence Strategic Update that recommended an emphasis on pre-emptive measures to prevent a hostile nation threatening Australia's soil. There would be more money for defence—which had already been set aside by Turnbull—and new missiles that could reach further to protect Australia's interests.[21]

Hidden in the text was a crucial phrase that reveals what Morrison had been planning all along: Defence would continue to strengthen its engagement with Australia's international partners in support of shared regional security interests, and would continue deepening 'our alliance with the United States'. That in itself was hardly a surprising statement, but what was missing was truly sensational, and no one picked it up and confronted Morrison with the lie he was spinning to the Australian public: France was not mentioned even once in the 69-page Strategic Update. Given that Australia was about to buy twelve submarines from the French, who had vast economic and political interests and a large military presence in both the Pacific and Indian oceans, France's omission revealed the true intentions of the Morrison government. Morrison could see no role for France in Australia's strategic future, no matter how good its submarines might turn out to be.

The day after the launch of the Strategic Update, Defence Minister Linda Reynolds, Secretary of Defence Greg Moriarty and Angus Campbell made their way to ASPI. Situated in the Canberra suburb of Barton, which is known as Lobby Central for its proliferation of organisations paid to influence government policy, ASPI is not far from Crosby Textor's Australian headquarters. Its utilitarian concrete and glass facade is as bland as what goes on inside is not. The organisation is one of the most influential think tanks in Australia. It might pride itself on being independent, but it would be difficult for it not to be influenced by those who fund it: the Defence Department and US arms manufacturers.

The troika at the heart of Morrison's nuclear gamble knew they would be on home turf as they began selling their message to the gathered crowd about an increased threat from new weapons and technologies, including hypersonic glide and long-range missiles, autonomous systems, space capabilities, artificial intelligence and cyber items. They warned that those weapons potentially aimed at Australia had increased range, speed, precision and lethality. Countries in the Indo-Pacific (China) were modernising their militaries, they said, and increasing their preparedness for conflict.

Not once did anyone ask what role France might play in the defence of Australia, or indeed what role Australia might play in the defence of French territory. It would have been a difficult question for them to answer, because Reynolds, Moriarty and Campbell were part of the group appointed by Morrison to the secret mission that would sink the French. The carefully crafted process of vilifying and excluding the French submarines was a brilliant example of manufacturing fear and massaging the media message. Morrison would sail on unchallenged as journalists followed in tow, awed by the threat of attack or even invasion. The drums of war were beating softly, but would soon become much louder.

By the end of 2020 Morrison had begun concentrating power even more into his own hands. He abolished the Naval Shipbuilding Advisory Board, which had been overseeing the submarine deal, and promoted its chairman, Donald Winter, to be his special adviser in PM&C. Winter was the kind of adviser Morrison wanted: he had not been in favour of building the submarines in Adelaide, and he supported the nuclear option. It was now, around October 2020, that the first approaches were made to the Trump administration for Australia to buy nuclear-powered submarines.

Morrison established a new Submarine Advisory Committee headed by former US naval secretary William Hilarides, whose security clearance still allowed him access to some of the US military's most tightly held secrets. Hilarides could even view SCI (sensitive compartmented information) items, which includes material so sensitive it holds a special classification above top secret. The links between the Morrison government and the United States were becoming stronger by the day, with Washington heavily represented at the highest levels of decision-making. US senior military officials were liberally sprinkled across the highest echelons of the administration.

Though the British were not so obviously present, Morrison did have a direct line to the United Kingdom through former prime minister Tony Abbott. A strong supporter of Australia opting for nuclear-powered submarines, UK prime minister Boris Johnson had decided a few months earlier to appoint Abbott as a UK trade adviser. Abbott quickly reaped the benefit of that position when the Morrison government gave him special clearance to travel overseas during COVID. The following month, September 2020, Abbott signed the Australian Government register as an agent of foreign influence in Australia, which meant he was legally free to lobby on behalf of the UK Government.[22]

In the final weeks of 2020, Morrison set up a special Cabinet subcommittee. Its members included Foreign Affairs Minister Marise Payne, Home Affairs Minister Peter Dutton, Defence Industry Minister Linda Reynolds and three other ministers. Morrison was the chair. Called the Naval

Shipbuilding Enterprise Governance Committee, its supposed role was to 'ensure the naval shipbuilding enterprise and each component of it is on track to deliver against Commonwealth agreed outcomes'.[23]

Though there were problems with other aspects of Australia's shipbuilding industry—especially its $45 billion Hunter-class frigates, which were over budget and behind schedule—the real focus of the committee was the French submarine deal. Morrison told the Department of Defence he was 'concerned' about the Attack class,[24] the new designation for the French Barracuda submarine.

Not surprisingly, the establishment of yet another investigatory committee greatly concerned the French. Reynolds has been quoted as saying that earlier in 2020 she had 'started to discuss with the PM "Is there an alternative if this falls over?"'[25] But if she was concerned that the biggest defence acquisition in the nation's history, and one of huge strategic importance, was going to fail, as defence minister why didn't she warn the French? The government clearly had other plans.

7

That Sinking Feeling

The French were vulnerable on a number of fronts in an Australian system that treated defence acquisitions as a political blood sport. Long before Scott Morrison took over as prime minister, Naval Group had been given a glimpse of what to expect.

Down by the docks at the Osborne shipyard, 20 kilometres north-west of Adelaide, the engineers and naval architects who had built the Collins-class submarines were rightly proud of their work. After a rocky start, they had managed to produce an outstanding submarine with the Swedish Kockums company and were looking forward to doing it again with the French. With the local car industry long gone, the Osborne shipyard was the biggest engineering employer in the state. It provided thousands of jobs and contributed substantially to the local economy.

Yet Osborne would also become a stark reminder of the mistake governments make when they mix national security and defence with political benefit. The politics of where to build Australia's submarines had already claimed one scalp when Malcolm Turnbull removed Tony Abbott, who had made the fatal error of suggesting Australia's future submarines might be fully built in Japan. Turnbull had resolutely resolved that the boats would be built in Adelaide, but even that sound political stance was not without its problems. With the Collins-class maintenance work slowing and ship orders running out, Adelaide faced what defence experts call the Valley of Death: a prolonged period when manufacturing slows and the skilled labour force moves out. Re-establishing the capabilities required in the highly technical business of weapons platform building is no easy task. It's better not to let the workers go in the first place.

Turnbull had staked a large amount of political capital on making Adelaide great again. It was just three weeks after his call to France to tell the then president that DCNS, which later became Naval Group, had won the contract for twelve submarines that Turnbull, along with Defence Minister Marise Payne and Minister for Defence Industry Christopher Pyne, arrived at Osborne to celebrate the good news about investment and employment.

Turnbull described his plan as the greatest recapitalisation of the RAN since World War II. It wasn't an overstatement. The government was about to splash out $89 billion on new naval ships and submarines—a national endeavour aimed at building and sustaining Australia's naval capabilities, creating economic growth through Australian industry participation, and securing jobs that would endure for decades to come. Osborne would get a large slice of the $1.6 billion the government had set aside to refurbish Australia's shipyards, part of the long-awaited Naval Shipbuilding Plan.

National industrial icons were sprinkled about to add colour to the announcement. It was the most significant national building project ever undertaken in Australia, Turnbull told the gathered media, larger and more complex than the Snowy Mountains Hydro Electric Scheme, which began construction in 1949. Strangely included was the National Broadband Network, which the Liberal Party had played a major part in nobbling. What also went unmentioned was that both those enterprises were Labor initiatives, though with the Snowy scheme the Liberals had supported the idea, aiming to solve the seemingly intractable problem of creating a long-lasting industrial base in Australia. Turnbull was walking down a nationalist, independent road—a dangerous route in a government so heavily weighted with views that ran contrary to his belief in a mixed economy where the state could play a significant role.

The project would not only produce the twelve French submarines: there would be nine frigates, twelve offshore patrol vessels and nineteen Pacific patrol boats. Standing on the dockside flanked by Payne and Pyne, Turnbull described the shipbuilding plan as a truly great national enterprise that would bring with it an enormous employment boost. It was, he said, 'unashamedly nationalistic'.[1]

Pressed on what percentage of the submarine build would be Australian and what percentage was mandated for the Adelaide build in the contract with the French, Turnbull explained that every dollar that was spent on defence procurement 'as far as possible' should be spent in Australia.[2] It was a neat sidestep to the question, but unfortunately for Turnbull it wouldn't go away. Pyne tried to reassure the locals, saying, 'We will not be bringing foreign workers in to build the ships or submarines.' He said a 'minuscule' number of trainers would be imported to 'transfer their intellectual property to our workforce' as part of the submarine project.

On the other side of the world in Paris, Naval Group CEO Hervé Guillou clearly had not been paying attention as President Emmanuel Macron staked out a new strategic frontier in Australia. Guillou made an astonishing faux pas for an executive so gifted at smoothing the passage of multibillion-euro French armament sales to the world. During a wide-ranging interview with Defense News, an authoritative online media organisation, Guillou boasted that DCNS (as it was then) had already celebrated that there would be thousands of extra jobs in France from the submarine contract. Though he pointed out it was too early to say exactly how many jobs, he estimated 4000.[3]

In the reporting of his comments the following day, the fact that it was only an estimate and it was too early to be precise was missing. The blunt news that while France would benefit from 4000 extra jobs, Australia would only get 2900 grabbed the headlines. It made no difference that Guillou had pointed out the deal with France was more than a contract to build boats but would help Australia create a sovereign naval capability, or that the deal that had been reached was an international partnering agreement that would see the French share their technical secrets, including the closely guarded details of the stealth capabilities of the submarines. He had declared perhaps too openly and honestly that there would be benefits for the French, too. Its nuclear-armed attack submarine was coming to the end of production, and the start-up phase for the Australian submarine would allow Naval Group and its subcontractors to avoid the Valley of Death that would otherwise have been beckoning for the French submarine builders, as it was for Adelaide. The work would involve technology transfer from France to Australia and 'adapting the infrastructure in Adelaide and the supply chain'.[4]

The submarines had a sophisticated combat information system that identified targets and fired its missiles. Sharing this information would need to be compatible with the International Traffic in Arms Regulations. What Guillou was signalling was the need to work with the US Lockheed Martin company to provide French and US classified material to Australia. When the details were worked through, the deal promised to make Australia a self-sufficient conventional submarine manufacturer, he said. Yet all the benefits he outlined were either ignored or drowned out by the outpouring of national anger in Australia. It was as though the French had pulled off a victory on the rugby field with a simple tally of who had 'won' the most jobs.

Even though there would be huge employment opportunities for skilled workers, Turnbull was open to criticism that he had oversold the prospect of jobs growth in a state where the rate of unemployment was double the national average. Try as he might to turn the conversation back to the significant partnership with France, which would benefit Australian defence, industry and the economy, the damage had been done. The ink was barely dry on the agreement and already those who could see the benefits of what would flow from the submarine deal with the French were fighting a rear-guard action.

In the prime minister's office in Parliament House, the phones were ringing like an off-key military medley. Politicians and industry groups were angry at what they saw as the export of Australian jobs. Over at the Naval Group offices, a senior official in the company received a call from PM&C. Those privy to the conversation said they could hear the 'anger' in the voices in the corridor outside.[5] The Naval Group executive board members were dumbfounded. The agreement with the Australian Government prevented them from commenting on what they saw as an unreasonable attack on the program, which they argued would have a lasting long-term benefit for jobs not only in Adelaide but throughout Australia.

Many at Naval Group were angry at Guillou for an insensitive and unnecessary boast. His comments about jobs provided ammunition for those who had opposed the French deal in the first place, such as Senator Rex Patrick. As a senator from South Australia, he also had a strong vested interest in any job creation program for his state, no matter that he had fervently opposed the French submarine deal and its much-lauded propulsion system.

Patrick not only wanted the subs built in Adelaide, he wanted the company that built them to be solely Australian-owned and -controlled. He pointed to the success of the Australian Submarine Corporation (ASC), which had originally been part-owned by outside interests but in 2000 was acquired 100 per cent by the government. In 2016 ASC was split up again, leaving it without a shipbuilding capacity. Yet Naval Group recognised ASC's expertise and had been keen to work with the company in partnership to build the new French submarines. Naval Group had made an offer in its original pitch to government, and reaffirmed wanting to work with ASC several months after winning the contract. But a directive from the government ruled out any such partnership. Instead, Naval Group was left dealing with the federal-government-owned Australian Naval Infrastructure (ANI), a company that found itself caught in a trap between its owner and a future customer.

It was ANI that had provided Naval Group with a quote for the cost of using the Osborne shipyard to build the submarines. But since ANI was owned by the government, if the government did not agree with the costing, it could reject the offer being made to Naval Group. And that's exactly what happened, not once but twice: first in August 2018 and again in June 2020. Each time, ANI and Naval Group went back to the drawing board to reduce costs. One way around the problem, to reduce the costs even further, was to arrange for Naval Group to share common manufacturing systems such as steel cutting, which was being used at Osborne for servicing the Collins-class submarines and building Australia's next generation of frigates. But even that wasn't enough.

The best way to slash the budget involved not just sharing facilities but taking them over, including land occupied by ASC where the company maintained the Collins-class submarines. As Gillis puts it, 'They wanted productivity and efficiencies, all those sorts of things. But it just didn't gel.

The whole design of the shipyard had to change because the government refused to agree to move the Australian Submarine Corporation's sustainment arm to Western Australia.'[6]

It's important to stop here and think about what was happening in the shipyard at Osborne. With an election coming, the government didn't want to move ASC, but at the same time it expected Naval Group to produce the high-quality work required for building extremely complex submarines. 'When we did assessments of what it was going to cost for the shipyard, the cost blew out by nearly a billion dollars,' said Gillis. 'The Commonwealth wanted the most advanced technology. They wanted a better shipyard than even the French had in France.'[7]

The Australian Government had Naval Group over a barrel. When the government asked why the costs had blown out from $1.6 billion to $2.47 billion for use of the shipyard, Naval Group pointed out that the original costing had been based on the intention of the government to move ASC out by 2024. Since the government had not announced that decision and there was no guarantee it would, Naval Group had to consider outsourcing work and even sending some of the production to France, which posed other problems on the job creation front.

In navigating Australia's treacherous political waters, Naval Group was clearly ill-equipped to meet the challenge. It naively clung to the notion outlined in the strategic plan that saw Australia and France operating as a government-to-government partnership. Naval Group internal correspondence stated that it was anxious to move its relationship with Australia from the 'current commercial state' to a 'strategic partnership' where there would be greater joint decision-making.[8]

There was a lack of grand vision from many on the Australian side, dominated by the idea of job creation schemes—or getting the biggest bang for your buck. Holding Defence to account for spending blowouts is one thing, but muddling weapons acquisitions with industry policy is a recipe for disaster. It's even worse when mixed with a form of pork-barrelling where the question isn't so much focused on how much the military is spending but on how much the local population (in this case, South Australia) will receive as a by-product of the spending of public money.

Back in Paris at the headquarters of Naval Group, a nondescript tower block not far from the River Seine, the head of the organisation, Pierre-Eric Pommellet, was becoming increasingly agitated. He had taken over as head in March 2020 and already, in an attempt to cool tempers and reset the relationship with Australia, a number of senior staff had been shown the door, most notably Jean-Michel Billig.

Almost a parody of the abrupt and haughty French executive, Billig's manner caused one observer to say, 'There wasn't a tear shed when he left.'[9] An ex-diplomat described Billig as a scapegoat: 'He was not a friendly type of guy you would invite to a barbecue, but [he was] a good technician.' Billig, chair of the executive board of Naval Group Australia, had a particularly abrasive relationship with the head of the Australian submarine task force, Greg Sammut, the likeable ex-submariner who at times unsurprisingly struggled to deal with the complexity of demands from the Australian Government. A person close to the negotiations told me Billig had not helped his Australian counterpart and had repeatedly tried to undermine him.

But Naval Group pointed out that it wasn't the only party at fault. The SPA signed in 2019, the cornerstone of the relationship designed to produce the complete integration of Australian and French industry to build the submarines, was showing signs of falling apart. Naval Group used particularly direct language to tell the Defence Department secretary, Greg Moriarty, that it believed there was 'little sense of partnership' in the submarine program.[10] There were few signs that the Australian Government and the Defence Department were at all interested in what were supposed to be 'strategic ambitions'.[11] They were not being 'practiced' in the 'delivery or execution' of the program, Moriarty was told. The relationship between Naval Group and the Department of Defence was under such strain that one Naval Group executive told Moriarty if it were left on its current trajectory there was the potential for cost escalations, schedule delays, negative outcomes for Australian industry and, in the worst case, '[a] halt [to] the submarine program'.

In response to these dire warnings of a potential breakdown in the entire submarine deal, Morrison took an aggressive stand that astounded both those in Naval Group and those in the Defence Department who had been working for years to build what they believed would be the best submarine possible. Sometime between December 2020 and January 2021, he ordered the Australian Government to stop paying Naval Group for its work.[12]

The impact of Morrison's directive was immediate. Australian workers who had been scheduled to travel to France for training were reduced to video calls to learn new skills, and the staff budget was slashed. With Naval Group Australia running out of money, it asked the French company for help. Pommellet agreed to bail it out but insisted this was a short-term measure.

There was little doubt in the Naval Group team that if the submarine timetable was to be put back on track, Pommellet would have to travel to Australia. He needed to speak to the prime minister face to face. As he weighed up what to do next, a crucial meeting on the other side of the world helped him make up his mind.

In early 2021 Pommellet received an important email from the Australian Naval Group senior executive team. It had held a meeting, he was told, over a 'very productive, if confronting few days'. Naval Group Australia was getting close to an operating model that could most effectively deliver 'the [difficult] customer's needs', Pommellet was told. But there were also dire warnings. On the issue of local Australian content, Naval Group warned that the Australian Government's patience to 'take our word on promises is running out'. The government appeared obsessed with forcing a minimum of 60 per cent Australian content into the contract, even though that had not been included in the original document.

This was a call from the frontline trenches to the general back at headquarters. The relationship with the Australian Government had all but broken down. Pointing out that Morrison was intimately involved in the program, the email said that Pommellet needed to be careful with any comments because 'we have to try to avoid any public knee jerking by him'. The team were particularly aware how prickly the prime minister could be, but had finally got a handle on his style.

Morrison was playing tough with Naval Group, but what the executive team from the French company didn't know was that there were other plans afoot. Morrison was spoiling for a fight. The French had a strong argument that local Australian companies lacked the expertise to build the submarines. Australian firms also had either low-level or non-existent security clearances. For Naval Group it appeared that the Australians were not concerned if low-quality material was used in the submarines. Security considerations were waved aside. Many pointed to the capability of engineers and Australian companies who had performed way above expectations in building the Collins-class submarines, but the French submarine, with its stealth capabilities and highly classified propulsion technology, was in a different class.

For Pommellet the vision of the strategic partnership meant lifting Australian industry up and improving the quality of its production, not dragging down the quality of the submarine to appease the government. There was another consideration: Naval Group would be held accountable for any failure in the reliability of the boat. Australian industry involvement could not be included to the overall detriment of the program.

Pommellet, a tough arms dealer not known for his sentimentality, was shocked at the way the Australian Government was interpreting the SPA, which was supposed to maximise Australian industry input without increasing costs or causing lengthy delays. He told people close to him that when discussing the agreement with Sammut, who was leading the Australian submarine team, and others in the government, they completely changed the sense of the SPA to introduce what he called a 'hard' performance base, which set a fixed percentage of Australian industry involvement in advance. Pommellet said Sammut and others in the Australian Defence Department should instead have recognised that there would be challenges that France and Australia would manage together. An exasperated Pommellet told colleagues, 'The interest of Australia in the first years of the program is to grab and take the maximum from Europe to create the competencies for producing and sustaining the submarine.' There was little sense of partnership.

To understand how Australia could have got itself into such a pickle and such confrontation with a nation with which it had decided to form a strategic partnership, it's necessary to focus on the core of the problem: the federal government's demand for Australian industry involvement. The contract to build the submarines included the necessity to maximise Australian content but did not contain a fixed percentage. Since the submarines were mainly going to be built in Australia, that seemed a straightforward proposition. But Naval Group ran into trouble when it suggested there were problems with Australian industry being able to provide cyber and security capabilities that would prevent them from tendering for work on the French submarine. It was estimated that only 2 per cent of Australia's industries qualified for this high-level requirement. Later figures showed the situation to be even worse. Of 2333 Australian companies that had registered to work on the submarine, only 578 (24 per cent) were assessed as ready by Naval Group; only 344 of the 578 had experience in naval defence work—only 138 (6 per cent) of suppliers currently held the appropriate accreditation, and only fifteen (1 per cent) held the necessary cybersecurity accreditation.[13] 'We couldn't even send out specifications for them to quote on, because they didn't have their security clearances,' Gillis said.[14]

Naval Group Australia had first raised its concerns in relation to Australian industry readiness with the minister for defence industry and the two Department of Defence deputy secretaries in December 2019. Despite a commitment for Defence to come forward with options to address these issues, no obvious action had been taken by the department or the government.

The French pointed out that they were trusting Australia with high-quality intellectual property for their most closely guarded military secrets. It was to be expected that they would be cautious. With the argument that the submarines were already over price, in 2021 Linda Reynolds—directed by Morrison, who was running the program—demanded that the French include 60 per cent local Australian content.[15] Since the submarines were still in the 'design phase', the French argued it was impossible to know exactly which Australian industries would be capable of producing the necessary hardware and technology, and whether they would have sufficient security qualifications.

Yet the French had made serious errors of judgement. In 2019 local businesses had been led to believe they could take part in a procurement program for large items of hardware. Instead, over the following months the procurement failed to eventuate. It had simply been wishful thinking that the design phase of the boat would be far enough advanced for tenders to be placed. As one insider put it, 'The maturity of the design and availability of sufficiently mature technical specifications was not at a level required for early industry engagement.'[16] Having raised Australian industry expectations, the inability to follow through led to significant political and industrial pressure for more Australian content earlier in the program. This pressure ultimately translated into the media narrative that Naval Group was not committed to Australian industry participation.

What worried the French was that Reynolds had suddenly demanded a guarantee that 60 per cent of the submarine work would be carried out in Australia, and Naval Group was being set up to fail if it did not reach it. There would be huge financial penalties and potentially a loss of profitability.

It was in this heated environment about Australian content that Reynolds ramped up the rhetoric, pointing to a comment that had been made when the French first pitched for the submarine business. She said the government had been swayed to go with France because they had promised that much more than 60 per cent of the project would be built by Australian companies. The figure had been as high as 90 per cent, she insisted.

There was nothing in writing, but importantly, even a cursory examination of the 90 per cent 'promise' made by Sean Costello when he headed Naval Group Australia in 2016 exposes the true intent of what was said.[17] It was the 'build' that the 90 per cent referred to—putting the pieces of the submarine together. And 90 per cent of what? It certainly did not include the Lockheed Martin weapons system with its highly secret technology, which is nearly a third of the submarine's total cost.

Naval Group's case that it had never given an undertaking involving fixed percentages of Australian content might have been helped if its Australian arm's chief executive, John Davis, hadn't told the *Australian* that the capability of Australian suppliers was presenting so many unforeseen challenges and the company was unsure whether the value of contracts to local firms would even reach 50 per cent. 'We didn't know the Australian market before we joined the program,' Davis said. 'Now we have a much deeper insight.'[18] A late admission by the French, and clearly a problem that needed to be fixed.

In late December 2020, Gillis received an unexpected call from Pommellet. Gillis had been in charge of Defence acquisitions and with Turnbull had worked assiduously to get the French submarine ready for production. By the middle of 2018 it had looked as though the biggest problems had been solved, and Gillis had decided to retire. But now Naval Group Australia asked him to return: they needed his help. Gillis says he was excited about being involved again in 'Australia's most complex and challenging program'.[19] But he took the job—sanctioned by the submarine team in the Defence Department—with 'some trepidation' because what he had heard and read about the program in the media was negative. His role went to the heart of the sensitivities of the SPA. This was more than just an agreement to build twelve diesel-electric-powered submarines: it involved the highest levels of government in a state-to-state relationship sanctioned by the president of the French Republic and the prime minister of the Commonwealth of Australia.

Gillis arrived at Naval Group Australia just as Macron demanded that the new French ambassador, Jean-Pierre Thébault, act with 'ambition' in expanding the relationship with Australia. But the ambassador was having trouble even getting access to Parliament House. Thébault wanted France to be treated like other close security partners of Australia—the so-called Five Eyes countries of the United States, New Zealand, the United Kingdom and Canada, whose ambassadors receive an 'open pass' that allows them to freely enter the parliament building. Repeatedly he wrote to the prime minister's office asking for a pass. He was told, 'No, only Five Eyes' have an open pass.[20]

Thébault, known to be a thoughtful and careful diplomat, is also renowned for his quiet determination. When he wrote to Morrison asking for a meeting, according to those with knowledge of the affair, he was told, 'The prime minister is not available.'[21] Next he tried Payne; he got a positive reply and then there was no response. He also tried to meet with Donald Winter, Morrison's US adviser on submarines, but again he was stonewalled.

Gillis must have felt like he'd walked through the looking glass. Given a slot on the Naval Group board, he tried to understand what was happening. 'I'm sitting in the middle of this going, "How? Why can't we defend ourselves?"' He believes he now understands: 'The minister was telling the department to tell us, "Don't make any announcement. We will sort it out."' He pointed the finger at Scott Morrison: 'The prime minister was saying, "Don't give any positive news out of this."'[22]

At Russell Hill, Gillis sat down with senior Defence officials in an attempt to thrash out a solution to the 60 per cent local content problem. They told him they had been instructed by the government to include the hard 60 per cent Australian content even though it wasn't in the original agreement. Gillis produced a whiteboard and, according to those present, proposed a solution that might solve the problem. The first boat would not meet the 60 per cent content. However, the following boats would contain more Australian content to make up for the 'lost' percentage in the first boats. The French agreed to include the 'averaged 60 per cent' Australian content in the agreement, provided Australian industry could provide the material.

Discussions of those proposals did not break the deadlock. Morrison was still refusing to pay Naval Group Australia for the work it had already done. On top of that, COVID-19 was running rife in the Adelaide shipyard offices where Naval Group was running its scaled-back training sessions by video to upskill Australian workers. The situation was becoming bleaker by the day for Naval Group and Australia's submarine project.

In the second week of February 2021, on a sunny but cold day in Paris, Pommellet took the long ride out to Charles de Gaulle Airport for the even longer trip to Australia. Once he arrived in Adelaide, he would have to spend two weeks isolating in a hotel. COVID had shut Australia's borders, and he had been lucky to get in. He would have to hope that he could reach the person who could make or break the submarine deal: Scott Morrison. The Adelaide Naval Group team had been hard at work trying to arrange an appointment. The plan developed by Gillis might smooth the relationship with Australia. Though 60 per cent Australian content had not been in the original contract, Pommellet was prepared to negotiate. Since Morrison had taken over complete control of the submarine deal, Pommellet was hopeful he would get a hearing, but Morrison was keeping his distance. On top of that, Defence Minister Reynolds was unavailable, in hospital with a heart condition. Even the temporary minister, Marise Payne, was unavailable.

After weeks of waiting and negotiation, Pommellet was relegated to a meeting with the defence industry minister, Melissa Price. Even the most optimistic member of Naval Group could sense that the signs of a rapprochement between it and the Australian Government were not good. As Pommellet emerged from the meeting he was noncommittal about whether he was close to finalising an agreement. Pursued through the underground car park at Canberra's Parliament House, he deflected questions from ABC defence reporter Andrew Greene. Pommellet tried to sound upbeat, saying he had had a very productive engagement with the government, but that wasn't how Price reported the meeting in a press release. She issued a terse statement pointing out that she had explained to Pommellet, drawing on what she described as her extensive credentials as a 'construction lawyer', the 'finer details of a contract matter'.[23] It was tough talking about a contract that did not exist, a statement designed to bolster the government's credentials as a job creator and to belittle her French visitor.

Pommellet kept his views of Price's legal capabilities to himself as he hopped into the back of a small white car. If he had looked to his right as he was driven out into the warm February afternoon, he might have glimpsed Defence headquarters at Russell Hill and a representation of an American eagle atop a 70-metre tower. Built with public donations, it honours the US soldiers who served in the Pacific during World War II and is emblematic of the ties that have bound the two nations together, perhaps too tightly, for seventy years.

What Pommellet could not have known is that, not far from the symbol of how strong the relationship is between Australia and the United States, work was well underway in the Defence Department to cement it even further. The senior leadership in the department had been ordered to carry out a feasibility study (see Chapter 6) to produce the evidence needed for a decision already well in the pipeline. For the past year the department had been secretly working on a nuclear submarine deal. Though the instruction had come from Reynolds, by now all major decisions regarding the submarines and Naval Group needed the authority of Morrison. He was now totally in charge, marshalling both his arguments and those supporters who would be by his side in the war of words to come. He had a formidable army behind him.

8

The Media and the Message

The Gothic Revival architecture of Sydney University, with its thick sandstone walls and high towers, is designed to portray a sense of academic freedom and strength. But the grandeur can be deceiving. Even the best universities can struggle to maintain their financial independence. They rely on fee-paying foreign students to top up the finances, and donations from former graduates who have done well and want to be remembered.

In 2005 the then prime minister, John Howard, who had gained a law degree at Sydney, joined the list, giving $25 million to help establish a new centre for US studies. It wasn't his personal money, though: it was a donation from the federal government. What is surprising, though, is where the idea of the centre was conceived.

In 2004, with the United States embroiled in the disastrous Iraq War, President George W Bush met with Howard in the Oval Office of the White House. The fiction of weapons of mass destruction that both Bush and Howard had pedalled as a reason for the war was finally unravelling. In Australia, public opinion, which had been heavily against the invasion even before it started in March 2003, was now questioning the US alliance itself. Howard was anxious, telling Bush that if the alliance were to survive, America's voice should be heard more clearly in Australian academic institutions. Howard had been caught relaying the fabricated stories cooked up in the White House to justify Australian troops fighting alongside Americans, and now he was suffering political damage as the war dragged on. He told Bush of his plans to fund an Australian institution that would correct what many in the Liberal Party believed was left-wing bias in the media.

Standing alongside Bush and Howard on that day, a long-term Republican diplomat, Dr Michael Green, took detailed notes of what was said.[1] Green had been appointed to the powerful US National Security Committee (NSC) in April 2001 as director of Asian affairs, with responsibility for Japan, Korea and Australia/New Zealand. Green knew all too well the pressure Howard and the US alliance were under. His job was to act as the go-between for Bush and the Australian prime minister. He didn't know it at the time, but he would play a significant role in moulding Australian public opinion in the years to come to correct that 'left-wing bias'.

Howard left the White House concerned that his political gamble on the war might destroy his prime ministership. But help would soon be at hand. In the following year, 2005, at News Corporation's headquarters in New York, chairman and chief executive Rupert Murdoch hosted a lunch. The guest list was a who's who of conservative Australian business leaders: Steven Lowy, the head of Westfield America; David Mackay, the Kellogg Company chief operating officer; Geoff Bible, former Philip Morris CEO; Qantas Airways chief executive Geoff Dixon; two of News Corp's New York–based Australian executives, Leon Hertz and Andrew Butcher; and Anthony Pratt, the head of Visy Industries America.

Pratt's right-wing credentials were faultless. In 2019, as he expanded his package-manufacturing company in the United States, he would publicly tell President Donald Trump that his election gave him 'incredible faith in investing in America'.[2] Trump responded by taking Pratt into his confidence, inviting him to parties at his Florida home and whispering secrets only a handful of people in the United States knew. Trump apparently boasted about the firepower of the nuclear submarines under his command, their stealth and the number of missiles they carry.[3] Though the US prosecutors who raided Trump's home in 2022 looking for highly classified documents illegally removed from the White House showed great interest in his conversations with Pratt, they took no further action.

Trump's rise to power was still a decade away as the Australian conservatives settled down for lunch with Murdoch to discuss how to counter what they saw as growing anti-Americanism in Australian society. The solution they came up with was audacious and simple: if they weren't happy with the output of Australia's universities, they should create their own department, called the United States Studies Centre (USSC). Pratt was the first to put his hand in his pocket. 'We'd like to put in a million dollars,' he said. News Corp agreed to contribute $2.5 million, and Howard later committed the $25 million of federal government money.[4]

When the USSC finally opened at Sydney University in 2007, it remained relatively unaffected by the ebb and flow of political discourse despite its right-wing backers. Howard would soon leave parliament, Lucy Turnbull was its patron, and her son-in-law worked there as research director.

With the removal of Malcolm Turnbull as prime minister a decade later, in 2018, and the arrival of Scott Morrison, the centre started coming under sustained attack, accused of being too left wing. The right was particularly unhappy with the centre's academic investigations of white supremacy and delving into failures of the capitalist system. At the height of the battle, conservative commentator Tom Switzer resigned from the centre and a poisonous atmosphere permeated the organisation. Many believed the USSC would not survive, but Morrison had other plans. The centre wouldn't perish, but its direction and leadership would change dramatically. As pressure mounted to replace the CEO, Professor Simon Jackman, waiting in the wings was a person who had been present in 2004 at the centre's conception in the Oval Office: Dr Michael Green.

Green, who had impeccable US Republican credentials, was also a close confidant and friend of Andrew Shearer. As soon as he took over as CEO of the USSC, the coverage of US–Australia relations on its website developed a level of unquestioning support for US foreign policy very much in keeping with Howard's self-proclaimed campaign to draw Australia closer to Washington. Green said the idea of the centre was to focus on 'shaping the foreign policy agenda'.[5] The question was: In whose interest was he shaping it?

Articles on the USSC website include 'America is still Australia's best bet'[6] and 'Australia's role in supporting democracies as a middle power'.[7] A republished report from the US-funded, Washington-based CSIS titled 'Full knowledge and concurrence: Key questions for US-Australia extended deterrence and escalation management consultations' gives advice on how the Australian Government should best manage 'public messaging' over China and deal with the possibility of a conventional war that goes nuclear.⁸ And then there is 'AUSMIN 2023 explained'—a not so snappy headline that reads like a PR handout from the Australia–US ministerial meetings of Australian Deputy Prime Minister and Defence Minister Richard Marles and Foreign Minister Penny Wong in Brisbane with their American counterparts, Secretary of Defense Lloyd J Austin III and Secretary of State Antony Blinken.⁹ In answering a *Quarterly Essay* by Hugh White that pointed to flaws in US strategic thinking in dealing with China, Green suggested, without producing any evidence, that Australia would have to face a binary choice of either US dominance in South-East Asia or a region dominated by China where Australia's free speech would be curtailed.¹⁰

Green's takeover of the USSC dovetailed neatly with the Morrison government strategy. In early 2021 the government was already softening up the public for an extraordinary shift in Australia's foreign policy, and it wasn't just the academic world that would be brought to heel. Journalists were to be secretly briefed under what are known as Chatham House rules, where information—including classified information from government security organisations—can be used but the source must not be directly named. It's a ruse oft-used by governments to influence reporters and, in doing so, attempt to shape the views of the population.

The Albanese government has used the same strategies. In February 2023 it held a roundtable with media managers and senior journalists in Parliament House under Chatham House rules. The Attorney-General's Department, which is responsible for ASIO, Australia's domestic spy agency, championed the meeting as a roundtable for 'discussion about press freedom issues in Australia and options for reform',¹¹ but the contacts for the meeting included the attorney-general's assistant secretary for the National Security Information Branch and a director of the Information Protection Section. Either Mike Pezzullo, the head of the Home Affairs Department, or a representative of his department was at this meeting.

Back in 2019 the Morrison government's actions were even more blatant. Pezzullo openly boasted to the Parliamentary Joint Committee on Intelligence and Security that he had two dozen 'trusted' journalists he spoke with. He said he talked to them only to confirm or deny the veracity of information they had already gathered, and did not leak material himself. Pezzullo would not name the journalists or explain how they reacted if he felt the material they wanted to publish or broadcast was against Australia's national security interests or might be embarrassing for the government.[12]

On 25 April 2021, as Australia began its detailed discussions with the United States about nuclear submarines, Pezzullo in an Anzac Day email to staff issued a stark warning of the inevitability of war. It is inconceivable that he would have been able to utter such ominous warnings without being sanctioned by Morrison, who was secretly taking over ministries, covertly developing a nuclear-powered submarine project, and manipulating the media with strategically placed leaks. In his email, entitled 'The longing for peace, the curse of war', Pezzullo said that free nations

> continue still to face [the] sorrowful challenge [of militaristic aggression and] tyranny's threat to freedom ... In a world of perpetual tension and dread, the drums of war beat—sometimes faintly and distantly, and at other times more loudly and ever closer. We must search always for the chance for peace amidst the curse of war, until we are faced with the only prudent, if sorrowful, course—to send off, yet again, our warriors to fight the nation's wars.[13]

Pezzullo noted the 'sorrow of Europeans after the horror of the First World War' but said their 'revulsion at the thought of another terrible bloodbath' had meant they 'did not heed the drums of war which beat through the 1930s—until too late they once again took up arms against Nazism and Fascism'. Pezzullo did not mention the economic war waged by the World War I victors against Germany through the Treaty of Versailles, which impoverished millions of Germans and aided Hitler's rise. He could also have spoken of China's concerns about having its sea-lane access to world trade strangled by the United States. But he didn't. His speech was designed not to encourage debate but to sow fear. Though Morrison kept his distance from Pezzullo's more bellicose warnings, there's little doubt he had sanctioned Pezzullo's words. Pezzullo would have lost his job if they weren't.

For Peter Dutton on that Anzac Day, the answer to any coming conflict was Washington's protection. 'China is militarising ports across our region. We need to deal with all of that, and that is exactly what we are now focused on,' he said. Channel 9 reported that Dutton paid tribute to the 'amazing effort' of the tens of thousands of Australians and other Allied service personnel who had fought in the Middle East over the past two decades. Without irony, it reported Dutton as saying the military action had saved Australia and other nations from terror attacks.[14]

The invasion of Iraq, in fact, had made the world a more dangerous place and led directly to terrorist attacks on Australian citizens.[15] Dutton would say later that year, in relation to whether Australia would send troops to fight alongside the United States in any war over Taiwan, 'It would be inconceivable that we wouldn't support the US in an action if the US chose to take that action.' He added that there may be 'circumstances where we wouldn't take up that option, (but) I can't conceive of those circumstances'.[16]

Why was Australia so keen to play itself into Washington's desire to contain the rise of China and fight a war over Taiwan as a pretext for protecting democracy? There are plenty of examples where the United States has supported authoritarian regimes and interfered to topple democratically elected governments. Democracy is not the issue, nor human rights: this is a battle being waged by the United States to prevent not just the military rise of China but its economic advance, too. For Australia it is a similar proposition. Australia supports the suppression of China's rise not because Beijing is undemocratic, or even authoritarian, but because Australia benefits from the economic advantages that flow to it as a sub-imperial power of the United States. Aided by a compliant media, the Morrison government was readying the Australian people to support the United States in a strategic war over Taiwan.

Pezzullo, Dutton and Morrison continued carefully laying the groundwork, playing to what the late Allan Gyngell, senior adviser to Prime Minister Paul Keating, described as Australia's fear of abandonment.[17] Few media outlets pushed back against the campaign. It was left to the minnows of the media to challenge the government. The most notable independent journalism came from online outlets. *Crikey*—which had shown its mettle by staring down Fox Corporation CEO Lachlan Murdoch in a defamation case—investigated the financial beneficiaries of AUKUS; *Pearls and Irritations*, established by a former head of PM&C, John Menadue, and Michael West Media, produced fact-based analysis and commentary. All were outraged at the secrecy and duplicity that surrounded AUKUS.

The nation's national broadcaster, the ABC, seldom veered from the safety of the Labor–Liberal embrace of AUKUS and the views of Australian Government and US-funded think tanks.

The *Australian* newspaper amplified the drumbeat of war, with the late senator Jim Molan—a former major general—writing an op-ed on Australia's preparedness for a war that he said was 'likely'. It wouldn't start as a direct conflict between Australia and China, but would more likely be a war that Australia could find itself fighting on behalf of its most powerful ally, Molan wrote. 'Many ordinary Australians, not just those who have personally experienced global conflict, are awakening to the sombre reality that war is not just possible in our region, but likely.'[18]

The *Sydney Morning Herald* and the *Age* reported details of a confidential briefing of special forces soldiers in which one of the nation's top military commanders told his troops that Beijing was already engaged in 'grey zone' warfare against Australia and they must plan for the high likelihood this would spill over into actual conflict in the future.[19]

Nobody was listening to former Labor prime minister Kevin Rudd, an acclaimed China expert and linguist, who warned that the escalating rhetoric 'serves zero national security purpose' and risked inflaming tensions with Beijing.[20] What Rudd didn't know then was that the rhetoric might not have served national security interests, but it certainly helped Morrison's grand plan. He was exploiting a theory first developed in the 1970s by two American academics that said that while the media might not be able to tell people what to think, it can direct them what to think about.[21] With the threat of the old red and yellow peril once again re-established in the Australian public's mind, Morrison would produce the saviour: AUKUS.

As the government beat the drums of war in Australia, Shearer took his trip to Washington to talk to senior US government figures (see Chapter 5). The official story is that he was on other business. Having been briefed on the possibility of Australia dumping the French and switching to nuclear submarines, Shearer, it was reported, asked Morrison if he should raise the issue with Biden's national security adviser, Jake Sullivan. It is implausible that the head of Australia's ONI should almost as an afterthought drop in to Washington to mention the possibility of the United States sharing its nuclear technology secrets with Australia. Yet that is the way the *Sydney Morning Herald*'s international editor, Peter Hartcher, reported the meeting.[22] What seems more likely is that this was Shearer making the running and pushing his agenda to drop the French and switch to the Americans.

Hartcher's report provided intriguing details of the meeting but also had the whiff of news management by the government. Incredibly, he wrote that to get to the United States, Shearer had managed to 'sidestep the Russian roulette' of Australia's vaccine rollout with the help of doctors at the Department of Foreign Affairs and Trade. As if the prime minister's senior security adviser would have had trouble leaving Australia on such a vital mission!

Hartcher described Shearer as a 'softly spoken Australian spy'. Though Shearer is undoubtedly intelligent and affable, this endearing description belies the fact that he is perceived by many to be a right-wing ideologue, obsessively pro-American and anti-Chinese. What is not in dispute, as Hartcher reported, is that when Shearer walked into the West Wing of the White House, his American interlocutors knew only that he wanted to discuss a matter of 'the utmost sensitivity'.

In Sullivan's chandeliered office, Shearer met with his close friend Kurt Campbell, a senior member of Sullivan's team and Biden's Indo-Pacific coordinator. Shearer explained what Australia wanted. 'As China's capability advances, we need to have submarines capable of meeting it. We need to be able to operate without the risk of easy detection by the Chinese,' he said, according to the participants. Feeding their own strategic rhetoric back to them, Shearer told the Americans that the security circumstances (in the Indo-Pacific) had changed dramatically. It wasn't just submarines he wanted, though.

A closer investigation would have revealed just how complicit the Americans were in deceiving the French. Philippe Étienne, who had been appointed French ambassador to the United States in 2019, turned up a few weeks after Shearer's visit, and spoke to the same people. The French had concerns about the bad press they were getting due to leaks from the Morrison government. The French thought they could trust the Americans, and told them the submarine deal was 'an essential part of their strategic presence in the Indo-Pacific'. Étienne says it was stressed 'again and again and again. So it is not that the Americans did not know it was important for us, because we just kept repeating [it to them].' But the United States, having talked to Shearer just a few weeks earlier about Australia buying US nuclear-powered submarines, said nothing: 'They did not answer. They took note,' Étienne said.[23]

It wasn't just at meetings in the Eisenhower Building that the French raised the issue of the submarine deal in June and July 2021, and the conversations weren't just with Jake Sullivan, but also with Secretary of State Blinken and the French foreign minister, Jean-Yves Le Drian; the French defence minister, Florence Parly, met with Secretary of Defense Austin at the Pentagon, where cooperation between France and the United States in the Indo-Pacific was discussed.[24] Le Drian also met with Sullivan and talked of coordination on issues in the Indo-Pacific. But the Americans said nothing about their talks with Australia at any of these meetings.[25]

The narrative from the *Sydney Morning Herald* revealed zero about this disastrous deception that has left Australian defence exposed, instead focusing on the argument put forward by Shearer to the United States that the only way Australia 'can remain strategically relevant in highly contested circumstances is if we have the ability to launch cruise missiles over long distances'.[26]

The idea that Australia was going to threaten China with the ability to sit off its coast in submarines armed with cruise missiles lacks any credibility, yet this comment is reported uncontested by Hartcher. Former prime minister Paul Keating was closer to the mark when he later described Australia's strategic ambition as like 'throwing a handful of toothpicks at the mountain'.[27] Keating may have used hyperbole to make his point, but it was also true that the submarines could help damage China's radar and what are known as anti-access/area denial systems (A2/AD)—though acting alone, without the United States, it would probably be the Australian submarines' last act.

For many decades in Australia the Fairfax Group of newspapers, as they were known, represented a politically liberal view and carried the usual shibboleths of journalism—reporting without fear or favour, speaking truth to power. Since 2018 the newspaper group has been owned by Nine Entertainment, which runs, among other media outlets, a television station, the *Age* newspaper in Melbourne, the *Sydney Morning Herald* and the *Australian Financial Review* (*AFR*). Since Nine took over the Fairfax Group, the news organisations have shifted markedly to the right. The chairman of Nine is former Liberal Party treasurer Peter Costello; James Chessell, a former media adviser to Coalition government treasurer Joe Hockey, was managing director of Nine Publishing from mid-2021 until December 2023, when he stepped down.

Though the pro-business *AFR* has taken a more moderate view of China, Nine Entertainment and its other two major newspapers have been beating the drums of war against China for years, strongly echoing the view from Washington. In March 2023 they published a report entitled 'Red Alert' in three parts over three days. A huge front-page illustration showed a blood-red map of China and a squadron of fighter bombers heading for Australia. The newspapers had assembled a panel of what they called national security experts to weigh up the situation. The panel comprised:

- Lavina Lee, a senior lecturer in the Department of Security Studies and Criminology at Macquarie University, a non-resident fellow of the CSIS in Washington and a senior fellow (non-resident) at the USSC
- Peter Jennings, former deputy secretary for strategy in the Defence Department, former executive director of ASPI (funded by the Defence Department and arms manufacturers) and senior adviser on strategic policy to former prime minister John Howard

- Mick Ryan, a retired major general in the Australian Army, a graduate of the US Marine Corps' School of Advanced Warfighting, and an adjunct fellow at the CSIS
- Professor Lesley Seebeck from the ANU, an expert on cybersecurity and national intelligence who in May 2021, as domestic political problems plagued the United States, called for Australia's military to be more self-reliant
- Alan Finkel, former chief scientist of Australia, neuroscientist, engineer, entrepreneur and philanthropist.

Three of the five members of the panel were either a national security adviser to Howard or affiliated to the USSC or CSIS. Unsurprisingly, the panel agreed that Australia faced the prospect of 'armed conflict in the Indo-Pacific within three years'. They said the most serious risk would come from a Chinese attack on Taiwan that 'sparks a conflict with the US and other democracies, including Australia'.[28] The sentiment was clear: China takes back Taiwan, and Australia joins in the war.

The problem with this kind of reporting is it presumes that Australia will join the United States in any fight over Taiwan. It also fails to accept that China fears being hemmed in by a string of US bases designed to hamper what it sees as its rightful place in the world. The real danger of a war in the Indo-Pacific involving Australia is a miscalculation. The United States is pushing hard up against China's borders, not the other way around. Under the pretext of 'freedom of navigation', the United States and Australia fly spy planes and drop sonobuoys as close as 12 nautical miles (22 kilometres) off the Chinese coast to identify China's coastal defences and submarines, in order to destroy them at the start of hostilities.[29] An investigation of exactly what the United States is doing would have better informed the Australian public of the dangers they face.

The 'Red Alert' report was in line with the view from the US administration. As Hartcher reported, when Shearer visited Washington he told the Americans that Australia needed submarines to attack China, but everyone in the room knew that Australia would only attack China if it was fighting alongside the Americans. There is no stronger evidence that the United States believed Australia was prepared to sacrifice its sovereignty than a comment made later by Kurt Campbell. He indicated that whichever US submarines were eventually provided to Australia, they would always remain in US control. 'When submarines are provided from the United States to Australia, it's not like they're lost,' he said. They would simply be deployed by an allied force (Australia).[30]

Unsurprisingly, both Jake Sullivan and Campbell were extremely interested in Shearer's proposal: Australia would buy a yet-to-be-specified number of ageing US Virginia-class submarines and the United States would be able to use them as Washington saw fit.

Campbell's comments revealed much about the true relationship between Washington and Canberra. 'What most countries do when grappling with relevance, when risks and costs are enormous, is they just opt out. Australia chose relevance.' It was 'a bold and important idea', he said.[31] This condescending commentary from Campbell went unremarked by Hartcher.

Sullivan and Campbell had lots of questions about Australian technology and personnel and the country's financial capacity to fund the nuclear program but, according to Hartcher, the potential killer at the meeting was Australian politics. 'We asked lots of questions about politics,' said Campbell. 'Would this be contentious? Would this hold?' The bipartisan commitment of Labor and the Liberals was a prerequisite for any agreement, the Americans said. 'This would be a military marriage. It would have to hold over decades,' Campbell told Shearer.[32]

It was a tricky situation for the Americans. For decades the Australians had been pursuing them to bolster their local presence; now that the United States needed Australia, it faced the real possibility of pushback. The problem was how Labor would react. Washington called on career diplomat Edgard Kagan, senior director for East Asia and Oceania on the NSC. Kagan had spent three years in Australia as a political and economics officer at the US embassy in Canberra and knew how the system worked. WikiLeaks cables reveal that in August 2009, while Kagan was at the embassy, senior ALP leaders backgrounded the American chargé d'affaires on Julia Gillard's plot to overthrow Prime Minister Kevin Rudd. Former ALP leader and defence minister Kim Beazley spoke glowingly of how Gillard had shed her left-wing credentials to embrace the US alliance, and the current defence minister and deputy prime minister, Richard Marles, described by the United States as 'right wing' in another cable, told the US embassy that Gillard hadn't put a foot wrong since becoming deputy prime minister.[33]

It is known from the WikiLeaks cables that embassy staff in Canberra spend an inordinate amount of time and money cultivating politicians who provide insider information for Washington, and the biographies they build over the years help guide them in their dealings with politicians at a later date. Marles, for example, is described in a classified US cable marked 'not to be read by foreigners' as a 'rising star'. He was assessed by the embassy as 'a realistic moderate who, along with his "peacemaker" characteristics, will tend to seek the middle ground on issues'.[34] We also know from WikiLeaks that Labor members are particularly keen to pledge their allegiance to the United States behind the embassy's doors.

The US embassy was suspicious of anyone perceived to be on the left of the ALP, like former prime minister Gillard. 'Although warm and engaging in her dealings with American diplomats, it's unclear whether this change in attitude reflects a mellowing of her views or an understanding of what she needs to do to become leader of the ALP,' the embassy wrote. 'It is likely a combination of the two. Labor Party officials have told us that one lesson Gillard took from the 2004 elections was that Australians will not elect a PM who is perceived to be anti-American.'[35]

To whom in Labor did the US embassy in Canberra talk as they tried to assess whether AUKUS would be accepted? Whoever it was had a very sound idea of what Labor's position would be. The American embassy knew that Labor was neurotic about being wedged politically on any issue of national security, and that many in the party rightly feared antagonising the Americans. Kagan reported back favourably that if Labor baulked, Morrison would use it as a wedge against Opposition Leader Anthony Albanese in the approach to an election, to frame him as weak on national security. In May 2021, the US embassy in Canberra understood more about the most important decision affecting Australia's future than many members of the Cabinet, the government, the Opposition and the entirety of the Australian population.

Labor, though, constantly reflected on Australia's relationship with the United States and how to handle it. Their concern has a long history. Even before the Whitlam government was elected in 1972, the CIA's chief of counterintelligence, James Jesus Angleton, reportedly 'shuddered when he was told [Australia was] about to fall into the arms of a "party that has extensive historical contacts with Eastern Europe", a party whose constitution commits it to socialism'.[36] The hostility became palpable as Whitlam shifted Australia towards the Non-Aligned Movement of nations, opposed nuclear weapons and ordered that his staff should not be 'vetted or harassed' by ASIO.[37] When government ministers publicly condemned the US bombing of Vietnam as 'corrupt and barbaric', a CIA station officer in Saigon said, 'We were told the Australians might as well be regarded as North Vietnamese collaborators.'[38]

Though it first began operations more than fifty years ago, Pine Gap is still emblematic of the ALP's tortured relationship with American power. Theodore Shackley, who had run the CIA's Saigon office at the height of the Vietnam War and was about to become chief of its East Asia Division, which included protecting North West Cape and particularly Pine Gap, was also gravely concerned when Whitlam indicated that his government might not renew the lease on the US bases when they fell due in a few years. Whitlam told parliament: 'The manipulation of unions, the financing of political parties, the deception over the CIA and the activities of foreign installations on our soil all affect Australia's independence and sovereignty. There is a need for parliamentary scrutiny of foreign intelligence activities in this country. The need is urgent.'[39]

On 4 November 1975, Shackley sent a message to ASIO saying, 'The CIA cannot see how this dialogue with continual reference to the CIA can do other than blow the lid off those installations … particularly the installation in Alice Springs.' He added, 'The CIA feel that if this problem cannot be solved they do not see how our mutually beneficial relations are going to continue.' CIA officer Victor Marchetti, who had helped set up Pine Gap, was blunt: 'This threat to close Pine Gap caused apoplexy in the White House ... a kind of Chile [coup] was set in motion.'[40]

On 11 November 1975, the Whitlam government was dismissed by Governor-General Sir John Kerr. In Whitlam's account of his time in office,[41] he says the United States' role in his dismissal was all but confirmed by an emissary sent to Australia in 1977 by then US president Jimmy Carter. Whitlam described a breakfast meeting with the US assistant secretary of state for Asia and the Pacific, Warren Christopher, at the Qantas VIP lounge at Sydney Airport on 27 July; other officials were present. Christopher made it clear to Whitlam that he had 'made a special detour in his itinerary for the sole purpose of speaking to me'. Christopher told him that the 'US Administration would never again interfere in the domestic political processes of Australia'. He added that President Carter would 'work with whatever government the people of Australia elected'.

As mentioned in Chapter 5, the ALP has good reason to be greatly concerned about the influence of Washington in the nation's politics. The events surrounding the election and dismissal of the Whitlam government might have taken place fifty years ago, but the same rules of politics in Australia applied in 2022. Four months after Labor won office, in July, Washington appointed the sole surviving child of President John F Kennedy as its ambassador to Australia. If the destruction of the Whitlam government had been brutal, Caroline Kennedy's appointment was seen by many as a charm offensive. But visions of Camelot were illusory.

Though Australia's Coalition governments had repeatedly voted with the United States against joining a new United Nations treaty banning all nuclear weapons, it had long been the ALP's policy that it would support any moves in that direction. Signatories to the Treaty on the Prohibition of Nuclear Weapons promised not just to renounce nuclear weapons but to renounce any activity that supported them. This places Australia in a bind, because the US military in Australia plays a central role in Washington's nuclear attack systems. Being careful not to confront this issue head-on, the new Albanese government decided to abstain in the United Nations vote in October 2022 rather than follow the United States and vote to oppose the treaty.

If Labor thought it had done enough to assuage Washington's concerns about its fealty by signing up to AUKUS and abandoning the French, it got a rude shock. Even abstaining in the vote was not enough. Underneath the smooth veneer of the new Kennedy administration in Canberra was the heavy hand of US power. As the *Guardian Australia*'s Daniel Hurst revealed, 'The US has warned Australia against joining a landmark treaty banning nuclear weapons, saying the agreement could hamper defence arrangements between the US and its allies.' Hurst quoted the US embassy in Canberra as saying the treaty 'would not allow for US extended deterrence relationships, which are still necessary for international peace and security'.[42] In other words, Australia would not be able to rely on the so-called US nuclear umbrella for protection. The threat was implicit: it was bad enough for Australia not to vote with the United States against the treaty, but if it were to move from abstaining to supporting and signing the treaty, Washington would have to take action. There were echoes of 1975 in what it might do.

With Morrison, though, the United States had no problems. Continuing the Howard legacy, Morrison's government was keen to reinforce the US relationship. The National Security Committee of Cabinet accepted the transactional nature of the relationship (where Australia lost some of its independence); as flawed as that thinking is, it believed it was a price worth paying for what it saw as Washington's protection. The fact that the increasing US military presence in the Indo-Pacific could draw Australia into a conflict seemed of little consequence in Morrison's desire to wedge Labor on national security.

Morrison was working at achieving what successive Australian prime ministers had tried and failed to do: draw the United States more closely into the fabric of Australia's defence. The closer alliance might cause problems of sovereignty, but Australia would become indispensable to the United States. As a bonus for Morrison, if Labor did not give the deal 100 per cent support, he could portray the ALP as being weak on national security and anti-American.

No one could accuse Peter Dutton of that. In May 2020 he appointed new members to the Submarine Advisory Committee whose brief was to provide 'independent critical peer review of the current and projected submarine capability'.[43] The committee was stacked with ex-US military people still working for US nuclear submarine and shipbuilding industries: Jim Hughes was a former vice-president of submarines at Newport News Shipbuilding, the company that constructs the nuclear-powered Virginia-class submarines, and Kirkland Donald was chairman of the board of Huntington Ingalls Industries, the company that owns Newport News Shipbuilding. Donald F McCormack was the former executive director, Naval Sea Systems Command, at the Naval Surface and Undersea warfare centres. The committee was a perfect fit for a decision already taken, looking for evidence to back it up.

Morrison was simply looking for any way he could find to circumvent the checks and balances that had long been in place to prevent governments making catastrophic decisions that had not passed proper parliamentary scrutiny. Not even the Queen's representative in Australia escaped his manipulation. In May 2021 he persuaded the governor-general to secretly swear him in as home affairs minister, giving Morrison direct access to Australia's security and defence intelligence apparatus. Those in the inner circle of his deceitful actions against the French Government didn't escape, either. Though Moriarty had been closely involved in running what he called plan B, the secret plan to scupper the French submarines, he said at the Senate estimates hearing into the cancelled French deal in October 2021 that he had no idea that Morrison was developing a formal partnership between the United States, the United Kingdom and Australia.[44]

And there was worse to come: Vice Admiral David Johnston, vice chief of the ADF, admitted at that Senate hearing in 2021 that the nuclear-powered submarines hadn't been properly investigated, and there was certainly nothing that proved Australia needed them.[45]

But that was of little interest to Morrison. The former marketing manager was working furiously on the public announcement of AUKUS, which would grab headlines and, he believed, help him win the next election. He was wrestling with how best to sell the product he was creating, or, as Moriarty put it, 'The prime minister was thinking about the framing.'[46] Once again Morrison was drawing on his marketing credentials to set the agenda—an agenda reinforced by think tanks and uncritically followed by much of the media. On the other side of the world, Morrison's flair for obfuscation and deception would serve him well.

9

In the Frame

In June 2021, in Cornwall's idyllic countryside on the south-west coast of England, Scott Morrison secretly laid out his plan to deceive the French. US president Joe Biden and UK prime minister Boris Johnson were co-conspirators. They both understood that Australia was buying twelve conventionally powered submarines from France, so why else would they be secretly discussing transferring nuclear technology to Australia to equip nuclear submarines?

Implausibly, Biden later said he understood that the French, just across the English Channel from where they were hatching their plot, had been told what was going on and that the Labor Opposition in Australia would support the deal.[1] The truth is that Biden had been deeply involved in the nuclear submarine project from the start, and his administration had deliberately not told the French about the secret discussions with Australia. He saw a strategic role for Australia in the containment of China, using US—not French—submarines. According to the *New York Times*, he told aides that 'those French-made submarines would not do'.[2] Biden said the French submarines 'did not have the ability to range the Pacific and show up unexpectedly off Chinese shores—adding an element of military advantage for the West'.

As Biden and Emmanuel Macron sat shaking hands in Cornwall, posing for the cameras, Biden continued his well-practised act of deception. As the *New York Times* reported: 'In meeting after meeting with their French counterparts—some including Mr Biden and Secretary of State Antony Blinken—the Americans did not give France a heads-up about their plans to step in with their own designs.' It was yet another example of how the United

States was deeply involved in what should have been an independent strategic decision for Australia.

If Morrison had wanted a distraction from his covert plans, he couldn't have hoped for better press coverage. The media reported that his office had spent weeks planning a secret G7 side trip for the prime minister to explore his convict family roots.[3] Morrison's team had even sworn the grave-keeper at the local church to secrecy about the visit to discover the final resting place of his great-grandfather. Unable to find the exact grave, he placed flowers on that of another relative and moved on. Morrison grabbed a ham sandwich and half a local brew at a nearby pub before heading off to see the prison where his fifth-great-grandfather had been held before being transported to Australia in the year 1787 for stealing 5½ pounds (2.5 kilograms) of yarn.

Morrison's decision to take what amounted to a mini diversion for family reasons caused an uproar. There are few things Australians question more than a politician taking a trip overseas. Mixing it with a dash of personal enjoyment was beyond the pale, particularly as the country was still suffering the effects of COVID-19—unprecedented lockdowns and the use of biosecurity laws that barred Australians from leaving the country without a good reason.

The TV breakfast shows couldn't get enough. Was it okay for the PM to take time off while overseas? Was it wise politically after his ill-fated secret holiday trip to Hawaii at the heigh of the bushfires in 2019–20? The questions were unstoppable, but luckily for Morrison nothing of any relevance to what was really going on was raised. Later, the more observant members of the media began focusing on why he had failed to get a one-on-one meeting with Biden during the G7. After all, Australia and the United States were close partners in upholding the 'rules-based order' in the Indo-Pacific. Why had he had to meet with Johnson as well? Only later did it become all too apparent. Nothing had leaked apart from the graveyard trip, and only then because a local newspaper got the story.

Morrison's office had prepared the ground well. Aware of the dangers of being seen overseas enjoying yourself, politicians are more wary of visiting one place than any other: Paris. Two weeks before he travelled to Cornwall, Morrison announced he had turned down an invitation to visit the Élysée on his way to the United Kingdom. He would not need to go to Paris until after the Cornwall meeting. To the casual political observer, it might have appeared that he was forgoing a visit to Paris because it was a bad look for a travelling PM.

But as with much of Morrison's behaviour, nothing was what it seemed. There was another, more surreptitious reason. Morrison had turned down Macron's offer because he hadn't yet met with Biden and Johnson to discuss the details of AUKUS. Only after the meeting in Cornwall did he head off to France for the dinner with Macron. On 15 June 2021 in the Élysée Palace the two leaders sat down to dine, alone. There were no note-takers to record the conversation, and no translators; Macron spoke perfect English.

In a nearby dining room Morrison's Australian team—the deputy secretary of the ONI, Michelle Chan, and the ONI head, Andrew Shearer—dined with Macron's advisers; among that group was the French ambassador to Australia, Jean-Pierre Thébault. Understanding what happened during this two-hour dinner is crucial in measuring the level of duplicity employed by Morrison to hoodwink the French.

Macron believed that Morrison had accepted the dinner meeting to talk about the newly forming Australia–France strategic partnership, and to iron out the inevitable problems involving the biggest single defence contract either country had signed in its respective history. Morrison said he wanted to meet Macron so he could share with the French president 'where Australia's thinking was'. He wanted to let Macron know 'after the meeting with the trilateral partners about where we were at'.[4] Since there was no trilateral partnership in existence at the time, it was a strange phrase to use. As the dinner broke up, Macron still had no idea what Morrison was planning. Morrison had made some forceful points, but nothing of great note. Macron looked calm and relaxed, according to one observer. As he chatted after the dinner, Macron said of Morrison, 'He's a tough guy. We have to make sure everything is okay.'[5]

Morrison's version of events—that he had raised concerns about the submarine program with Macron—remained unchanged until nearly two weeks after the public announcement on 16 September 2021 that the program had been axed. On 30 October, at a G7 meeting in Rome, Macron was walking through a group of Australian journalists when he was asked about the loss of the submarine deal. 'I have a lot of respect and a lot of friendship for your people,' he said. 'I just say when you have respect, you have to be true. And you have to behave in line and consistently with this value.' He was then asked by *Sydney Morning Herald* reporter Bevan Shields if he thought Morrison had lied to him. The answer has become infamous: 'I don't think—I know.'[6]

The barb stung Morrison, and his bullying response invoked victim status, demonstrating Samuel Johnson's famous point about patriotism being the last refuge of the scoundrel. He hadn't lied, and he wasn't going to cop any sledging about Australia, he said.[7] Morrison refused to acknowledge that the criticism had been directed at him personally and that Macron had gone out of his way to say how much respect he had for Australians. Two days later, on 1 November, at a press conference after the Glasgow Climate Change Conference (COP26), Morrison made an attempt to diffuse Macron's attack. Instead, it provided further evidence to understand why Macron had called Morrison a liar.

During the press conference, Morrison laid out his version of what had happened at the dinner. 'Now, at that point I made it very clear that a conventional diesel-powered submarine was not going to meet Australia's strategic requirements,' he said. 'We discussed that candidly. I did not discuss what other alternatives we were looking at.'[8]

The problem for Morrison was that if he had told Macron that conventionally powered submarines were no longer of any use to Australia, then the French deal would have been scuppered at that very moment. No amount of extra work by the French could have saved the deal: they were offering conventional boats. Morrison could not have said those words unless he had led Macron to believe he was considering French nuclear-powered submarines. And Morrison has never suggested that as his defence.

Boxed into a corner and exposed for his falsehoods, he (or someone with access to his encrypted phone) leaked a text message from the French president that Morrison said proved that Macron knew after the Élysée dinner that there was doubt about the submarine going ahead. 'Should I expect good or bad news for our joint submarines ambitions?' the French president texted.[9] By leaking the private correspondence, Morrison hoped it would bolster his argument that he had signalled to Macron that the deal might be cancelled. But if, as Morrison asserts, he had already indicated to Macron that diesel-powered submarines were 'not going to meet Australia's strategic requirements',[10] why would Macron be asking if there was any good news? He would have expected the cancellation. As Philippe Étienne explained, it was 'understandable' for Macron to be worried because of the media campaign against Naval Group.[11]

There is another problem with Morrison's account of the conversation with Macron. Morrison said that as a result of that meeting, the French defence system 'swung into gear'. Again, if he had told Macron the diesel subs were not up to the mark, why bother? Morrison says that his argument to Macron is validated by the fact that after the meeting the French president sent one of his top admirals to Australia to deal with the problems Morrison had raised. Morrison described that action as a 'full court press' operation by the French because, he argued, Macron was so anxious about losing the deal. But the question that gives a lie to Morrison's version is: Why would the French admiral have travelled to Australia if the submarines the French were offering were not fit for purpose? There would have been no point. Obviously Macron was left with the impression that there were problems and it was possible to sort them out.

Neither publicly available information nor Naval Group internal records nor briefings from French diplomatic sources support Morrison's version of events. Only one week after the Élysée dinner, on 23 and 24 June, a number of meetings occurred in Canberra between Naval Group and government officials. There was no particular crisis that Macron had sent his admiral to sort out. In fact, after the tumultuous earlier months, all appeared to be calm and Naval Group was on track to deliver Australia's submarines on time.

Kim Gillis says that the Defence Department's submarine project team was bemused by the arrival of the French admiral. The admiral asked them what the problem was and they said, 'It's okay, we're back on track.'[12] With that, the admiral returned to France. With all the deception, leaks to the press about often non-existent problems, and the fact that Morrison had a record for being untrustworthy, in June 2021 the Australian Senate called retired US admiral William Hilarides, who served as chairman of Australia's Naval Shipbuilding Expert Advisory Panel, to give evidence at a hearing into the submarine project. Australian senators wanted answers. Had the American consultants urged the Australian Government to consider modifying, or even killing, the Attack-class submarine deal? The senators didn't know it then, but they were closer to the mark than anyone else.

Testifying remotely from the United States, Hilarides refused to answer the question. 'Because that advice is used to support government decision-making, it's confidential,' Hilarides said.[13] It might have been a moment of outrage that a former US admiral who was employed by the Australian Government would refuse to answer a question from the Australian Senate, or his silence might have given the government pause for thought. But it did nothing of the sort. The lies and the secrecy were part of a grand plan.

Just how much the US administration was involved in Morrison's deception was still a matter for debate in 2023.

Not far away from where Hilarides runs his consulting company, 25 kilometres south-west of Washington in Fairfax Station, Virginia, famous for its pristine picturesque environment, Kurt Campbell had been mulling over how to shift Australia's nuclear submarine project forward. The biggest obstacle was the Biden administration's concern over the proliferation of nuclear weapons. For fifty years, ever since the United States had shared some of its nuclear secrets with the United Kingdom to power British submarines, no one else had been granted access to its secrets of nuclear propulsion. Even the South Koreans had been rejected. Greatly concerned that the spread of HEU might end up in the hands of terrorists, the United States believed that the sealed reactor it uses in its submarines might solve the problem. It would be a way around the non-proliferation argument. Australia would never be able to access the uranium. There were plenty of other issues that would haunt the submarine project, but this was the biggest concern that might stop the deal getting off the ground.

If anyone could help the Australian Government get what it wanted, it was Campbell, the White House's Indo-Pacific coordinator. He's a friend of former Labor leader and defence minister Kim Beazley and is known as 'Mr Australia' in Washington. In August 2021, Campbell called representatives of the United States, the United Kingdom and Australia together for a meeting at US military headquarters, the Pentagon.

It should have been a relatively straightforward get-together, but the Australian delegation had been issued with strict instructions. They were to make themselves as inconspicuous as possible. As they made their way to a side building away from the main entrance to the Pentagon, Australia's admiral Jonathan Mead and the other military personnel wore civilian clothes. They had been specifically told not to dress in their uniforms. Secrecy was paramount.

Exactly who were these meetings being kept secret from?

In what later appeared to be a ruse, the United States let it be known that Washington had been so concerned that the French had been told about Australia's discussions with the Americans that they demanded proof.[14] Australia had even sent a list of the dealings that had taken place between Canberra and Paris involving the submarine issue to the White House, supposedly to reassure President Biden. Representatives from the United Kingdom were at the meeting, so obviously London was in the loop.

There was only one other group that might have questioned the project: the ALP. Was the United States party to Morrison's plan to wedge Labor on national security? Was it breaking the pledge President Carter had made five decades ago that the United States would 'never again' interfere in Australian domestic politics?[15] Kagan virtually admitted this was the case when he accepted that Morrison would use any opposition to the deal as a wedge against Anthony Albanese in the approach to the Australian election due the following year, framing Albanese as weak on national security.

'The government has clearly thought this through, and we should submit to their judgement,' Kagan argued.¹⁶

Over the following four days, the director of the US Naval Nuclear Propulsion Program, Admiral Frank Bowman, worked with Campbell, Mead and Vanessa Nicholls, the British Government's director general nuclear, to build what would end up as the foundation of AUKUS. According to various versions of what happened, experts on the NPT were consulted.¹⁷ They argued that if the reactors on the submarines were run as sealed units, installed and later removed by the United States or United Kingdom at the end of their 35-year life, then the treaty would not be breached. They pointed out that Australia may have use of, but not access to, the nuclear technology and materials. Morrison and Marise Payne met with the IAEA's director-general, Argentinian Rafael Grossi, to reassure him.

The Americans also had reservations over Australia's finances and politics. Even if Labor accepted the deal, would future governments? And could Australia sustain the cost, which would be a high percentage of the nation's gross domestic product?

Another, even bigger question remained: Exactly how would Australia manage to acquire the submarines in the first place? Clearly it couldn't build the nuclear-powered submarines itself. The United States was going to provide the reactor to drop into the planned UK-designed and Australian-made submarines once they were completed. But that was years away—into the 2040s, and maybe even longer.

By cancelling the French deal, Australia had created a huge gap in its submarine capability. The ageing Collins class could be kept going for a few more years, but that was still not sufficient. Morrison faced an acute dilemma of his own making. He had beaten the drums of war with China to argue the case that only nuclear-powered submarines could defend Australia, but the submarines would not be ready for another twenty years. By any reckoning they would be too late for any coming conflict with China. Since Morrison had determined that Australia needed nuclear submarines to face off against China, Canberra asked the United States to provide at least three—and up to five—Virginia-class nuclear-powered submarines to fill the gap. Yet with the French deal ended, Australia had lost any power to negotiate with the Americans. It was up to the Americans whether they would help or not, and even the terms and conditions of what that assistance might be.

With the best will in the world, it would be no easy task for the United States to help Australia. It had problems of its own.

The sprawling shipyards at the Huntington Ingalls–owned facility on the banks of the James River north of Norfolk and the General Dynamics Electric Boat yards in Connecticut and Rhode Island, where America's nuclear submarines are built, look impressive. The order books are full. The US Navy can't get enough of their submarines, and want the shipyards to deliver two a year in an attempt to outpace China's submarine production. The trouble is that for the past few years they've only been turning out 1.4 per year. The shipyards are flat out trying to fill the orders for the US Navy, and Australia is at the end of a long queue.

In an attempt to overcome this problem, the United States came up with a novel solution: instead of ordering new submarines, Australia should buy a couple of second-hand ones from the US Navy. They might be old, but they would still have more than twenty years of their 35-year life span left on the clock. There are, however, a number of problems with this solution. Older submarines often need spare parts and there's a chronic shortage of those; they can sometimes take up to two years to be supplied. This ongoing problem has had a knock-on effect. As the United States struggles to boost the number of its submarines on active duty, it's been relying on the Cold War–era Los Angeles–class submarines to plug the gap. And they too have had problems sourcing spare parts. In an attempt to deal with this cascading spare-parts catastrophe and underproduction issues, the US Government is pouring billions of dollars into its shipyards and manufacturers.

The problem facing the US Navy was so huge as it raced to build up its stocks to challenge China that Washington began searching for different ways to solve it. In centre frame was how to maintain a higher level of submarine production and at the same time honour its deal with Australia.

On Washington's Capitol Hill the influential Congressional Research Service, which provides senators and Congressional representatives with detailed statistics and analyses of major issues, produced a report called *Navy Virginia (SSN-774) Class Attack Submarine Procurement: Background and Issues for Congress*. The title was as bland as the contents were explosive. It pointed out what must have been obvious from the start of negotiations between the Morrison government and the United States: 'The Navy anticipates building additional Virginia-class SSNs [nuclear-powered submarines] in the 2030s as replacements for submarines sold to Australia.'[18]

This was the crux of the problem, and the report laid it out like a dead body on a mortuary slab. The navy's thirty-year plan involved the procurement of twenty SSNs during the ten-year period from 2030 to 2039. If Australia was to be sold between three and five submarines during that period, it meant the shipyards would have to turn out either twenty-three or twenty-five boats, lifting the yearly rate to around 2.5 boats per year—a big hike from the present rate of 1.4. Selling between three and five Virginia-class boats to Australia by 2045 and not replacing them through the construction of additional Virginia-class boats would reduce the projected number of nuclear-powered submarines in the water by 2045 to fifty, fifty-two or fifty-five boats—way behind one estimate of the sixty-six boats the navy says it needs.

The report pointed out that it was difficult enough for the United States to hit its sixty-six nuclear-powered submarine target by 2045. Staff shortages and bottlenecks were causing major problems at both shipyards. In a desperate attempt to win over American support, the Australian Government larded its plea with a $4.5 billion down payment to the United States.[19] The money, budgeted over the following four years, might help speed up US submarine building, but it would not guarantee a solution to the problem.

Significantly for Australia, the Congressional report posited a number of scenarios questioning whether it would even be in America's interests to sell the Virginia-class submarines to the Australians. The most critical analysis rested on whether or not Australia would support the United States in a war over Taiwan. Australia might 'use the transferred Virginia-class boats less effectively than the US Navy' or 'might not involve its military, including its Virginia-class boats, in US-China crises or conflicts that Australia viewed as not engaging important Australian interests'.[20] The report pointedly drew attention to comments by Australian defence minister Richard Marles that in exchange for the Virginia-class boats, Australia's government 'made no promises to the United States that Australia would support the United States in a future conflict over Taiwan'.

In a country gearing up for a war with China, any loss of military firepower—particularly to a country that might not side with it in a coming conflict—was hugely problematic for US legislators, who would ultimately have to sign off on the sale. What the report raised as an alternative to the proposed sale of Virginia-class SSNs (the description used for nuclear-powered submarines) to Australia might have solved the problem for the Americans, but it stripped away Australia's sovereignty. It involved what the United States termed a military division of labour. The US nuclear-powered submarines would 'perform both US and Australian SSN missions', while Australia invested the money it would have spent on the submarines in military forces for performing other missions for both itself and the United States. The report points out that this division of labour is similar to an agreement that exists between the United States and its NATO allies.

The plan would boost the number of boats under US Navy control by at least three to five, the report argued. In other words, the United States would keep its submarines, because it couldn't rely on Australia backing its fight against China. The money Australia saved on not buying the submarines would be spent on other joint military ventures with the Americans. As a trade-off, the United States would carry out Australia's nuclear-powered submarine patrols. What the Congressional report proposed was a stopgap. The Americans would share their nuclear propulsion and submarine technology with Australia, allowing it to build its own AUKUS submarines—the new UK model that is still being developed—while 'reducing at that point the need for US nuclear-powered submarines to perform Australian nuclear submarine missions'.

Another proposal would see the United States 'continue to carry out submarine missions on behalf of the Australian Navy'. Australia would continue investing in other joint US–Australia military capabilities. Under this variation, the size of the US submarine force would eventually be expanded above previously planned levels by about eight boats—the number of nuclear-powered submarines that Australia had planned to buy.

It was obvious the United States was examining every option that would help it keep control of as many submarines as possible. Selling them to even a friendly ally like Australia would have to come with strings attached, as Campbell had indicated earlier.

For Labor, this was their worst nightmare. Having been ambushed the night before the AUKUS deal announcement and wedged on national security, they had to deal with the shifting sands of an agreement with the United States that turned out to be not much more than a public relations announcement. No amount of smiling and handshakes in the US port city of San Diego when the latest phase of the AUKUS deal was announced by Albanese, Biden and new UK prime minister Rishi Sunak in March 2023 could shake off the feeling that the United States and the United Kingdom were the great winners.[21]

Australia had already committed to make a $4.5 billion down payment to help the overstretched US shipyards speed up production, but greater complications emerged when the United States shifted focus to its new nuclear-armed Columbia-class submarines (see Chapter 10). Building the Columbia submarines put pressure on the ability of the US naval yards to maintain the number of Virginia-class subs in production. This change in US scheduling priorities showed just how vulnerable Australia had become to the vagaries of American submarine production. The premature axing of the French submarine deal left Australia with no leverage in Washington. It would have to take whatever America offered.

Australia would also splash money across the Atlantic at the UK submarine shipyard at Barrow-in-Furness, on the Cumbria coast. It, too, would receive a huge cash injection from the Australian taxpayer, but by the end of 2023 no one was sure exactly how much. Rex Patrick accurately described the payment as an open cheque.[22] Barrow would be delighted with any help it could get: like the United States, the UK yard had problems. Barrow's stemmed not from huge demand, but from not enough work.

The Australian AUKUS submarine had come to the rescue of the United Kingdom's own version of the Valley of Death. The AUKUS subs would be built in both Barrow and Osborne, with a predicted delivery from the late 2030s to the early 2040s.[23] Nobody was talking about how many jobs were now being exported to the United States and the United Kingdom, or how many companies had been thrown on the scrap heap, or how many workers were now unemployed in Australia following the decision to drop the French deal, which would have cut its first steel for the Australian submarines in 2023.

The level of incompetence in the government of Australia was breathtaking, as were the repercussions. The United States would be calling all the shots on what kind of submarines would be sold to Australia, how old they would be, how many there would be, when they would be delivered, and even if they would be sold at all.

It was to be expected that Washington would act in its own best interests. What is extraordinary is the possibility that Morrison truly believed that what was best for the United States was best for Australia. Just as extraordinary is the fact that the Labor Party, perhaps fearful of history, embraced a deal that made Australia so vulnerable, undermining its independence and sovereignty. It would be a hard sell to the party faithful.

10

The Sting

On 15 September 2021—a full eighteen months after the nuclear submarine venture had officially begun—Scott Morrison phoned the then Opposition leader, Anthony Albanese. It's not often that the Opposition gets this kind of personal attention from the prime minister, but Morrison had important business to discuss and wanted to meet Albanese and his team face to face for a secret briefing.

What Morrison told the Labor leaders—Albanese, Foreign Affairs spokesperson Senator Penny Wong, Deputy Leader Richard Marles and Defence spokesperson Brendan O'Connor, was designed to shock, and it did. Morrison said that at 7 a.m. the next day he would be announcing that the French submarine deal had been terminated. Instead, Australia was going into partnership with the United States and the United Kingdom for Australia's new submarines. If that wasn't a big enough surprise, he added that the submarines would be nuclear-powered.

Morrison had lured Labor into a trap, confronting Albanese with an agonising choice: the status quo, where Labor maintained its sixty years of opposition to nuclear power in Australia and rejected a deeper US alliance, or embrace nuclear power and risk a loss of sovereignty that many on the left of his party would bitterly oppose. Morrison must have secretly wanted Albanese to reject the AUKUS plan, leaving him free to fight a 'khaki election' the following year focused on national security—an area where the Coalition believed it had an advantage over Labor.

The details of what the Labor leadership discussed as they retreated to digest what Morrison had just sprung on them are not known, but there would have been much heart-searching, particularly from Wong. She was not only a strong defender of Australia's sovereignty, but also the person who would have to defend the nuclear decision to Australia's allies in Asia if Labor won the coming election. That night Morrison called Emmanuel Macron to break the bad news. In what can be seen as a metaphor for the whole AUKUS debacle, the Australian Government also sent two letters to the French Government. The first told the Élysée the contract was being terminated; the second congratulated the French for meeting all the requirements for the submarine contract to move to the next stage. Philippe Étienne is still baffled: 'How can you understand that those two letters were sent out on the very same day?'[1]

Armed with the cancellation letter, Étienne headed for the White House to confront one person who had been so deeply involved in the deception of France. He handed Jake Sullivan a copy of the letter from Australia cancelling the contract. Étienne said Sullivan was 'a bit surprised' that Australia had already told France it would not be going ahead with the submarine program. The White House was busy making plans for the AUKUS announcement in a few hours' time with Morrison and Boris Johnson, and the Americans clearly believed they had time to spare, before France would be alerted.

Étienne had one last point to make before he left Sullivan. He told him that President Macron would be recalling him to France: 'I insisted on telling him before it was public.' Étienne was not alone in being recalled: the French ambassador to Australia, Jean-Pierre Thébault, who described the submarine decision as a 'stab in the back',[2] was also on the next plane back to Paris.

Yet it could not possibly have come as a surprise, either to Kurt Campbell, the coordinator for the Indo-Pacific on the US National Security Council, or Jake Sullivan, his immediate superior. The French had repeatedly told them of the importance they attached to the submarine project. For their part the Australian team may have felt elated at their AUKUS 'win' but the question was, could what happened to France happen to another valued US ally such as Australia? By March 2024 there were strong signs that the United States could not be trusted to keep its side of the AUKUS deal. The Pentagon announced it would only be building one Virginia-class submarine in 2025 instead of the promised two, making it even less likely there would be any spare subs to sell to Australia.

Turnbull says he did his best to mitigate the damage to the Australia–France relationship. 'I kept on saying to Emmanuel, "We have a deceitful prime minister, but we are not a deceitful nation,"' he said. 'To which Macron would always say, "Yes, I understand, my friend." You know, he was always very good about that. But the reality is that even if Emmanuel was convinced that this was all Morrison's work, the damage was done in France.'[3]

The White House said publicly it believed the French had been kept informed about the submarine decision, when clearly they hadn't. About whether the Americans were involved in misleading the French, Turnbull isn't sure: 'I mean, Biden has said, whether you entirely believe him or not, [that] he was misled.'[4] By way of an apology, Biden told the French their treatment had been 'clumsy'.[5] Since the United States said it believed Labor, too, had been kept informed when it had not, Biden might have publicly extended an apology to Labor—or, better still, made a call to Albanese earlier. But that might have put AUKUS in jeopardy. As Australia's ambassador to the United States, Arthur Sinodinos, said, if Albanese had said no, the deal would have been 'dead'.[6] Instead, Morrison's brinkmanship and deception worked, with the help of the United States.

A tri-national launch that had all the look of an international publicity campaign, with intertwined flags draped across the nations' respective platforms, delivered AUKUS to the world via a bank of video screens—Biden in Washington, Johnson in London and Morrison in Canberra.

The announcement began smoothly enough, with Morrison invited to open the proceedings. 'Good morning from Australia,' he said. 'We have always believed in a world that favours freedom, that respects human dignity, the rule of law, the independence of sovereign states, and the peaceful fellowship of nations.'[7] Others may disagree with this rosy view of Australia's foreign policy, but nobody in the Washington or London administrations was going to argue. Boris Johnson, though, cared less about the big picture and more about his electoral chances. Seemingly oblivious to how his statement might undermine Morrison's claim that jobs would be created in Australia, Johnson boasted that AUKUS would create 'hundreds of highly skilled jobs across the United Kingdom, including in Scotland, the north of England, and the Midlands'—areas where his ruling Conservative Party was losing support. It got worse for Morrison when it came to Biden's turn to speak. The US president turned first to the British prime minister. 'Thank you, Boris,' he said. Then, looking towards a TV monitor with Morrison's face beaming in from Australia, Biden hesitated. 'And I want to thank that fella down under. Thank you very much, pal.' He added, 'Appreciate it, Mr Prime Minister.'

Biden's failure to remember Morrison's name was an appropriate metaphor for Australia's submarine acquisition program: no one had any idea what was going to happen next. It also pointed to the question of how much—despite all the hoopla—the president was really committed to the deal, if he couldn't remember his partner's name.

In Biden's defence, he may have had other matters on his mind. He might not have been thinking of the next war the United States would fight, with China, but the one it had just lost, in Afghanistan. The images of a strong president taking a global stand on national security with the United Kingdom and Australia (like Johnson, Biden was keen to play up job creation in his country) played well against the alternative vision that was still dominating US TV screens: pictures of the desperate US withdrawal from Afghanistan just two weeks earlier, an eerie echo of America's last days in Vietnam.

AUKUS was also a welcome distraction for the United States at the State Department the following day, when Peter Dutton and Marise Payne appeared alongside their opposite numbers, Lloyd Austin and Antony Blinken, at a press conference. The US media was still hounding the Biden administration about Afghanistan, but as Austin tried to switch the focus he ran into trouble. In thanking the Australians for 'coming all the way to Washington',[8] he identified Washington's biggest strategic weakness in the Indo-Pacific: its huge distance from the mainland United States and the consequential lengthy supply lines necessary to maintain US influence and military power.

The submarines were barely mentioned. And when they were, it was hardly a ringing endorsement of their acquisition, or even the United States' ability to deliver them. Blinken spoke only of US 'efforts to help Australia acquire nuclear submarines'. Austin repeated the message of assistance but went no further. As a public relations exercise it was strong on rhetoric—Austin spoke of 'standing together as mates' ready to face what he called the challenges and opportunities of the future—but did little more. The bottom line was this: We'll see what we can do to help you get nuclear submarines, but no promises. The Americans were more interested in stationing extra troops and aircraft in Australia—Austin spoke of contributing to what he called 'integrated deterrence in the region', military jargon for countries aligned with the United States to confine China's influence inside what is known as the first island chain (from Taiwan to Japan to the Philippines to part of Indonesia).

The press conference gave an insight into Washington's grand plans for the Indo-Pacific, even referencing NATO as a contributor to military operations. In this context, where NATO provides a seamless interchange between countries, allowing nuclear weapons to be stored by non-nuclear countries, what Dutton had had to say was extremely illuminating. He spoke of enhanced cooperation, increasing interoperability between the United States and Australian militaries and deepening alliance activities in the Indo-Pacific. Significantly, he talked of 'greater air cooperation through rotational deployments of all types of US military aircraft to Australia'. By stating 'all types', he left room for the controversial B-1 nuclear-capable supersonic bomber. The nuclear-capable US B-52s already had their parking spots being built at RAAF Base Tindal in the Northern Territory.

Dutton also outlined what he called 'defence industrial base integration', which would bind Australia even closer to a single source of production for military equipment. There were also secret plans for how Australia would fight a war alongside the United States. Dutton didn't take the Australian public into his confidence about whether they agreed with this decision. Instead, he spoke of 'signing a classified statement of intent on strategic capabilities, cooperation, and implementation'. Exactly what he was committing Australia to without parliamentary debate, or any public discussion, remains secret, like much of the AUKUS deal.

Whether it was deliberate or just the excitement of the occasion, Dutton did let out one piece of information: he spoke of what he might decide to do if, in his opinion, Australia's security was at stake. He said of US weapons: 'If that includes basing and includes the storage of different ordnances, I think that is in Australia's best interest, in our national interest ... that's something that I'll be continuing.' He indicated that the storage of 'different ordnance' had been part of the AUKUS agreement. Australia and the United States had an 'in-principle agreement' related to the storage of these weapons, he said.

By 'different ordnances' it's reasonable to believe that Dutton meant nuclear weapons. Why he should have raised such a sensitive issue in public is unclear. Was he trying to bait Labor on nuclear issues? His statement was not lost on many in the Labor Party, but they decided to let it slide rather than get into what they saw as a nuclear trap set by Morrison and Dutton.

Buried in the speech was another detail that bound Australia closely to America's war-fighting plans. Dutton said that the Australian Department of Defence and the United States National Reconnaissance Office (NRO) had committed to a broad range of cooperative satellite activities. To listen to Dutton, you could believe this was an innocuous system that would involve Telstra improving telephone communications in Australia. But despite its name, the NRO is not merely involved in reconnaissance: it works closely with the United States Space Force (USSF) and Space Command—a catch-all organisation responsible for all military action high above the earth. Australia has set up its own version of Space Command, which Dutton believed was necessary to maintain peace. While that might be true, Donald Trump gave a different and perhaps more accurate explanation when he launched the US Space Force in December 2019. 'Space is the world's new war-fighting domain,' he said.[9] Though there was a new US president in January 2020 when Biden took over the White House, the nation's military strategy did not change.

On 10 September 2023 at 8.47 a.m., the USSF and NRO launched an Atlas V rocket from Cape Canaveral, Florida carrying a secret satellite payload code-named Silent Barker.[10] The NRO did not reveal how many satellites were deployed, but Silent Barker's role is to spy on communications and intelligence-gathering satellites, mainly those belonging to Russia and China. It provides the United States with a close-up view of an adversary's space-based capabilities, which is a great advantage—the difference between simply knowing that a surveillance or intelligence satellite is gathering information, and understanding exactly what it is capable of transmitting back to earth. It's like having a cup to the wall rather than hearing muffled sounds from the room next door. In the event of war, identifying and then destroying or disabling an opponent's satellite surveillance or communications system would give the United States a huge strategic advantage.

Silent Barker joined other spy satellites launched by the NRO three years earlier. The office gave no details of their capability, either, but said they had been 'designed, built, and operated by the National Reconnaissance Office in partnership with the Australian Department of Defence'.[11] Australia was being increasingly drawn into America's plans to wage war in space.

Just as it had not been entirely honest with the Australian public about the role of Space Command, the United States was equally misleading about what was being installed on land next to the North West Cape submarine communications base in Western Australia—a vital part of the US war-fighting capability. In 2018, in the shadow of the 387-metre-high North West Cape antennas, the United States began planning for the arrival of what it called the Space Surveillance Telescope (SST). The US military was preparing to shift the 232-tonne piece of equipment halfway across the world from White Sands Missile Range in New Mexico—famous as the site of the Trinity atomic bomb test in 1945—to the far west coast of Australia.

The SST has the world's biggest parabolic mirror, which enables its ground crew to scan the heavens in a single 360-degree sweep and therefore to photograph objects in geosynchronous orbit approximately 22,000 miles (35,000 kilometres) above the earth. It is so powerful that it can observe an area of sky the size of the United States in seconds and detect a tiny laser point on New York's Empire State Building from Florida. The data processing system is so fast it can filter through more than a terabyte of data per night as well as receive and process images in real time to determine precise satellite positions.

The big selling point by the Pentagon for Australia was that the telescope would be able to detect and track 'faint objects in deep space and to help predict and avoid potential collisions as well as detect and monitor asteroids'.[12] But it would be misleading to believe the telescope is just chasing space debris. According to the Pentagon's own statement, it provides information for the USSF to be 'combat ready' to 'fight to protect and defend the US and Allies from attack in, through and from space'.[13] The telescope's main function is to detect any attack from space, but more importantly to identify and pre-emptively target an adversary, even if they are not attacking, and knock them out, giving the United States superiority in any confrontation. The fact that the SST is being operated by the US Space and Missile Systems Office strips away the pretence that it is only watching for space junk.[14]

Asked in Congress whether the United States was developing a 'directed energy' weapon capable of shooting down satellites, US Chief of Space Operations General Jay Raymond responded, 'Yes, sir, we are.'[15] Raymond refused to go into more details because the information was highly classified. Space Operations also runs satellites with an arm that can pull other satellites out of orbit and send them into deep space—an action that puts an adversary out of action without creating space debris that might harm the Americans' own satellites.

Though the United States and Australia say they are working together on the SST, there is no doubt who controls it. The Pentagon has formally stated that it is totally owned by the United States.

Just a few metres away from the SST at North West Cape is another piece of equipment the United States recently shipped in, from the island of Antigua in the Caribbean. For several decades, the Mission Control Center of the National Aeronautics and Space Administration (NASA) used a giant radar to track US rocket launches from Cape Canaveral. Now it has a new role in Australia, tracking low-orbiting satellites and missile launches as part of a worldwide network of optical and radar sensors supporting the US Space Operations Center. While the radar relied on radio waves to build a picture of a satellite and its electronic functions, the SST provides a crystal-clear picture for ground staff to analyse. Together, the SST and the radar are a formidable duo for the US military's war-fighting capabilities.

There is no doubt the US military appreciates the access it has to real estate down under. Former Space Force director Lieutenant-General Nina Armagno told a media briefing, 'Australia is sitting on a pot of gold at the end of the rainbow for our common national security interests.'[16] The radar station's former manager, Lieutenant Colonel Steven Melvin, was more forthright, saying the radar gave the 'war-fighter' a clearer view of where threats—a euphemism of whatever you want to attack—were coming from in space.[17]

The radar and the high-quality telescope integrate Australia further into the US military in a particularly dangerous area: where America and China are facing off in space. It's where a nuclear war could start. As US Space Force Deputy Chief of Operations Lieutenant General B Chance Saltzman said in November 2021, 'We are seeing a shift to where the first strike advantages are encountered in space … They're the first mover advantage: whoever can go first on the offense has an advantage.'[18]

According to an Australian Parliamentary Library report, the ability to attack satellites without killing adversary personnel may lead to miscalculations that make conflict more likely.[19] For example, a belligerent might calculate that an attack on its adversary's satellites that kills no one is less likely to prompt retaliation than an attack on a satellite ground station operated by personnel. Similarly, 'soft-kill' techniques, such as using a laser to dazzle a satellite, might be considered by an attacker to be less escalatory than destroying a satellite.

Until recently, the United States has skirted around the issue of whether or not it is researching the ability to kill satellites, preferring instead to concentrate on the threats posed by the Chinese and Russians. But in April 2023 Air Force Secretary Frank Kendall, explaining the details of the US military budget for 2024, confirmed for what appears to be the first time in public that the Americans are also preparing for a satellite war in space. 'There are hard kill and soft kill capabilities, if you will, that we're funding,' he said.[20]

What is often missing from analysis and reporting in the media is any mention of what the United States is doing in this area, even though it has a direct impact on Australia. The entire focus is on what the Chinese and Russians have done, shooting down their own satellites and creating space junk. The Americans have in fact carried out an attack on one of their own satellites, but the official explanation from Washington that it needed to be destroyed for safety reasons was accepted without question. As the Australian Parliamentary report points out, 'Of great concern is that nuclear powers typically rely on satellites for early warning of missile launches, communications, geo-positioning, navigation, and timing and synchronization of NC3 [nuclear command, control and communication] systems and networks. Such satellites also commonly serve tactical and strategic, nuclear and conventional roles.'[21] Once targeted, even in a non-nuclear confrontation, there is a risk that the enemy is attempting to 'blind' them as a precursor to a nuclear strike, the report said. The US refusal to rule out the first use of nuclear weapons if the country believes it is under attack only makes the situation more precarious.

In Australia's case, the AUKUS agreement binds the country close to this doctrine. With vast areas of the Northern Territory and Western Australia being close to the equator, Australia is an ideal location not only for satellite surveillance, as is happening at North West Cape, but also for firing rockets into space.

In 2022 NASA launched three suborbital rockets from Australia's Arnhem Space Centre in the Northern Territory to conduct astrophysics studies of the stars and planets that NASA said could only be done from the Southern Hemisphere. 'We're excited to be able to launch important science missions from the Southern Hemisphere and see targets that we can't from the United States,' said Nicky Fox, director of NASA's Heliophysics Division.[22]

But NASA is not merely a scientific organisation that sends astronauts into space and for years ran the US Space Shuttle program. Evidence emerged in 2022 that it has worked with US intelligence agencies, particularly the CIA. A secret document dated 29 July 1965, declassified in 2022, headlined *Guidelines Governing the Serving of Officials of the National Aeronautics and Space Administration (NASA) as Consultants on Advisory Panels of the Central Intelligence Agency (CIA)*, revealed that the CIA and NASA met twice a year. Meetings were instigated and chaired by the CIA to discuss, among other things, 'launch and test facilities', 'manned Space Flight', 'Advanced Research and Technology' and 'Scientific and Technical Satellites'.[23]

The Northern Territory Arnhem Space Centre is ideal for US military use. Because it is close to the equator, the distance a rocket needs to travel to reach orbit is shorter than elsewhere on the planet. It's the reason the United States uses Cape Canaveral and the French launch site is at Guyana in South America. The rockets use less fuel, whose weight is a critical limitation on breaking free from the earth's gravitation. The Australian spaceport would also make an ideal launch pad for rockets designed to kill or disable satellites that the United States determines to be a threat or need to be destroyed before a strike against China.

Australia's integration with the US military was, of course, well underway before the AUKUS agreement. As already noted, Pine Gap and North West Cape are part of this. But there is also the basing of thousands of US marines in Darwin, the stationing of nuclear-capable B-52s at Tindal with its US weapons storage facilities, and the stationing of US military throughout the ADF, including from the NRO at the military headquarters in Canberra.

How much control, or even influence, the Australian Government has over the US presence in Australia is difficult to say. As former defence minister Stephen Smith, one of the two people who wrote the report charting the future road for Australia's relationship with the United States under AUKUS, acknowledged, full knowledge and concurrence means that Australia knows about but doesn't necessarily approve of everything the United States does at its bases in Australia.

It's against this background that Australia embarked on its perilous course to abandon the French submarine deal, and in the short term rely on the United States to supply Virginia-class nuclear-powered submarines to fill the gap in the country's defences. Even if the boats arrived, there was only one place in the whole of Australia where, because of safety concerns over their nuclear propulsion, they could anchor: the RAN's high-security island base off the coast of Fremantle. Known as HMAS *Stirling*, it is linked to the mainland by a dual-carriageway road and a high-level bridge; only military-authorised traffic is allowed in.

In 2022, two months after taking office, Deputy Prime Minister and Defence Minister Richard Marles introduced a new description for Australia's defence relationship with the United States. US and Australian military personnel would no longer be just interoperable, where the services worked alongside each other: the new relationship would mean they were interchangeable, creating in effect a large single military entity. 'We will move beyond interoperability to interchangeability,' Marles said. 'And we will ensure we have all the enablers in place to operate seamlessly together, at speed.'[24] Morrison could not have expressed the relationship better himself.

US submarines began increasing their port visits to *Stirling* and so, too, did politicians. Marles—who constantly publicly refers to himself as the next in line for the Labor leadership and not just the minister of defence—welcomed the nuclear-powered USS *Asheville* in early 2023. A few months later, Treasurer Jim Chalmers arrived in Western Australia to announce that the government would spend $8 billion on HMAS *Stirling*, upgrading wharves and maintenance facilities to be ready for the arrival of more US and UK submarines—a first step in training Australian naval officers in how to manage the complexities of commanding a nuclear-powered submarine. By 2027 HMAS *Stirling* will host what the Defence Department calls the 'rotational presence' of UK and US nuclear-powered submarines.[25]

The word 'based' is studiously avoided in government statements. Yet there is no reason why the United States and, eventually, the United Kingdom will be using *Stirling* other than for a base. It provides an open route to the Indian Ocean, through which 70 per cent of China's oil is imported. Chinese oil tankers travelling from Africa, the Middle East and as far afield as Venezuela have to pass through the Indian Ocean before heading for a narrow 'choke point', the Malacca Strait, which separates the northern part of the

Indonesian island of Sumatra from Malaysia. In any conflict with China, the tankers would be a primary target for the submarines based at *Stirling*.

Along with Australia's Collins class, the US submarines have been using fixed underwater sonar arrays throughout the area to track Chinese submarines and oil tankers. Spy planes—maritime surveillance aircraft—drop sonobuoys as part of the targeting process. In the event of hostilities, US submarines using conventional weapons would attack Chinese radar and communications systems, clearing the way for a full attack, potentially from the main US nuclear strike submarines, the Ohio class.

The Ohio has been the backbone of the US nuclear strike capability since the 1980s, able to survive undetected during the opening salvo of any nuclear conflict and then strike its target. In 2020 the Americans laid the keel of an even bigger submarine, the Columbia class. Each Columbia-class submarine—the US plans to build twelve of them—has sixteen bays holding nuclear missiles that themselves have multiple warheads. One estimate says they are capable of destroying more than 200 cities. Unlike the Ohio, Columbia submarines can carry more accurate missiles, which gives them the capacity to be used as a first strike option. Instead of wreaking revenge on an opponent by flattening entire cities in response to an attack, the Columbia would be able to hit a defined target, giving the United States the capability of being the first to use a nuclear weapon in the hope of controlling and winning a nuclear conflict.

The US administration is a firm believer both that a nuclear war can be fought and won, and that nuclear weapons can be legitimately used. The Trump administration's Nuclear Posture Review (NPR) in 2018 reiterated America's right to be the first to use nuclear weapons against any opponent, including those who launch cyber attacks against the United States. Significantly for Australia, the NPR says that the United States is keen to share the burden of what it calls its 'nuclear deterrence mission'.[26]

As the United States is the only country to have used nuclear weapons (against civilian populations in Hiroshima and Nagasaki in 1945), its threat to use them again must be taken seriously. This position sits oddly with the country posing the greatest threat to US hegemony, China, which is the only nuclear-weapon state to maintain an unconditional no first use (NFU) pledge since it first tested a nuclear weapon, in 1964. China has also consistently called on the United States to negotiate an NFU agreement either bilaterally or with all five nuclear states. At a UN Security Council meeting in March 2023, China reiterated its NFU stance and its support for the NPT. In addition, it rejected any attacks against nuclear weapons facilities and power plants.[27]

The fear of war with China might have been good for the argument that the RAN needed nuclear-powered submarines, but it has also put the navy on the defensive. In August 2023 the RAN's Sea Power Centre published a lengthy list of US naval visits to Australia since the 1960s, arguing that it was quite normal for the number of visits to rise and then fall depending on the strategic circumstances.[28] It charted a large increase in the number of port visits to Australia during the Cold War and the Iraq and Afghanistan wars. The question was: Were any of the vessels nuclear-armed? Undoubtedly some of them were, but with the US policy of neither confirming nor denying the presence of nuclear arms, it's not surprising that the RAN identified no nuclear-warhead-carrying US ships or submarines.

What is significant, though, is that the one point the navy was keen to stress had nothing to do with the vast number of US surface ships that might have been nuclear-armed. The navy focused on whether or not any nuclear submarines, known as SSBNs, had visited Australia. ('SSBN' identifies a submarine capable of carrying nuclear-armed ballistic missiles.) With rising opposition to the AUKUS deal, which would see US nuclear-powered submarines entering Australian ports, the author of the report was keen to dampen fears of nuclear-armed submarine visits. To allay these concerns, the author made a categorical statement of denial, stating that there had never been a visit to Australia by an SSBN. Since ballistic submarines are the mainstay of the US nuclear strike force, the implication of this statement is that no nuclear weapons have ever entered Australian ports on US submarines.

Arguing that the United States has never sent an SSBN to Australia might be correct, but it is misleading. It gives the impression that only

SSBNs are capable of being nuclear-armed and, more importantly, that no US submarine has ever brought nuclear weapons into an Australian port. Neither of these statements is true.

In May 1960, at the height of the Cold War, the submarine USS *Halibut* sailed into Sydney Harbour. The crowds who lined the shores were there to mark the anniversary of the Battle of the Coral Sea, where Australian and US forces had turned back a major Japanese advance in the South Pacific during World War II. Eighteen years later it was still viewed as a defining moment when the United States had helped 'save' Australia from the Japanese.

Back in 1960 few of the people who saw the *Halibut* arrive would have known that the submarine was nuclear-powered. If they did, it would have been viewed as a novelty. What is certain is that none of them knew what lay below the steel-grey hump on the deck of the submarine. On its maiden voyage, the *Halibut* sailed from the United States to New Zealand before heading for Australia. It carried five Regulus I cruise missiles. At the time they were state-of-the-art weapons that could be steered remotely, able to hit a target 800 kilometres away.

To the delight of the estimated 5000 people gathered on the Domain overlooking the main naval fleet base at Garden Island, the captain of the US sub opened the dome on its deck and hoisted a Regulus onto the launch ramp.[29] Probably no one in that crowd—or even the RAN—knew that those missiles were armed with nuclear warheads, the world's first lightweight strategic nuclear bomb. The Regulus was carrying either a W27 or W5 warhead; the W5 had an explosive power three times greater than the Fat Man bomb dropped on Nagasaki.

The Sea Power Centre report did hail the USS *Halibut* as the US Navy's first 'nuclear-powered cruise missile armed submarine', and added that the Regulus was the forerunner of the Polaris. But it left out the fact that the Regulus I, like the Polaris missile, carried a nuclear payload.[30] In its efforts to make nuclear-powered submarine visits seem normal, Sea Power had drawn attention to a provable example that the United States had indeed brought nuclear weapons into Australia in the past.

Along with the *Halibut* on that autumn day in 1960, the USS *Canberra* also sailed into Sydney Harbour. All US cruisers were named after a US state capital, but the USS *Canberra* was an exception—a tribute from the United States for HMAS *Canberra*'s role in the Pacific War, and its loss in 1942. Eighty-one years later, on 21 July 2023, another USS *Canberra* sailed into Sydney Harbour to be commissioned, continuing the historical connection. On its bow the RAN bolted a sign carrying the emblem of a kangaroo with the US stars that they called the star-spangled kangaroo. History was repeating itself as the United States prepared for a new war. What the *Halibut* had helped create with a nuclear-tipped cruise missile might also be new again.

During his term in office, President Trump instructed the Pentagon to examine the possibility of putting nuclear warheads on submarine-based cruise missiles. Until then, only SSBNs had carried nuclear weapons. The Pentagon supported the idea and began working on a proposal. Only in 2020, when Joe Biden was elected president, did it drop the plan. But the RAN wasn't interested in engaging the Australian public with the fact that the cruise missiles on the US submarines could be easily switched to carry a nuclear weapon—particularly if Trump, or someone like him, is elected president in the future.

Misleading by omission is a tactic used by successive governments and administrations to blunt the impact of the US presence in Australia. Even some of those who support increasing military ties to the United States oppose language that hides the truth. In an opinion column on the ASPI website, contributor Euan Graham called for plain language that 'eschews euphemism' when talking about the US military.[31] But successive Australian governments prefer slippery words that do not confront the hard reality of the American presence.

In 2011, when Prime Minister Julia Gillard first invited American troops to be stationed in Australia after President Barack Obama announced the US 'Pivot to Asia', she called them the Marine Rotational Force and they numbered just 200. In 2023 the Australian Defence Department boasted that the numbers were 'now ten times that size each year'.[32] Moving more than 2000 US marines in and out of the Northern Territory every six months is done for just one reason: it allows the Australian Government to say that the US marines are not 'based' in Darwin but 'rotated'. According to the Australian military, their presence allows Australian and US troops to be interoperable and even interchangeable with each other—in other words, to fight as a single unit.

There are many in the Australian military who are not happy with US troops being in Australia. They see it as a breach of sovereignty and a dangerous precedent that could allow Australia to be sucked into a war of America's choosing, particularly over Taiwan.[33] But such is the overwhelming Americanisation of the upper levels of the ADF establishment that the detractors remain silent, afraid that speaking out would be a career-ending act and would make little difference anyway.

Two men who had the opportunity to speak their minds are former ADF chief Sir Angus Houston and former Labor defence minister Stephen Smith. In 2022 they were commissioned by the Albanese government to produce a report examining how to implement AUKUS and protect Australia's national interest. In their *Defence Strategic Review*,[34] Houston and Smith came to the conclusion that the best way Australia could defend itself was to adopt what has long been the Chinese military strategy that goes by the cryptic acronym A2/AD—in other words, a focused force aimed at defending Australia's vital sea and air corridors to the near north. The focused force concept recommended that the government cut down on armoured vehicles and artillery purchases; instead, it should spend its money on the navy, 'which must be optimised for operating in Australia's immediate region'. The report came down heavily in favour of nuclear-powered submarines, but it is unclear exactly why.

As a former analyst with the Office of National Assessments—the forerunner of the ONI—Sam Roggeveen argued, quoting the *Defence Strategic Review*, that if the navy should be optimised for operating in our immediate region, why do we need submarines optimised for operating thousands of kilometres north of that region? And why is a naval base in Western Australia being upgraded so that the United States and United Kingdom can operate submarines along China's coast? Why is RAAF Base Tindal being modernised so the United States can operate long-range bombers from there? These are significant questions that no one in the government has adequately addressed.

With regard to the Tindal modernisation, the six parking bays being built for the B-52H aircraft—the H marks it as a nuclear-capable bomber—will allow the long-distance aircraft to operate in pairs: two loading bombs, two on the bombing mission, and two waiting. A lengthened runway will permit a fully laden B-52H to fly to the coast of China and back without refuelling.

The role of the B-52H at Tindal is particularly significant. For decades the B-52H used what are known as gravity bombs, which meant that the aircraft had to fly close to the target before releasing its weapons. Fitted with cruise missiles several years later, it was then able to remain at a distance but was often still too close to the possible enemy and risked being hit in a retaliatory strike. To overcome this problem, in 2019 the US military announced a major upgrade to the B-52H as it improved its nuclear arsenal to face down China. The USAF Nuclear Weapons Center awarded Boeing a US$250 million contract to give the B-52H an even longer reach. It would now be capable of carrying twenty Long Range Stand Off nuclear-armed cruise missiles. The new missiles are fitted with an internal navigation system that allows them—at least theoretically—to be pinpoint-accurate in hitting a target. They are also more elusive, flying low over the land or water, hard to track by radar and other weapons detection systems. This is one reason why the United States will be installing the long-range missiles on its B-52H bombers: they need to keep their distance from militarised islands and be able to hit them and the Chinese mainland without putting their aircraft in danger.

The former Liberal prime minister Malcolm Fraser originally allowed B-52s into Australia four decades ago to carry out navigation training exercises.[35] Back then, it was the fear of a Soviet threat that drove the policy. Significantly, under the 1981 agreement signed by Fraser, the United States needed prior approval for the aircraft to be used for any other purpose. Now the agreement over the use of America's most potent strategic weapon, based at an Australian airfield where it has its own hangars, munitions dumps and fuel storage areas, is unknown. As Professor Richard Tanter at Melbourne University's School of Political and Social Studies and an acclaimed expert on Australia–US military and intelligence points out, 'We know nothing of the implementing agreements under the Morrison and Albanese governments allowing the Tindal deployment.'[36]

Tindal is also the base for the RAAF's F-35 fleet—the trouble-prone, overbudget, US-made fighter bomber that John Howard signed up for in 2001 after the Twin Towers attack. It was another step by the former prime minister to mesh Australia into the US military. The F-35 was originally designed as a conventional fighter bomber, but the Pentagon was keen to make it dual use, capable of carrying nuclear weapons, too. Its supersonic speed and stealth characteristics would make it difficult to detect as it made its way over a target. Unlike the lumbering B-52, the F-35 could use the B61 gravity bomb. In October 2021 at a test range in Nevada, two F-35s dropped an imitation nuclear bomb that mimicked what the US military called a 'real-world tactical gravity nuclear weapon'.[37] With the F-35s and the B-52s alongside each other, Tindal has become Australia's frontline nuclear-capable airfield.

During the Cold War in the 1960s and 70s, the benefits of Tindal's relative isolation put it in the frontline of strategic thinking. Calculating that the main target for a nuclear strike would be Darwin, it was estimated that Tindal was far enough away from that city to escape the blast and, with luck, the ensuing radiation cloud. With much of the infrastructure still in place from the decades of preparing for a Soviet attack, Tindal's role has changed. No one is talking about it being used for defensive purposes today. It's a symbol of how Australia's military has returned to the days of 'forward defence'—a euphemism for expeditionary wars that saw Australian troops fighting alongside the United States in Vietnam to prevent what Washington called the domino theory, where country after country in Asia would fall to the Red Peril of communism. At the time, in July 1966, Australian prime minister Harold Holt told US president Lyndon Baines Johnson that Australia's commitment over Vietnam was unrelenting. 'All the way with LBJ,' he said.[38] Now, with a new Red Fear, it is 'All the way with the USA' over fears of China's expanding influence in the Indo-Pacific.

At Tindal there are storage areas set aside explicitly for United States use; marked for munitions, they are purpose-built shelters for housing the weapons. The question of ownership of those munitions is important. According to the agreement signed as part of AUKUS, the United States agrees to abide by Australian law. But if there is a secret agreement that allows the Americans to retain ownership of those weapons, Australian law may not apply, as was the case in the Netherlands with the storage of nuclear weapons. As revealed by WikiLeaks in 2010,[39] and later confirmed by former Dutch prime minister Ruud Lubbers,[40] the Netherlands Government allowed the USAF to store nuclear weapons at its Volkel Air Base during the Cold War and for many years after. It was a deliberate decision by the Dutch Government to hand over sovereignty to the United States.

There are several interlocking treaties between the United States and Australia dealing with the Americans storing their weapons and military hardware in Australia. One, signed in 2014 by the Abbott government, allows the United States to import and remove any material it wishes. Although Australia has the right to decide whether that material comes in, there appears to be no direct process by which it is told. Furthermore, the treaty states that the United States will maintain 'title' over the material, leaving the way open for Australia to argue that any nuclear weapons aren't legally Australia's but the property of the United States, and that Australia is not in breach of either the NPT or the Pacific Nuclear Free Zone Treaty. None of the treaties prevent Australia from allowing nuclear weapons to 'transit' its ports or airfields, such as Tindal. As shown by the Netherlands' storage of nuclear weapons, even the NPT does not stand in the way.

In other words, there might be a legitimate argument that the United States can keep any weapons (including nuclear weapons) it wishes at Tindal. They may not be held there permanently, but in a time of crisis they could be brought into Australia.

The question of what Australia knows about the inside operations of the 'joint facilities' is compounded by the question of exactly what 'joint' means. The Australian Government has identified three joint US–Australia facilities: North West Cape, Pine Gap and the USAF-operated Joint Geological and Geophysical Research Station. The geological station, near Alice Springs, on the face of it appears to be a benign operation providing seismic data on nuclear testing as part of Australia's support for nuclear non-proliferation, recording the seismic shock waves from both China's first nuclear test in

1964 and the Chernobyl nuclear meltdown in 1986. The seismic sensors, buried securely in a metal pipe 30 metres underground, register even the tiniest shock wave anywhere in the world. Inside the pipe, a free-floating magnet is surrounded by a metal coil. When the earth's crust moves, the coil around the magnet moves with it, creating an electrical signal that is relayed to Geoscience Australia and two other organisations that track compliance with the Comprehensive Nuclear-Test-Ban Treaty.

But those are not the only organisations that receive the data. It's also passed on to the Florida headquarters of the USAF's secretive Technical Applications Center (AFTAC), whose military staff run the entire operation near Alice Springs. While Australia has the right to locate staff at the station, according to the Australian office of the Nautilus Institute for Security and Sustainability, that hasn't happened. AFTAC, which is part of the Twenty-Fifth Air Force, also known as Air Force Intelligence, is controlled by a branch of the USAF that would provide command, control, computing and communications (C4) services to the US president aboard Air Force One in the event of a nuclear war. It also operates hundreds of highly sensitive detection systems throughout the world designed to pick up the fallout or shock waves from any low-yield or dirty nuclear bomb detonated inside the United States. This is Australia's contribution to a nuclear club that Canberra joined decades ago.

Exactly what the United States does in Australia is not transparent. As Stephen Smith told the parliament in 2013, Australia could only get a 'detailed understanding' of what was happening 'by having Australian involvement in operations; having access to products; and through provision of briefs'.[41] In other words, Australia would know what was going on by working alongside the Americans. Only after the event would it be able to have 'reviews of activities when they occur'. The mangled syntax makes it difficult to understand exactly what this means, but it appears to give Australia the possibility of reviewing at a later date something the United States has done without Australia's knowledge. In other words, unless it was directly involved in a military operation, it would have no idea what was happening inside the joint facilities on Australian soil.

Paying a high price for protection from a powerful ally has long been part of the history of Australia, but it wasn't always the prevailing wisdom. As we shall see, in the 1950s there were many in Canberra who wanted Australia to acquire its own nuclear weapons.

11

The Bomb

On a summer's day in 1958 the prime minister of the United Kingdom, Harold Macmillan, arrived at Canberra Airport. He was met by his Australian counterpart, Robert Menzies. Leaders only travel halfway across the world to speak to each other face to face if there is something extremely important to discuss, and few things are more important than a nation's security. What Menzies wanted to talk to Macmillan about was of the utmost sensitivity: nuclear weapons.

Menzies was no particular fan of the latest fashion in destructive capability. He preferred to rely upon the United Kingdom for protection. But others in Australia—and his government—disagreed. Memories of World War II, when the British had abandoned Australia, leaving it to fight largely alone, were still fresh. Many in the government and the Defence Department wanted an independent nuclear weapons force that could act in Australia's national interests without having to rely on the British.

Leading the charge was Sir Philip Baxter, chair of the Australian Atomic Energy Commission (AAEC), who wanted to build a facility for the production of weapons-grade plutonium in the mining town of Mount Isa in outback Queensland. It was an ideal site: remote, but close to some of the richest seams of uranium in the world. Baxter appealed to the British: if they would help, in return they would get guaranteed access to uranium for their own nuclear industry. The collaboration would allow Australia to have its own nuclear bomb.

Baxter's plan was too audacious for Menzies, who opted for a far simpler and less hazardous road to nuclear weapons: Australia could buy them from the British. But there were problems with that course of action, because the United Kingdom would need to get permission from the United States to pass on weapons that used US nuclear technology. The British were worried that if they asked the Americans for permission to share nuclear weapons with Australia, it might disrupt the sensitive negotiations that were underway with Washington at the time to share US nuclear secrets with London.

Despite the delicate situation, Baxter and the heads of the three armed services in Australia, the air force, navy and army, continued secretly pressing the United Kingdom for access to nuclear weapons. These covert discussions have an eerie echo, more than sixty-five years later, of the secrecy surrounding the AUKUS nuclear deal. And as now, once again the Defence Department was deeply involved in acts of deception.

When he discovered what the nuclear watchdog, the AAEC and Defence had been up to, Menzies was infuriated. He issued a stern warning to the Defence Department and chiefs of staff that they were no longer to 'initiate discussions with the United Kingdom authorities concerning the possibility of nuclear weapons being made available to us until specific approval is given by me'.[1]

In the end Menzies changed his mind, but he was careful not to offend the United Kingdom with any grandiose Australian strategic plans for South-East Asia. He made it clear that the nuclear weapons Australia wanted were tactical, not strategic. He was particularly interested in what his government called the 'means of delivery'—nuclear-capable bomber aircraft.[2]

In Whitehall, the UK seat of government, the British saw an opportunity. Despite the problem of having to get clearance from the United States before transferring American nuclear information and technology to Australia, the British were keen to help. They had strong strategic interests in Australia, particularly its nuclear test sites in the Montebello Islands off the coast of Western Australia, and Maralinga in South Australia. Though the Australian Government had allowed them to explode increasingly powerful nuclear weapons since the early 1950s, the British had refused to share any of the technical information derived from the tests.

Keen to maintain its strong nuclear relationship with Australia, the United Kingdom came up with a novel solution that benefited both countries.

The UK military would support the sale of tactical nuclear weapons to Australia with one major proviso: Australia must buy a number of British-made aircraft to deliver the weapons. Known as V bombers, the Vulcan, Victor and Valiant aircraft were the backbone of the UK nuclear strike force; capable of travelling at supersonic speed, they were able to hit targets deep inside the Soviet Union. The Australians had already witnessed the V bombers' capability when a Valiant was used to drop an imitation British nuclear bomb at Maralinga. Their sale would be a great boost for the British aerospace industry and tie Australia closer to the United Kingdom, heading off competition from US plane makers who were keen to sell Canberra the nuclear-capable F-111 fighter bomber.

In the end the bomb program did not go ahead, largely stymied by a hardening of Australian public opinion against the possession of nuclear weapons. In November 1959, Cabinet even decided against asking the British to share information from a new round of nuclear tests that were planned for the coming months. The government made a decision to shelter under the United Kingdom's nuclear umbrella and support the limiting of nuclear weapons to a few major powers.

Even so, Australia's desire for nuclear weapons did not completely evaporate. The AAEC had opened a nuclear reactor in 1958 in the south-western Sydney suburb of Lucas Heights, the first to be built in the Southern Hemisphere. Housed in a sealed circular steel building 21 metres wide and 21 metres high, its core contained twenty-five fuel rods and 280 grams of enriched uranium.

Lucas Heights' role was to test materials for use in future nuclear-power stations. The government had plans to build a reactor at Jervis Bay on the New South Wales south coast and a string of others across the country. In the 1950s, nuclear power was heralded as the most efficient way to produce cheap electricity. What the government wasn't so keen to point out was nuclear power's potential by-product: plutonium, the core component of nuclear weapons. Both the United States and the Soviet Union recognised the problem of nuclear power stations' bomb-grade plutonium and the potential creation of a host of nuclear-armed states. Together they negotiated the NPT to stop nuclear fuel being diverted to make nuclear weapons.

The Liberal Party, however, wanted to keep its nuclear options open and refused to sign the NPT. Under pressure from a public fearful of nuclear war, Prime Minister John Gorton finally did sign, but he made it clear that his government had not ratified the treaty, so it had no effect in law. In other words, Australia still planned to have the capability to produce a nuclear weapon. The Jervis Bay nuclear power plant would not be built just to produce electricity but would also serve the purpose the NPT was designed to stop: the siphoning off of plutonium from the uranium waste to make nuclear weapons. In an interview with *Sydney Morning Herald* reporter Pilita Clark in 1999, Gorton finally admitted that was the plan: 'We were interested in this thing [the power plant] because it could provide electricity to everybody and it could, if you decided later on, it could make an atomic bomb.'[3]

Only when the Whitlam government was elected in 1972 did Australia ratify the treaty and become bound by its rules of disclosure. But even that did not stop Australia's nuclear ambitions. For the next decade, after the Whitlam government was removed from office in 1975, the pro-nuclear lobby kept up the pressure. Inside a top-secret enclave at Lucas Heights known as Shed 54, a group called the Uranium Enrichment Team (UET) developed a new and novel way to enrich uranium, matching the most advanced system at the time—Europe's enrichment program, run by a consortium called Urenco. Though it was a brilliant scientific breakthrough, it posed a major threat to Australia's obligations under the NPT. The enrichment program might help boost Australia's uranium ore exports, but it was also a step towards the construction of a nuclear weapon.

In 1983 the incoming Labor government wasted no time in moving to shut down the enrichment process. Don Mercer, a senior member of the UET, remembers the day a government official arrived: 'He came in, flanked by two minders, walked through the plant, didn't ask a question, walked out and said, "You're closed down." Like that.'[4]

Desperate to keep the research going, Dr Clarence Hardy, a physicist and senior manager at Lucas Heights, developed a novel plan with his team.

They persuaded the Australian Department of Foreign Affairs to fund a program the IAEA could use to monitor uranium enrichment programs to ensure NPT safeguards were being honoured by all the signatories to the treaty. From the fifth floor of Hardy's office in Sydney's Kings Cross, the team monitored the enrichment process at Lucas Heights by remote control. Hooked up by video cameras, they could check everything that was taking place at the plant, including the rate at which uranium was being enriched. Under the cloak of developing better safeguards, the UET had been allowed to continue operating the uranium enrichment centrifuges. It was a stopgap measure, placing the project on life support until the election of a Liberal government, which the team assessed would allow full-scale enrichment to continue.

But Labor won the next election and, according to Hardy, when funding from the Foreign Affairs Department ran out, it wasn't renewed. All was not lost, though. A private technology company, Silex, which rented space at Lucas Heights adjacent to Shed 54, set up a uranium enrichment program with a partner company in the United States in 2001.[5] Silex didn't use centrifuge systems that relied upon rows of spinning tubes to create enriched uranium: it was developing a revolutionary system using lasers. Just what the connection, if any, was between Hardy's work and Silex has never been explained. And why should Silex—a private company—be allowed to operate inside the top-secret Lucas Heights facility?

A hint at what was going on came in November 1999, when President Bill Clinton told the US Congress that his administration had signed the so-called Silex Agreement (its full name was *Agreement for Cooperation with the United States of America Concerning Technology for the Separation of Isotopes of Uranium by Laser Excitation*) with the Howard government. Clinton told Congress he had assured the Australian Government that Silex technology would not be used to enrich uranium for nuclear weapons, but it was not a complete guarantee. He added, 'Yet, to ensure the enduring ability of the United States to meet its common defense and security needs, the United States must maintain its military nuclear capabilities.'[6] Clinton indicated that although Silex itself would not be involved in weapons production, the US Energy Department would be keeping an eye on the Australian company in case any of the processes it developed might be useful in making nuclear weapons. One matter Clinton was clear about: the Silex Agreement specifically prohibited the 'construction of a uranium enrichment facility in Australia'.[7] Silex would remain at Lucas Heights but the enrichment would be carried out in the United States.

The agreement was a big win for the nuclear industry, allowing Australia to outsource its obligations under the NPT to the Americans but still keep its foot in the door for a nuclear future. For its part, the United States agreed to send highly classified nuclear 'restricted data' to Silex at Lucas Heights,[8] with agreement from the Australian Government that it would be tightly held in a top-secret area.

There is a reason Silex technology is such a closely guarded secret. The system it developed is known as dual use. Though it's designed for only low-level enrichment, there is no guarantee the technology can't be used in weapons production. Its main disadvantage is its cost, but because it doesn't require large buildings and is easy to hide, it's a proliferation risk. The off-shoring of the Silex enrichment process in the United States leaves open the possibility of the system being imported back into Australia if the law prohibiting nuclear power is ever rescinded. Various Liberal Party leaders have been trying to do just that for decades.

In the dying days of his administration in 2006, John Howard commissioned a report to examine using Australian uranium to power electricity generation, this time as an answer to climate change. He had already personally inaugurated a new, more advanced reactor at Lucas Heights, and with an election less than a year away, the report was another attempt to wedge Labor on nuclear issues. In the end its author, nuclear physicist Dr Ziggy Switkowski, failed to produce the decisive blow Howard hoped would destroy Labor's anti-nuclear platform, and Howard lost the election.

Thirteen years later, with the Liberal Party once again in power and facing a difficult election, nuclear energy—which had barely been mentioned during the Liberals' previous terms in office—once again asserted itself. In December 2019, after a rapid four-month inquiry, a government-controlled House of Representatives committee called for Australia to consider the possibility of 'collaborating with and learning from international partners with expertise in nuclear energy'.[9] It was hardly a coincidence that the timing was perfect for the government, which for the several months had been secretly working with the United States and the United Kingdom on the AUKUS submarine project and an agreement to share nuclear technology with Australia. Once again a Liberal government was raising the possibility of ending a ban it had introduced in 1999 after a deal with the Australian Democrats and the Greens outlawing the construction of nuclear power stations, fuel enrichment and reprocessing.[10]

In 2023 the new Liberal Party leader, Peter Dutton, argued that technology had improved, particularly for smaller modular plants that could be used to fill gaps in the power generation system as Australia moved away from fossil fuels. Waiting in the wings to help fulfil the Liberal Party's latest dreams of a nuclear Australia was Silex. In August 2023 it boasted that its uranium enrichment process was ideal for Dutton's small modular reactors (SMRs).

Like Australia, Canada is a country with rich and cheap reserves of uranium. Supporters of nuclear power argue that it's a cost-effective, low-carbon alternative to wind and solar and can provide baseload power when those sources sometimes cannot. However, an investigation by Australia's chief scientific organisation, CSIRO, found that any form of nuclear power was more expensive than renewables, and the SMRs would take too long to build to have any impact on global warming.[11]

Alan J Kuperman perceives another agenda—a country where nuclear politics lurks below the surface of any discussion about the military or power generation—and a massive mining lobby that has extraordinary influence on government policy. Every country had different economic fundamentals, he said, but Australia's surely favoured renewables over nuclear. 'Any move to nuclear energy would either be a favour to industry or hedging for a bomb program—nothing else makes sense,' he told me.[12]

Whatever the arguments about nuclear and the safety fears of local communities where the reactors might be stationed, one of the biggest obstacles to its introduction is its highly radioactive nuclear waste. Dutton cited a decision by Canada, which already manufactures and uses nuclear reactors and was examining the use of SMRs, as an example Australia could follow.[13] But the safety and efficiency of SMRs—there are only two in the world, one in Russia, the other in France—is hotly debated. According to a peer-reviewed study published by the US National Academy of Sciences, founded in 1863 to provide independent objective scientific advice to the US Government, the small reactors create thirty times more radioactive waste per unit of electricity than conventional reactors.[14] The study singled out Dutton's preferred models, including the reactor type being proposed by Canada, as particularly problematic: this kind of reactor created waste that would need additional treatments to make it safe to store. The report added that the processes would also introduce significant costs, likely radiation exposure, and what it called 'fissile material proliferation pathways'. In other words, those extra treatments made the waste vulnerable to being converted to make fissile materials for a crude nuclear bomb.

Allison Macfarlane, a co-author of the study and former chair of the US Nuclear Regulatory Commission, said although it was important to know about the waste products and whether they were going to pose any difficulties in disposing of them and managing them, SMR designers 'don't pay that much attention in general to the waste ... because the thing that makes money for them is the reactor'.[15]

Over three decades from the 1970s, the United States spent nearly US$7 billion trying to find a location to store its nuclear waste. Its solution: bury it deep underground in Yucca Mountain in Nevada. As one of the most geographically studied sites in the world, chosen in part for its remote location, many were confident that the area was the answer to permanent nuclear waste storage. But though the nuclear regulatory bodies might have done their geological work in finding a place to dump the highly contaminated material, they made one fatal error: they failed to 'adequately consult and respect tribal perspectives and concerns' of the Western Shoshone and Southern Paiute peoples, the traditional owners of Yucca Mountain.[16] The plan to use Yucca Mountain was stopped by the Obama administration.

It's a similar story in Australia, where for the past forty years successive governments have been searching for a suitable nuclear waste dump site. By 2021 the Morrison government believed it had found one, in the remote Kimba district of South Australia. But the area's traditional owners, the Barngarla people, were highly suspicious that the nuclear site would be safe. They had a deep distrust and fear of nuclear waste after British bomb tests in the 1950s and 60s poisoned their land and left many suffering from the effects of radioactive fallout. In 2023 the Federal Court blocked plans for the site at Kimba, ruling in favour of the Barngarla people, who had argued they were not properly consulted by the former Coalition government about the decision to pick the site.[17]

What will happen to the waste from Australia's nuclear submarines is a vexed question. Despite all the hype surrounding their acquisition—and the dangers posed by their waste—no provision has been made. There is currently no national facility, and the waste pile is growing. Much of it is stored in hospital basements and universities, on defence and mining sites and in research laboratories. The vast majority from Australia's sole nuclear reactor is stored at Lucas Heights, but the storage space there is not infinite. In the foreseeable future a site will have to be found, if only to cater for Australia's low-level waste from nuclear medicine.

The AUKUS deal only complicates the issue. The US and UK naval reactors that will power both the Virginia-class subs and the future UK AUKUS boats are fuelled by highly enriched uranium. Once removed and decommissioned, any spent fuel from naval reactors is reprocessed to extract usable nuclear fuel for civilian power generation. The problem is that this nuclear waste also contains plutonium, the component of nuclear weapons. Since Australia has said it will not reprocess its nuclear submarine fuel, the question is: Where will it go? It could be sent to the United States, with the extraneous waste being sent back to Australia to be stored here. But that is problematic.

As David Gould, the former UK Ministry of Defence adviser who oversaw the final selection for the original Australian submarine deal with the French, explained, 'All of that on the inside [of the submarine reactor] will have been contaminated. It's got a half-life of ninety years, 100 years. So you have to let it cool down. And the best thing to do with it is bury it. Environmentalists don't like it, but it is a very good thing to do with it. The other thing to do with it is cover it in concrete.'[18]

Even during the life of the submarines, nuclear power being used by a non-nuclear country like Australia is a complex problem for the IAEA to unpack. It is understood that Australia wants to discuss options to verify that the nuclear material remains in the nuclear-powered submarines.[19] The IAEA may demand that it makes physical inspections to make sure no HEU goes missing, but this, too, is a tricky area. Who owns the reactors on the submarines Australia is trying to buy from the United States? Who owns the enriched uranium? It might be useful for the IAEA to be told the reactors and uranium remain the property of the Americans, but what does that say about Australia's sovereignty? If the United States owns the reactors and the fuel, who really owns the submarines?

Maintaining ownership might solve one problem but create another for the Americans. As a nuclear-armed state, the United States has never had to allow the IAEA to inspect its submarines' reactors, with their highly classified propulsion systems. It would be a first if the Americans allowed that to happen in Australia. The precedent it creates is dangerous. As respected nuclear physicist Frank N von Hippel revealed,[20] in 2013 during the hardline administration of Iranian president Mahmoud Ahmadinejad, the head of the Atomic Energy Organization of Iran suggested Tehran might require uranium enriched to 45–56 per cent for a nuclear submarine program. After the AUKUS deal was announced in 2021, two journalists from the *New York Times* interviewed aides accompanying Iran's new foreign minister to the United Nations and reported that the aides noted that HEU 'could be used in naval reactors, suggesting they might want to use it for that purpose. And they cited Biden's new deal with Australia, which calls for [the United States and the United Kingdom] to supply Australia with the technology for nuclear-propelled submarines,' which use HEU.[21] The argument that Iran could run was simple. If Australia can use HEU to run its submarines and not be in breach of the NPT, why can't we? The problem for the IAEA would be to keep track of the HEU in Iran and prevent it being diverted into a nuclear weapon.

Professor von Hippel has a stark warning over the AUKUS deal: '[It] highlights the fact that the United States and United Kingdom are undermining the nuclear non-proliferation and anti-terrorism regimes by fuelling their naval reactors with weapons-grade uranium. Now they propose to export these reactors to a non-nuclear-weapon state.' He argues that if the United States does not switch to using LEU naval fuel by about 2060, when its excess stock of weapons-grade uranium is projected to run out, it will have to restart production of weapons-grade uranium for the first time since the end of the Cold War.[22]

The irony of this strategic and nuclear mess is that the answer to Australia's nuclear quandary lies in the very country whose submarines it rejected. Within days of Scott Morrison cancelling the French submarine deal, Naval Group drew up a plan to sell Australia its nuclear-powered submarines, the same submarine class the French had redesigned so their nuclear reactors could be removed in order to meet Australia's demands for conventional propulsion. The French Barracuda class uses LEU, not HEU. There would be no need to worry about nuclear proliferation, and the problems of waste storage would be greatly reduced. And the French deal meant Australia would be able to build an independent nuclear industry that in time could service and maintain the submarine fleet—an independent and sovereign nuclear-powered submarine fleet unencumbered by the foreign policy objectives of the United States, and all that entails.

Instead, Australia is struggling with how to maintain its maritime defence with Collins-class submarines that should be retiring; with United Kingdom's Astute class, which won't probably come on stream until 2040 at the earliest; and with the possibility that the United States will renege on its deal to sell Australia Virginia-class submarines in around 2030.

In his 'War in 2025' speech at the ASPI conference in 2019, ADF head Angus Campbell talked of 'looking ahead to war in 2025; to be interested in war, interested in a war so near it will definitely and personally be interested in me and all of you'. Ironically, this inflammatory language from the head of Australia's armed forces, clearly aimed at China, was part of an address designed to warn the Australian population about the use of propaganda. It's doubtful, though, that Campbell saw the contradiction, as he went on to talk about US 'Congressional investigations shut[ting] down covert operations, much to the chagrin of embittered advocates of the dark arts'.[23] For Campbell, it appeared that the 'dark arts' were only bad if they were practised by countries that didn't share 'Western values'. He didn't point out that a Congressional investigation revealed the CIA's involvement in coups and assassinations around the world, including in the destruction of the democratically elected government of Chile in 1973.[24]

It is extraordinary, given the level of concern in ALP ranks about the feared role of the CIA in destabilising the Whitlam government, that Campbell kept his job when Labor formed government. And then there was Andrew Shearer. Many in the ALP wanted him gone when they took office, but he was kept in place to calm Washington's worries that Labor might be too left-leaning. History has revealed there was little risk of that happening.

Labor was aware that antagonising the United States could have painful repercussions, which is one of the reasons the leadership embraced AUKUS and the increasing US military presence in Australia. But not everyone in the party was happy.

12

No Way Out?

The presence of the US military in Australia and the United States' influence on the country's foreign policy have been major irritations in the Labor Party for decades. The debates have often been rowdy and bitter. AUKUS, with its nuclear-powered submarines and an even closer relationship with the US military, threatened to be double trouble for new prime minister Anthony Albanese.

One of the party leader's toughest jobs is to face the membership every three years at the annual national conference. It's even more difficult when the party is in power and decisions made at the conference have a real impact. As he walked into the Brisbane Convention Centre in August 2023, Albanese had already worked the numbers to embrace AUKUS in the party platform, but that didn't mean AUKUS wouldn't get a raucous reception.

Though the public face was one of ALP unity, with opposition pushed to the political fringe, behind the scenes there was anything but cordial agreement, even in the mainstream of the party. Party cohesion wasn't helped by the comments of the defence industry minister, Senator Pat Conroy, who told the conference, 'Strength deters war, appeasement invites conflict.'[1] Some members of the Labor Cabinet did not take kindly to the description of them as 'appeasers'. They'd kept quiet for the sake of unity but had been talking privately about the disastrous consequences of the AUKUS deal.

After Scott Morrison ambushed Labor in September 2021, Rex Patrick, who was still a senator at the time, spoke with several senior members of the ALP about how to handle the nuclear submarine issue. Patrick was the go-to person in Parliament House for a no-nonsense assessment of the project.

Even before the deal was announced he'd received a call from the deputy prime minister, Barnaby Joyce, asking him to explain the workings of nuclear submarines: What was their role, and how different were they from conventionally powered boats?

Only after the AUKUS announcement did Patrick understand why Joyce had called him. Morrison had been so secretive about his discussions with the Americans that even the leader of the National Party, whose support kept Morrison's government in power, had been shut out until the last moment.

Once the deal was announced, Patrick began a vigorous lobbying campaign against it, meeting senior members of the ALP and hoping to persuade them to change the policy. If Labor won the election in 2022, he saw an opportunity for the new government to take a second look.

Patrick's activities reveal what was hidden from public view on the floor of the ALP conference: there had been great concern among a number of newly appointed Labor Cabinet ministers that AUKUS was an expensive disaster in the making. Patrick tried to persuade them it wasn't too late to prevent the deal from going ahead; they were sympathetic to his arguments and wanted it stopped. 'Their difficulty was that they viewed it as: How do you stop this thing now?' Patrick said.[2] He advised them to make a submission to the inquiry being led by former head of the ADF Angus Houston and former Labor defence minister Stephen Smith, which was due to report in eighteen months on the viability of AUKUS. Whether or not the submission happened Patrick doesn't know, but there were no complaints from the ministers—not even when the $368 billion nuclear submarine price tag was revealed. A Cabinet decision had been made, and they were bound by it.

The Australian political system was faced with one of its greatest challenges. Fearful of being accused of being weak on national security, Labor had embraced a decision taken after a deeply flawed process. With the major parties in lock step on AUKUS, the most complex and expensive spend in Australian military history would never be publicly investigated. The closest the Australian public got to any kind of accountability for the disastrous AUKUS process came just six weeks after Morrison had ambushed Labor—well before the federal election in May 2022.

In any other circumstances, what came out of Senator Penny Wong's detailed grilling of the secretary of the Defence Department and members of the military at the Senate estimates hearing in October 2021 would have produced grounds for a royal commission. Since Labor's full embrace of AUKUS on 15 September 2021, any opposition to the submarine project was now out of the question. But by forensically examining the process by which they were being acquired, Wong could make life very difficult for those who had been deeply involved in Morrison's extraordinary act of deception. Were they serving the public, as public servants are required to do, or were they aiding their political masters?

Wong chose her target carefully, with her questioning focused on the process. Had Defence done its due diligence on the need for nuclear-powered submarines and the creation of AUKUS? She meticulously unpicked Morrison's skirting around and undermining parliamentary process with the support of the Australian military.

Wong asked Greg Moriarty to explain how Defence usually goes about making a risk assessment or acquisition plan before sending it to government ministers for consideration. In his reply he stated what should have been obvious to any mildly informed onlooker: 'A requirement is identified.'[3] In other words, is there a problem that needs fixing or a threat that needs to be countered? It might not have sounded like much of a reply to an important question, but it went to the heart of the matter: Had anyone in Defence thought AUKUS was necessary for the defence of Australia? Well, no, they hadn't. If they had, what would have been the process? Once a decision had been made that Australia needed an agreement like AUKUS for its defence, 'the idea would be worked through the parliamentary committees', Moriarty told the Senate. The proposal would go to the investment committee (to assess the cost) and the Defence committee (to see how it worked), and then it would be taken to the defence minister 'for his or her consideration'.

The fact that none of that was done meant that either the Defence Department didn't know about AUKUS and was blindsided itself, or it did. And if it did, was it conniving with the government to breach parliamentary process?

Moriarty told Wong that it was in May or June 2021 that Prime Minister Morrison was thinking about 'the framing' of the way in which he wished to approach this engagement with the United States and the United Kingdom. Senator Wong: 'This framework, as you describe the partnership—was that the Prime Minister's idea?' Moriarty: 'I believe it was.'

So Morrison had come up with the idea of AUKUS, but no reason for its existence had been identified.

The decision-making process for switching to nuclear-powered submarines and dumping the French was embarrassing for the Defence Department. In the normal process, before making any decision to go ahead with a military acquisition, the government and the department must go through a number of parliamentary committee hearings known as 'gates'. Gate One scrutinises the concept and the necessity; Gate Two mainly examines the cost and benefits. The nuclear submarine proposal had not even passed Gate One.

Senator Wong put it to the vice chief of the ADF, Vice Admiral David Johnston, that there was 'no Gate One approval for the acquisition of nuclear-propelled submarines'.

Vice Admiral Johnston: 'That's correct.'

Senator Wong: 'Thank you—and therefore, obviously, no Gate Two.'

Vice Admiral Johnston: 'Yes.'

Senator Wong: 'It's an interesting way to do it, isn't it? You do a public announcement and you message that you're going to get nuclear subs, but actually you've not made any decisions other than to consult about it and to cancel a contract.'

It was a devastating analysis. The Defence Department had not only been party to deceiving the French, it had connived with the Morrison government to breach the basic rules of process necessary for the defence of Australia. Senator Wong's work laid the groundwork for what inevitably lay ahead in understanding the catastrophic fallout of the shambles created by Morrison—a disaster that Labor would have to deal with if it won the election.

Though the US Congress voted in December 2023 to support the sale of at least three Virginia-class boats to Australia, a presidential veto could always sink the agreement—not an impossibility given the fractured state of the US political system. What is more alarming is the comment made after the vote by the Senate majority leader, Chuck Schumer, who described AUKUS as 'a game changer' that would create 'a new fleet of nuclear-powered submarines to counter the Chinese Communist Party's threat and influence in the Pacific'.[4] There is no doubt what he and many other high-ranking officials in the United States see as the primary role of the Virginia-class boats, if they ever arrive in Australia.

Meanwhile, there are serious questions about how Australia will cope with the US military strategy to contain the rise of China. A more farsighted national security view would have invested heavily in the nations of the Indo-Pacific instead of abandoning them after the end of the Cold War, when Australia felt their usefulness had run its course, or, in the case of Timor, spying on and exploiting the oil reserves of an impoverished country. Though Defence Minister Richard Marles has ruled out automatic support of the United States in any war over Taiwan, it is difficult to see how Australia won't be involved. Pine Gap, Tindal, North West Cape and Perth will all be integral to the battle.

Labor not only has to manage the disastrous nuclear submarine acquisition program and pay the French $835 million compensation for Australia's failing to honour the submarine contract, it also has to deal with another legacy of the Morrison government: the arrival of more B-52s, and their nuclear capabilities. Australia could give clear and categorical assurances to the Australian public and the IAEA that any nuclear-powered submarine under its control would not be nuclear-armed, but it can give no such assurances involving the US military. In the Senate in February 2023, Greens senator Jordan Steele-John asked the obvious question: 'I'm seeking on behalf of the community to get a firm commitment from the government that the B-52s cycling through Australia will be solely conventionally capable, not nuclear-capable.'[5]

It was a question to which Steele-John already knew the answer—the B-52H is nuclear-capable—but that wasn't his point. His intention was to expose Labor's anti-nuclear credentials as highly questionable. In this theatre of the absurd, the Greens understood only too well that the South Pacific Nuclear Free Zone Treaty specifically did not prevent the transit of nuclear weapons through Australia or any other part of the Pacific. They also knew that Labor, both in and out of government, accepted that the United States needed to neither confirm nor deny any position on nuclear weapons.

Wong's job as the government leader in the Senate and Australia's foreign minister meant that she had to mount an awkward and tortuous defence to Steele-John's question. There was no straightforward reply, just the repeated line about the government's acceptance of the US policy of neither confirm nor deny, and treaty obligations that allow US military aircraft to enter Australia.[6] A simple answer would have been: There is nothing under Australian law or any treaties the government has signed that prevents the United States from bringing nuclear-capable or nuclear-armed ships or aircraft into Australia. There is, however, an agreement that nuclear weapons will not be 'stored' in Australia.

But the Australian public will never hear those words from any government. Politicians are fearful that if the public suspects there are nuclear weapons travelling in and out of Australia, they will raise moral objections or fear being part of a nuclear war in which they have no say.

The Greens have an unusual ally in their attempts to make governments more accountable for their nuclear policy. In my interview with former Liberal Party leader and prime minister Malcolm Turnbull, I asked him if the Australian people had a right to know if nuclear weapons were stored in their country. He replied, 'I think if we were to have nuclear weapons stored in Australia, that's something that would be a legitimate matter of public concern.'[7] That, of course, does not mean he is opposed to the 'neither confirm nor deny' position of the United States if they carry nuclear weapons through Australian ports and airfields, but it is a firm belief that if the Americans ever want to store nuclear weapons in Australia, the Australian people have a right to know they are there. The question is: Would they ever be told? And what sort of legal fiction might be constructed to bypass Australia's treaty obligations, as happened in the Netherlands? If history is any guide, it will be difficult to get clarity on the issue. Obfuscation is the normal response to any question about nuclear issues in Australia. The truth will remain under lock and key and only seep out, if at all, decades into the future.

Turnbull's anxieties go to the heart of Australian sovereignty. Successive governments have clearly decided that Australia's independence is not diminished by US nuclear weapons moving through the nation's ports, but as Turnbull points out, storing them on Australian soil is a matter of much greater significance.

As Sam Roggeveen of the Lowy Institute says, 'There is, of course, a deeper question hanging over Australia's escalating military build-up and the consequences of its increasing role in international affairs. Australia has never before gone so dramatically on the offensive in its weapons acquisition, buying a weapon expressly designed to hem China's navy in along its coastline and strike targets deep inside Chinese territory.' He says it's not just a question of 'military strategy but of how Australia defines itself as an international actor, and as a nation. Australians should be asking themselves: is this really who we are?'[8]

It's a big question about how governments make decisions and the processes that are supposed to protect the population from government overreach. All governments are secretive, trying to promote their achievements and bury their failures. They also try to push through policy that may have questionable legal foundations. The role of the public service is to stand in the way of these grievous misadventures, to protect the population from the idiocies of the executive arm of government. The road to this catastrophe can be, in part at least, traced back to the failure of a weakened public service, too keen to please its political masters.

One of the great ironies of this tragic saga is that it was Paul Keating—one of the biggest critics of AUKUS—who took the first step to ending tenure, introducing fixed contracts for public service departmental secretaries in 1994. It was true that entrenched mandarins could be a problem, but the subsequent Howard and Abbott governments took to Keating's changed rules with gusto, destroying any notion of tenure, outsourcing work and stacking the public service with their ideological supporters. Thirty years later, compliant public servants put up no resistance to Morrison's and Dutton's disastrous decision to dump the French submarines, leaving a gaping hole in Australia's most vital defences. Home Affairs Secretary Michael Pezzullo, who was banging the drums of war to do the bidding of his political masters, laid bare what had been apparent for some time: the public service has been politicised to a point where it is difficult to see how public servants can give frank and fearless advice.

But Pezzullo had been doing more than following the government line. A series of text messages between him and Liberal Party insider Scott Briggs, a close confidant of Scott Morrison, showed that he had sought to undermine political and public service enemies and promote the careers of right-wing politicians he considered allies. His texts contained derogatory comments about former foreign affairs ministers Julie Bishop and Marise Payne, both moderate Liberals.[9] For Pezzullo there appeared to be no line between being a public servant and being a politician—another legacy of the Morrison government. He was finally fired in November 2023 after the Australian Public Service commissioner announced that an independent inquiry had determined Pezzullo had breached the APS Code of Conduct fourteen times.[10]

The Australian Department of Defence is another prime example of the increasingly blurred line between the public service and service to the government, with ADF head Angus Campbell's public warning of the need to be prepared for a coming war strongly echoing the government line. Kim Gillis is not critical of Campbell but understands well how the system should operate. Having worked in defence acquisitions for the Australian Government and Boeing defence industries, he has reached the conclusion that only a strong public service can prevent another shambles like the Attack-class submarine. Gillis, who was deputy secretary for defence acquisitions under Turnbull, says it was his job to give frank and fearless advice to the executive branch of government. Public servants need to fight against what he calls 'the commercial naivety of governments of various persuasions'.¹¹ Gillis wants to see the return of tenure for public service heads of department, which will prevent the government of the day installing bureaucrats who simply agree with their policies. 'We don't have enough people telling the truth in the government.'

Gillis says that if he had been in his old job and Morrison was prime minister and told him to cancel the French deal 'in the way that that was handled', he would have resigned. Only 'an independent public service will stop the same mistakes being made again', he says. He points out that the Morrison government did not follow its own procurement rules, bypassing many of the commercial steps that should have been followed, and then made a decision to buy submarines from the Americans without any pricing. The United States and the United Kingdom have become 'sole source providers', which meant that Australia had 'limited political or commercial leverage'.

One senior diplomat who had experience both in government administration and intelligence said he believed it would have been reasonable for a public servant to blow the whistle on Morrison's nuclear submarine deal by offering to give evidence to the Senate—such was the breach of due process involving the public service.¹²

For Turnbull, the lessons for Australia go beyond the submarines. It's not just the impact that the submarine decision had on Australia's relationship with France: it also affected the way Australia was judged by its regional neighbours. 'The more we are seen as being a rubber stamp, wholly owned subsidiary agent, whatever, of the United States, the less influence we have. It's as simple as that,' he says.¹³ And there are other dangers from being seen by neighbouring countries as being too close to the United States: 'If we are just literally an echo chamber for Washington or an agent of Washington, then why [should they] not just talk to the head office?'

What rightly appalls Turnbull is that there has been no real public debate about such a radical shift to outsource a major component of Australia's defence to the United States by spending 'a couple of hundred billion dollars of defence expenditure on assets over which we will not have exclusive control'. He points out that 'it is fundamental that all of our military capabilities should be thoroughly sovereign. That's to say we should be able to maintain and sustain them ourselves. If you have a nuclear submarine that can only be safely operated under the supervision of the United States Navy, then it is not a sovereign capability.'

Turnbull is strongly supported by Professor Clinton Fernandes, a former Australian military intelligence officer who understands full well the meaning of sovereignty. Fernandes, who witnessed first hand the young nation of Timor-Leste fight for its independence during its brutal suppression by Indonesia, said he wanted to get on the record that he strongly disagreed with Albanese that Australia would have sovereign control over the Virginia-class submarines. 'I think this is disinformation that has been thought up for him by his advisers who are spin doctors.' He points out that sovereignty is more than whose flag is painted on the outside of a boat or who ranks above whom inside it. Sovereignty is about the purpose for which the boats are intended[14]—and the purpose for which these vessels are being used is interchangeability with the United States in order to threaten China's seaborne food, energy and trade supplies during a crisis. It's not just the submarines that are causing sovereignty problems.

Several sources have confirmed that Shearer gave advice to the Morrison government about 'the US submarines and the French contract' which, as cabinet secretary was reasonable, but something as director of national intelligence he should not have been asked to do, according to a former intelligence chief. His job was to manage the agencies and ensure they carried out the 'tasking' they were directed to do, such as intercepting phone calls or carrying out covert operations against foreign governments.

It must be remembered that Labor opposed Morrison's decision to appoint Shearer as head of ONI because of his partisan views, but he had signed a five-year contract and couldn't be sacked. One source said he was still too close to the Americans.[15] Whether or not Australia had become the de facto fifty-first State of the United States is hotly contested, but what cannot be disputed is that US influence is as strong now as it has ever been. Yet any attempt by Australia to become truly independent of the United States would require a huge shift in thinking. And unhitching from Washington could be extremely expensive.

Estimates say it would cost an extra 1–2 per cent of GDP,[16] lifting the rate to between 3 and 4 per cent —a considerable amount of money for sure. But as a price for keeping some distance from the foreign and defence policy of a volatile ally, there's no doubt it should be considered along with a major audit of defence spending.

And that is the problem. Any increase in spending would have to be carefully vetted. It's not just the former US military consultants who fed from the public purse during the creation of AUKUS. As Morrison left parliament in February 2024, he talked of God being his guiding path while in office, but when he walked out the door Mammon appeared just as attractive. Like Christopher Pyne, who'd joined EY as a defence consultant and Arthur Sinodinos, who had been appointed co-chair of the business group the AUKUS Forum, Morrison was keen to cash in on his inside knowledge.

Along with Trump's former CIA director, Mike Pompeo, Morrison became a strategic adviser to US asset management firm DYNE Maritime, which launched an AU$157 million fund to invest in technologies related to AUKUS. DYNE Maritime was established by an Australian former JPMorgan investment banker Matthew Kibble and an ex-US Navy surface warfare and intelligence officer Tom Hennessey.

Morrison also became vice-chair of American Global Strategies (AGS), headed by former Trump security adviser Robert O'Brien. AGS, stacked with former Pentagon, White House and State Department officials, boasts that it 'assists clients as they navigate US government processes', a useful addition to any company wanting to boost profits in the burgeoning area of military spending.

Less than two months after the AUKUS announcement, Joe Hockey, the former US ambassador and Coalition government treasurer, joined with investment firm Ellerston Capital to launch The 1941 Fund, named after the year that Australia turned from the United Kingdom to the United States for protection during the second world war. The founding of Hockey's company Bondi Partners in Washington in early 2020 coincided with the end of the Trump presidency and the first tentative steps towards AUKUS. It was a well-timed strategic move by Hockey, praised in the *Australian* as 'Australia's first pure private investment play into national security'.[17]

Sam Roggeveen, a former senior strategic analyst at Australia's peak intelligence agency, the former Office of National Assessments, points out that the financial feeding frenzy is a byproduct of a belief that more expensive weapons will make Australia safer. He believes that independence from the United States and its aspirations in Asia to contain the rise of China would provide Australia with better protection.

Independence, Roggeveen points out, will eventually be forced upon Australia either because the United States continues its decline as a regional power, or because it chooses to resist that decline, thus 'ensnaring Australia' in a conflict with China.

For the US alliance to make Australia more secure, America would have to triumph in its quest for dominance in Asia, Roggeveen argues. And that cannot happen without risking World War III. When Roggeveen published his views the executive director of the Lowy Institute, where Roggeveen is director of its international security program, issued a public rebuke. As Roggeveen pointed out:

'… our political class would do almost anything to avoid this conclusion. Indeed, we are rushing towards a position in which Australia is more committed to the American alliance, and to US leadership in Asia, than is the US itself. This is not sustainable.'[18]

Morrison left many legacies when he was driven from office by an irate public, and there was a chance after Labor took over in 2022 to reassess the AUKUS debacle, with all of its wishful thinking, and deal with at least some of the structural problems it threw up.

But Labor lost the one chance it had to identify itself as independent and courageous and put the interests of the country ahead of its understandable desire to win government. The consequences of the fear that drove the ALP leadership to embrace AUKUS with barely a second thought will haunt them for years to come. Just as Morrison was only too willing to trade Australia's independence for the chance to win an election, so too was Labor. Now it is left to make work a deeply flawed scheme that, more than ever before, ties Australia's future to whoever is in the White House.

Acknowledgements

Many people helped in the creation of this book, a great number of whom do not wish to be named, for all-too-obvious reasons. Some who helped were motivated by a wish that Australia had greater independence, others because they believe in government accountability and are greatly disturbed by the secrecy surrounding the AUKUS deal. Others saw more than a whiff of authoritarianism in the Morrison government and were worried about the future. Thanks, then, to all those who gave on-the-record interviews, and others who provided valuable information that could not be attributed, for what I hope is a significant contribution to the necessary debate about the need for open and accountable government so that the same mistakes will not be made again.

Thanks, in no particular order, to *France 24* presenter and journalist Annette Young, Australian historian Paul Ham, Australia's former ambassador to France, Brendan Berne, for his invaluable insights; *Declassified Australia*'s Peter Cronau; the *Australian Financial Review* international editor, historian James Curran; Peter Wilson; Harry Bernas; Wayne Harley; former *Le Monde* North Africa editor Florence Beaugé; Patrice Richard; Ben Cramer; General (Ret.) Bernard Norlain; Clinton Fernandes from the Australian Defence Force (ADF) Academy campus of the University of New South Wales; staff at the National Library, Canberra; Dr Nathan Hollier, the former MUP publisher who commissioned the book, and the current publisher, Foong Ling Kong, who continued MUP's commitment; senior MUP editor Louise Stirling; and Katie Purvis, who did such an excellent job editing the book. Having said that, all errors and omissions are mine and mine alone.

Finally, I thank my wife, Pamela, who managed to tolerate me throughout the process of writing this book and often provided wise counsel and encouragement.

Notes

1 Introduction

1. Malcolm Turnbull, interview with author, Sydney, January 2023.
2. 'Sous-marins: Six questions sur le contrat "historique" entre l'Australie et DCNS', *Le Monde*, 26 April 2016.
3. Ibid.
4. 'Howard plays down sheriff comments', *ABC News*, 17 October 2003.
5. Fred Brenchley, 'The Howard defence doctrine', *The Bulletin*, 28 September 1999.
6. Clinton Fernandes, *Sub-Imperial Power: Australia and the International Arena*, Melbourne University Publishing, Carlton, Vic., 2022.
7. Brendan Berne, interview with author, Paris, 24 August 2022.
8. Michael J Green and Andrew Shearer, 'Mr Turnbull goes to Washington', *National Interest*, 17 January 2016.
9. The Editors, 'The Strategist Six: Andrew Shearer', *The Strategist*, 20 May 2016.
10. 'Admiral slammed over "love sub" trip', *Canberra Times*, 12 January 2023.
11. The White House Visitor Logs, *The White House* website.
12. Informant with knowledge of Campbell's statement.
13. Clinton Fernandes, interview with author, Canberra, 2024.
14. Ibid.
15. 'Applied Field Experience: Economic and Foreign Commercial Affairs, Peter Dien (Class XIV)', *Peace Pieces*, Uppsala Rotary Peace Center, December 2016.
16. Jommy Tee, 'Where the bloody hell is it? Did Scott Morrison lie about the report that saved his bacon at Tourism Australia?', *Michael West Media*, 18 November 2020.
17. Edward S Herman and Noam Chomsky, *Manufacturing Consent: The Political Economy of the Mass Media*, Pantheon, New York, 1988.
18. Craig Whitlock and Nate Jones, 'Former US naval leaders profited from overlapping interests on subs deal', *Washington Post*, 18 October 2022.
19. Berne interview.
20. Interview with author, not for attribution, 2023.

2 Murky Depths

1. Malcolm Turnbull, email to author, March 2024.
2. *Whaling in the Antarctic (Australia v Japan; New Zealand intervening)* [2010], International Court of Justice overview, n.d.
3. Tomohiro Osaki and Daisuke Kikuchi, 'Prime Minister Abe and Australian counterpart Malcolm Turnbull meet in Tokyo and agree to boost defence ties', *Japan Times*, 18 January 2018.
4. Lenore Taylor, 'Malcolm Turnbull's flying visit to Japan to include "special time" with Shinzo Abe', *The Guardian*, 16 December 2015.
5. Malcolm Turnbull, interview with author, Sydney, January 2023.
6. Mark Dodd, 'Australia's next submarine: Did we get it right?', *Asialink Insights*, 13 July 2020.
7. Jonathon Gul, 'Defence Minister says he "wouldn't trust" Australian Submarine Corporation to build a canoe', *ABC News*, 25 November 2014.
8. David Gould, interview with author, London, 2023. Other quotes from Gould in this section are also from this interview.
9. Clinton Fernandes, *Subimperial Power: Australia and the International Arena*, Melbourne University Publishing, Carlton, Vic., 2022.
10. Gould interview.
11. Ibid. Other quotes from Gould in this section are also from this interview.
12. Confidential source.
13. Ibid.
14. Naval Group document seen by author.
15. Malcolm Turnbull, *A Bigger Picture*, Hardie Grant, Richmond, Vic., 2020.

3 Champagne Days

1. 'Abbott calls for plan B on submarines', *9news.com.au*, 28 June 2017.
2. Pierre Tran, 'French Naval Group and the Australians: Working the cultural challenges', *SLDinfo.com*, 17 April 2019.
3. Ibid.
4. Ibid.
5. Bisalloy press release, 5 April 2018.
6. Confidential source.
7. Philippe Étienne, phone interview with author, 2024.
8. Brendan Berne, interview with author, Paris, 2022. Other quotes from Berne in this section are also from this interview.

9   'Speech of the President of France at the Sydney Naval Base, Garden Island', SciencesPo University website, 2 May 2018. Other quotes from the speech in this section are also from this source.

4   What Washington Wants

1   Michael J Green and Andrew Shearer, 'Mr Turnbull goes to Washington', *National Interest*, 17 January 2016.
2   Turnbull, *A Bigger Picture*.
3   Max Blenkin, 'France pitches nuke sub option for Australia', *InDaily*, 24 March 2016.
4   Malcolm Turnbull, interview with author, Sydney, January 2023.
5   Kim Gillis, phone interview with author, 2023.
6   Ingrid Fuary-Wagner, 'How Australia would actually use submarines in a war (in four maps)', *Australian Financial Review*, 24 March 2023.
7   Rex Patrick, phone interview with author, 2023
8   Statement to author by physicist Harry Bernas, former director of the Centre de Sciences Nucléaires et de Sciences de la Matière, CNRS, Université Paris-Saclay, France.
9   Shizuka Kuramitsu, 'US says shift to safer nuclear fuel would be costly', *Arms Control Today*, January/February 2024.
10 George Moore, *Life-of-Ship Reactors and Accelerated Testing*, Federation of American Scientists. Washington, DC, 2017.
11 Princeton University, 'Nuclear Princeton: The Manhattan Project', Princeton University website, n.d.
12 Professor Frank N von Hippel, email to author, March 2024.
13 International Atomic Energy Agency, *The Structure and Content of Agreements between the Agency and States Required in Connection with the Treaty on the Non-Proliferation of Nuclear Weapons*, INF/CIRC 153, IAEA, Vienna, 1972, p. 10.
14 Fredrik Dahl, 'Iran submarine plan may fuel Western nuclear worries', *Reuters*, 6 July 2012.
15 Gavriel Fiske, 'Avraham Burg panned for breaking "nuclear ambiguity"', *Times of Israel*, 8 December 2013.
16 Francois Murphy, 'AUKUS submarine deal "very tricky" for nuclear inspectors—IAEA chief', *Reuters*, 28 September 2021.
17 Statement to author by Harry Bernas.
18 'Petition of Alan J Kuperman for leave to intervene and request for hearing', before the United States Nuclear Regulatory Commission in the matter

of Edlow international company (export of 93.20% enriched uranium), 4 August 2016.
19. 'IAEA Director General's introductory statement to Board of Governors', IAEA website, 5 June 2023.
20. Alan J Kuperman, 'France can help Albanese fix AUKUS', *The Interpreter*, 27 July 2022.
21. Kim Gillis, interview with author, Canberra, March 2023. Other quotes from Gillis in this section are also from this interview.
22. Mark Kenny (host), 'Nuclear subs and the Aston fallout with Rex Patrick' [podcast], *Democracy Sausage*, Australian National University, April 2023.
23. Fuary-Wagner, 'How Australia would actually use submarines in a war (in four maps)'.
24. Quoted in Department of Defence, *Future Submarine Program: Transition to Design*, 14 January 2020, Auditor-General Report no. 22 of 2019–20.
25. The Editors, 'The Strategist Six: Andrew Shearer', *The Strategist*, 20 May 2016.
26. Green and Shearer, 'Mr Turnbull goes to Washington'.
27. Author interview with former Australian intelligence officer, April 2023. Other quotes in this section are also from this source.
28. Hamish McDonald, 'Nobody keen to answer the big Taiwan question', *Sydney Morning Herald*, 31 December 2011.
29. Author interview with former Australian intelligence officer.
30. Ibid.
31. Daniel Keane, 'Future submarine renamed "Attack class" but concerns remain about project rollout', *ABC News*, 13 December 2018.

5   France Overboard

1. Confidential author interview with former submarine commander, 2023.
2. Quoted in Peter Edwards, 'Another look at Curtin and Macarthur', paper delivered at *2002 History Conference: Remembering 1942*, Australian War Memorial, Canberra, 2002.
3. Peter Hartcher, 'Radioactive: Inside the top-secret AUKUS subs deal', *Sydney Morning Herald*, 14 May 2022.
4. Jane Cadzoe, 'The downfall of Arthur Sinodinos', *Sydney Morning Herald*, 4 October 2014.
5. David Hardaker, 'Morrison had evangelical Christian Mike Pompeo on speed dial for two years. Who knew?', *Crikey*, 7 February 2022.

6   Malcolm Turnbull, interview with author, Sydney, January 2023.
7   Kim Gillis, interview with author, Canberra, March 2023.
8   Ibid.
9   David Gould, interview with author, London, 2023. Other quotes from Gould in this section are also from this interview.
10 Department of Defence, *Future Submarine Program: Transition to Design*, 14 January 2020, Auditor-General Report no. 22 of 2019–20.
11 James Curran, 'Fighting with America: Facing up to the unpredictable', *The Interpreter*, 9 January 2017.
12 James Curran (@j_b_curran), 'And now for one take on the findings ... a thread' [tweet], 6 June 2023 (includes image of National Security Council Memorandum, 22 August 1974).
13 Nick Miller, 'Revealed: The room inside Pine Gap no Australian could enter, bar one', *Sydney Morning Herald*, 25 April 2018.
14 Australian House of Representatives, *Ministerial Statements: Full Knowledge and Concurrence*, 26 June 2013, p. 7071.
15 Ibid.
16 Hamish McDonald, 'What really happens at Pine Gap', *Saturday Paper*, 1 October 2016.
17 Ibid.
18 Australian House of Representatives, *Ministerial Statements: Australia-United States Joint Facilities*, 20 February 2019, p. 1087.
19 Ibid.
20 Australian House of Representatives, *Ministerial Conduct: Order for the Production of Documents*, 22 July 2019, p. 355.
21 Edmund Tadros and Tom McIlroy, 'EY and Pyne: Whatever were they thinking?', *Australian Financial Review*, 5 July 2019.
22 Ibid.
23 Department of the Prime Minister and Cabinet, *Code of Conduct for Ministers*, PM&C website, June 2022.
24 Craig Whitlock and Nate Jones, 'Former US naval leaders profited from overlapping interests on subs deal', *Washington Post*, 18 October 2022. Other quotes in this section are also from this article.
25 *Bloomberg Finance*, April 2024.
26 Centrus Energy Corp., 'Manufacturing, engineering and innovation', Centrus website, n.d.

6 A Secret State

1. Larry Rihta, 'As door opens for legal actions in Chilean coup, Kissinger is numbered among the hunted', *New York Times*, 28 March 2002.
2. Department of Defence, 'Australian Policy Institute International Conference, "War in 2025": General Angus Campbell AO DSC, Chief of the Defence Force' [speech], 14 June 2019.
3. David Hardaker, 'Mere coincidence? Crosby Textor is common link in Morrison's AUKUS deal', *Crikey*, 31 May 2023.
4. Ibid. The book is Simon Benson and Geoff Chambers, *Plagued: Australia's Two Years of Hell—The Inside Story*, Pantera Press, Neutral Bay, NSW, 2022.
5. Rory Sullivan, 'Eight awkward conversations facing Donald Trump at G20', *The Telegraph*, 27 June 2019.
6. Brendan Berne, interview with author, Paris, July 2023. Other quotes from Berne in this section are also from this interview.
7. Quoted in Senate Finance and Public Administration References Committee, *Inquiry into Government Advertising and Accountability*, tabled 1 December 2005, Department of the Senate, Canberra, 2005.
8. Ibid.
9. Matthew Tempest, 'Push me poll you', *The Guardian*, 27 April 2005.
10. Department of Defence, *Future Submarine Program: Transition to Design*, 14 January 2020, Auditor-General Report no. 22 of 2019–20. Other quotes in this section are also from this report.
11. Nicole Brangwin, *Managing SEA 1000: Australia's Attack Class Submarines*, Australian Parliament, 26 February 2020.
12. Marcus Hellyer, 'Has the cost of Australia's future submarines gone up? Part 2', *The Strategist*, 28 April 2020.
13. Department of Defence, 'Australia and France sign Future Submarine Inter-Governmental Agreement' [media release], Australian Government, 12 December 2016.
14. Peter Hartcher, 'Radioactive: Inside the top-secret AUKUS subs deal', *Sydney Morning Herald*, 14 May 2022.
15. FOI copy held. Other quotes in this paragraph are also from this source.
16. Naval Group document seen by author.
17. Ewen Levick, 'Who killed the Attack-class?', *Australian Defence Magazine*, 10 May 2022.
18. Defence Department document obtained via FOI and held by author.
19. Hartcher, 'Radioactive'.

20 Daniel Hurst, 'Labor retains Coalition-appointed shipbuilding adviser on $9000 for each day worked', *The Guardian*, 23 November 2022.
21 Department of Defence, *2020 Defence Strategic Update*, Commonwealth of Australia, Canberra, n.d.
22 Daniel Hurst, 'Tony Abbott registers as agent of foreign influence over UK trade adviser role', *The Guardian*, 9 October 2020.
23 Andrew Greene, 'Shake-up of naval shipbuilding as concerns grow over future submarines, frigates', *ABC News*, 22 March 2021.
24 Levick, 'Who killed the Attack-class?'
25 Hartcher, 'Radioactive'.

7 That Sinking Feeling

1 James Elton-Pym, 'Row over Adelaide shipbuilding as Pyne promises "miniscule number" of foreign workers', *SBS News*, 16 May 2017.
2 Department of Defence, 'Prime Minister the Hon. Malcolm Turnbull doorstop with Senator the Hon. Marise Payne, Minister for Defence and the Hon. Christopher Pyne MP, Minister for Defence Industry and Vice Admiral Ray Griggs AO, CSC, RAN, Acting Chief of the Defence Force', Australian Government, Canberra, 16 May 2017. Other quotes in this paragraph are also from this source.
3 Pierre Tran, 'Interview with Hervé Guillou, CEO of French shipbuilder DCNS', *DefenseNews*, 12 October 2016.
4 Ibid.
5 Naval Group internal correspondence seen by author.
6 Kim Gillis, interview with author, Canberra, March 2023.
7 Ibid.
8 Naval Group internal correspondence seen by author.
9 Andrew Tillett, 'French submarine boss exits troubled $80 billion project', *Australian Financial Review*, 24 March 2020.
10 Naval Group document seen by author.
11 Naval Group internal correspondence seen by author. Other quotes in this paragraph are also from this source.
12 Gillis interview.
13 Ibid.
14 Kim Gillis, phone interview with author, 2023.
15 *ABC News* (Australia), 'French submarine boss confronted over $90 billion defence project' [video], *YouTube*, 25 February 2021.

16 Confidential source.
17 'Submarines: 90 per cent of build to occur in Australia, DCNS says after securing $50bn contract', *ABC News*, 26 April 2016.
18 Ben Packham, 'French tell sub firms to shape up', *The Australian*, 13 February 2020.
19 Gillis interview.
20 Confidential source.
21 Ibid.
22 Gillis interview.
23 Andrew Greene, 'Visiting French submarine boss confronted over Australian industry content in $90 billion defence project', *ABC News*, 24 February 2021.

8 The Media and the Message

1 'United States Studies Centre appoints new CEO Dr Michael Green' [media release], USSC, 29 March 2022.
2 Katherine Faulders, Alexander Mallin and Mike Levine, 'Trump allegedly discussed US nuclear subs with foreign national after leaving White House', *ABC News America*, 6 October 2023.
3 Ibid.
4 Aaron Patrick, 'US Studies Centre academics specialise in movies, witches, fashion and sex', *Australian Financial Review*, 30 March 2017.
5 'United States Studies Centre appoints new CEO Dr Michael Green'.
6 Michael J Green, 'America is still Australia's best bet', USSC website, 15 July 2023.
7 Michael J Green and Victoria Cooper, 'Australia's role in supporting democracies as a middle power', USSC website, 4 July 2023.
8 Kelsey Hartigan, 'Full knowledge and concurrence: Key questions for US-Australia extended deterrence and escalation management consultations', USSC website, 22 August 2023.
9 Tom Corben and Alice Nason, 'AUSMIN 2023 explained', USSC website, 4 August 2023.
10 'Michael Green writes for the *Quarterly Essay*', USSC website, 6 September 2022.
11 Michael West, 'Secret government roundtable with media mates less love-fest than nat-sec', *Michael West Media*, 26 February 2023.

12   Josh Taylor, 'Home Affairs boss Mike Pezzullo reveals he negotiates with trusted reporters on sensitive leaks', *The Guardian*, 20 September 2019.
13   Paul Karp, 'Home Affairs secretary Mike Pezzullo urged to "tone it down" after "drums of war" speech', *The Guardian*, 26 April 2021. Other quotes in this section are also from this source.
14   Lara Pearce, '"China is militarising ports across our region": Dutton's stern warning for Australia', *9news*, 25 April 2021.
15   See, for example, Damien Murphy and Yuko Narushima, 'Unguarded statement was the beginning of the end', *Sydney Morning Herald*, 7 May 2009.
16   '"Inconceivable" Australia would not join US to defend Taiwan—Australian defence minister', *Reuters*, 13 November 2021.
17   Allan Gyngell, *Fear of Abandonment: Australia in the World since 1942*, La Trobe University Press in conjunction with Black Inc., Carlton, Vic., 2021.
18   Rohan Smith, 'Top Australian general warns of "high likelihood" of war with China', *news.com.au*, 4 May 2021.
19   Nick McKenzie and Anthony Galloway, 'Conflict with China "a high likelihood", says top Australian general', *Sydney Morning Herald*, 4 May 2021.
20   Thomas Wilkins, 'Australia's war drum to nowhere on Taiwan', *East Asia Forum*, 11 June 2021.
21   Maxwell E McCombs and Donald L Shaw, 'The agenda-setting function of mass media', *Public Opinion Quarterly*, 36(2), 1972, pp. 176–87.
22   Peter Hartcher, 'Radioactive: Inside the top-secret AUKUS subs deal', *Sydney Morning Herald*, 14 May 2022. Other quotes in this section are also from this source.
23   Philippe Étienne, phone interview with author, 2024. Other quotes by Étienne in this section are also from this interview.
24   'US, France extend special forces cooperation', *France 24*, 10 July 2021.
25   Informant with detailed knowledge of the meetings.
26   Hartcher, 'Radioactive'.
27   Daniel Hurst, 'Paul Keating blasts *Age* and *SMH* for provocative China war story', *The Guardian*, 7 March 2023.
28   'Red Alert', *Sydney Morning Herald* and *Age*, 7 March 2023.
29   Clinton Fernandes, interview with author, Canberra, 2024.
30   James Curran, 'America's Asia tsar doubted Australia', *Australian Financial Review*, 5 July 2023.
31   Hartcher, 'Radioactive'.
32   Ibid.

33   US Embassy Canberra, 'Gillard on track to become Australia's next prime minister', WikiLeaks cable 09CANBERRA545_a, 10 June 2009.
34   US Embassy Canberra, 'Bio Notes: Richard Marles, MP', WikiLeaks cable 09MELBOURNE87_a, 27 July 2009.
35   US Embassy Canberra, 'Deputy PM Julia Gillard star in Rudd government', WikiLeaks cable 08CANBERRA609_a, 13 June 2008.
36   Jonathan Kwitny, *The Crimes of Patriots: A True Tale of Dope, Dirty Money, and the CIA*, WW Norton & Company, New York, 1987.
37   John Pilger, *A Secret Country*, Vintage, London, 1992.
38   Richard Hall, *The Secret State: Australia's Spy Industry*, Cassell Australia, Stanmore, NSW, 1978.
39   Max Suich, 'Whitlam death revives doubts of US role in his sacking', *Australian Financial Review*, 14 October 2013.
40   Phillip Frazer, 'Dirty tricks down under', *Mother Jones*, February–March 1984, pp. 13–20, 44–5, 52.
41   Gough Whitlam, *The Whitlam Government 1972–1975*, Viking, Ringwood, Vic., 1985. All quotes in this section are from this source.
42   Daniel Hurst, 'US warns Australia against joining treaty banning nuclear weapons', *The Guardian*, 9 November 2023.
43   Ewen Levick, 'Who killed the Attack-class?', *Australian Defence Magazine*, 10 May 2022.
44   Parliament of Australia, Foreign Affairs, Defence and Trade Legislation Committee, 27 October 2021.
45   Ibid.
46   Ibid.

9   In the Frame

1   Peter Hartcher, 'AUKUS fallout: Double-dealing and deception came at a diplomatic cost', *Sydney Morning Herald*, 15 May 2022.
2   David E Sanger, 'Secret talks and a hidden agenda: Behind a US defense deal that France called a "betrayal"', *New York Times*, 17 September 2021. Other quotes in this section are also from this source.
3   'Morrison defends secret G7 side trips to delve into family history', *New Daily*, 21 June 2021.
4   Scott Morrison, 'Press conference: Glasgow, Scotland' [1 November 2021], PM Transcripts, Department of the Prime Minister and Cabinet, Canberra.
5   Confidential diplomatic source.

6   '"I don't think, I know": Macron accuses Scott Morrison of lying about submarine contract' [video], *The Guardian*, 1 November 2021.
7   Catie McLeod, 'Morrison says "I won't cop sledging on Australia" amid nuclear subs fallout', *news.com.au*, 1 November 2021.
8   Scott Morrison press conference.
9   Daniel Hurst, 'Morrison accused of worsening rift with French Government after leak of Macron text', *The Guardian*, 2 November 2021.
10 Morrison press conference. Other quotes in this section are also from this source.
11 Philippe Étienne, phone interview with author, 2024.
12 Kim Gillis, interview with author, Canberra, March 2023.
13 Parliament of Australia, Foreign Affairs, Defence and Trade Legislation Committee: Estimates, Defence Portfolio, Naval Shipbuilding Expert Advisory Panel, 1 June 2021.
14 Hartcher, 'AUKUS fallout'.
15 Gough Whitlam, *The Whitlam Government 1972–1975*, Viking, Ringwood, Vic., 1985.
16 Hartcher, 'AUKUS fallout'.
17 Ibid.
18 Congressional Research Service, *Navy Virginia (SSN-774) Class Attack Submarine Procurement: Background and Issues for Congress* (RL32418), CRS, Washington, DC, 15 August 2023.
19 Jade Macmillan, 'Australia nuclear submarines are a step closer to reality as AUKUS legislation clears US Senate', *ABC News*, 14 December 2023.
20 Ibid. Other quotes in this section are also from this source.
21 Rosa Prince, 'Sunak, Biden and Albanese announce new subs—and jobs', *Politico*, 14 March 2023.
22 Rex Patrick (@mrrexpatrick), 'In case you ever wondered what an Australian Govt blank cheque looks like …' [tweet], 4 December 2023.
23 Hon. Richard Marles MP, Defence Minister, 'AUKUS nuclear-powered submarine pathway, House of Representatives, Parliament House, Canberra ACT' [statement], 22 March 2023.

10 The Sting

1   Philippe Étienne, phone interview with author, 2024. Other quotes from Étienne in this section are also from this interview.
2   Tom Stayner, 'French ambassador savages Australia for "stab in the back" over scuttled submarine deal', *SBS News*, 3 November 2021.

3   Malcolm Turnbull, interview with author, Sydney, 2023.
4   Ibid.
5   'Biden tells France's Macron, US was "clumsy" in Aussie sub deal', *Al Jazeera*, 29 October 2021.
6   Peter Hartcher, 'Radioactive: Inside the top-secret AUKUS subs deal', *Sydney Morning Herald*, 14 May 2022.
7   The White House, 'Remarks by President Biden, Prime Minister Morrison of Australia, and Prime Minister Johnson of the United Kingdom announcing the creation of AUKUS', 15 September 2021. Other quotes in this section are also from this source.
8   US Department of State, 'Secretary Antony J Blinken, Secretary of Defense Lloyd Austin, Australian Foreign Minister Marise Payne, and Australian Defence Minister Peter Dutton at a joint press availability', 16 September 2021. Other quotes in this section are also from this source.
9   Associated Press, 'Donald Trump officially launches US Space Force', *The Guardian*, 21 December 2019.
10 Stephen Clark, 'US spy satellite agency isn't so silent about new "Silent Barker" mission', *Ars Technica*, 29 August 2023.
11 Sandra Erwin, 'NRO space missions mark new level of US Australia cooperation', *SpaceNews*, 2 February 2021.
12 'US Space Surveillance Telescope in Australia achieves initial operational capability', USSF Space Operations Command website, 30 September 2022.
13 Ibid.
14 Dorothy Ryan, 'Space surveillance telescope in Western Australia captures its first image', *MIT Lincoln Laboratory News*, 2 February 2021.
15 Nathan Strout, 'The Space Force wants to use directed-energy systems for space superiority', *C4ISRNET*, 17 July 2021.
16 Jack Norton, 'Australia the "pot of gold at the end of the rainbow" in new space race', *The Strategist*, 2 December 2022.
17 'Antigua Air Station inactivated', *Air & Space Forces*, 16 July 2015.
18 Sandra Erwin, 'Space Force official: Satellites in orbit have become pawns in geopolitical chess games', *SpaceNews*, 29 November 2021.
19 Stephen Fallon, 'The ongoing militarisation of space', Parliament of Australia Library, n.d.
20 Theresa Hitchens, 'Space Force's FY24 budget includes "offensive" options for space. What does that mean?', *Breaking Defense*, 13 March 2023.
21 Fallon, 'The ongoing militarisation of space'.

22 'Nasa conducting suborbital rocket missions in Australia in June and July', NASA website, 7 June 2022.
23 *Guidelines Governing the Serving of Officials of the National Aeronautics and Space Administration (NASA) as Consultants on Advisory Panels of the Central Intelligence Agency (CIA)*, US National Security Archive, approved for release 14 June 2002.
24 David Hardaker, '"Interchangeable": Richard Marles in lockstep with US Navy's holy grail of integrated forces', *Crikey*, 21 April 2023.
25 Australian Submarine Agency, 'Submarine Rotational Force—West' [fact sheet], Australian Government, n.d.
26 Office of the Secretary of Defense, *Nuclear Posture Review, February 2018*, US Department of Defense, Washington, DC, 2022.
27 United Nations Security Council, 'Risk of nuclear weapons use higher than at any time since Cold War, Disarmament Affairs Chief warns Security Council' [media release], SC/15250, 31 March 2023.
28 Sea Power Centre, *Port Visits to Australia by Nuclear-Powered Vessels: A Historical Context*, Royal Australian Navy, Canberra, 2023.
29 'Modern US naval units visit Australia', *Navy News*, 6 May 1960.
30 'The 1960s: Page 2—Overview', New Zealand History website (NZ Government), n.d.
31 Euan Graham, 'Time for a more honest conversation about foreign basing in Australia', *The Strategist*, 1 March 2023.
32 Department of Defence, 'Australia welcomes United States Marines back to Darwin' [media release], Australian Government, 22 March 2023.
33 Author conversations with several ADF personnel, 2023.
34 Australian Government, *National Defence: Defence Strategic Review 2023*, Commonwealth of Australia, Canberra, 2023.
35 Australian House of Representatives, *Questions Without Notice: B52 Bombers*, 2 April 1981, p. 1234.
36 Richard Tanter, 'Prepping for a China war: The United States and the new arc of militarization across Northern Australia', *Asia-Pacific Journal: Japan Focus*, 20(18), 2022.
37 Abraham Mahshie, 'F-35 completes final test for nuclear-capable B61 series weapons', *Air & Space Forces Magazine*, 5 October 2021.
38 National Archives of Australia, 'Harold Holt: During office', NAA website, n.d.
39 Slobodan Lekic, 'NATO condemns WikiLeaks', *Sydney Morning Herald*, 1 December 2010.

40 'US nuclear bombs "based in Netherlands"—ex-Dutch PM Lubbers', *BBC News*, 10 June 2013.
41 Australian House of Representatives, *Ministerial Statements: Full Knowledge and Concurrence*, 26 June 2013, p. 7071.

11 The Bomb

1 Australian Archives (ACT): A 7941/2, N15: Note by Defence Department, Question of nuclear capability for the Australian forces, 2 June 1961, p. 1 (Top Secret), cited in Jim Walsh, 'Surprise down under: The secret history of Australia's nuclear ambitions', *Nonproliferation Review*, 5(1), 1997, pp. 1–20.
2 Ibid.
3 Pilita Clark, 'PM's Story: Very much alive … and unfazed', *Sydney Morning Herald*, 1 January 1999.
4 Don Mercer, interview with author for ABC Investigative Unit, 2007.
5 Greenpeace, *Secrets, Lies and Uranium Enrichment: The Classified Silex Project at Lucas Heights*, Greenpeace Australia, Sydney, 2004.
6 US Government Publishing Office, *Public Papers of the Presidents of the United States: William J Clinton (1999, Book II)*, 3 November 1999.
7 Ibid.
8 Greenpeace, *Secrets, Lies and Uranium Enrichment*.
9 House of Representatives Standing Committee on the Environment and Energy, *Not Without Your Approval: A Way Forward for Nuclear Technology in Australia*, December 2019.
10 Fred Brenchley, 'Nuclear balance of power', *Australian Financial Review*, 26 October 2006.
11 CSIRO, 'The question of nuclear in Australia's energy sector', CSIRO website, 20 December 2023.
12 Statement from Dr Alan J Kuperman to the author, March 2024.
13 Institute of Public Affairs, 'Peter Dutton address to IPA members on Australia's energy security and nuclear energy, 7 July 2023' [video], *YouTube*, 7 July 2023.
14 Lindsay M Krall, Allison M Macfarlane and Rodney C Ewing, 'Nuclear waste from small nuclear reactors', *Proceedings of the National Academy of Sciences*, 119(23), 2022.
15 Timothy Gardner, 'Small nuclear power projects may have big waste problems: Study', *Reuters*, 2 June 2022.
16 'Nuclear waste storage', Nuclear Princeton, Princeton University, n.d.

17 Tory Shepherd, 'Traditional owners win court case to stop nuclear waste dump in South Australia', *The Guardian*, 18 July 2023.
18 David Gould, interview with author, London, 2023.
19 Daniel Hurst, 'Australia seeks talks with global nuclear watchdog to allay Aukus fears', *The Guardian*, 15 May 2023.
20 Frank N von Hippel, 'The Australia-UK-US submarine deal: Mitigating proliferation concerns', *Arms Control Today*, 51(9), 2021.
21 Ibid.
22 Ibid.
23 Department of Defence, 'Australian Policy Institute International Conference, "War in 2025": General Angus Campbell AO DSC, Chief of the Defence Force' [speech], 14 June 2019.
24 Central Intelligence Agency, 'CIA activities in Chile: Report to Congress', 18 September 2000.

12 No Way Out?

1 Paul Karp, 'Labor thrashes out AUKUS position at party conference with dissent from MP and unions', *The Guardian*, 18 August 2023.
2 Rex Patrick, phone interview with author, September 2023.
3 Parliament of Australia, Foreign Affairs, Defence and Trade Legislation Committee, 27 October 2021. Other quotes in this section are also from this source.
4 Chuck Schumer (@SenSchumer), 'With the Senate passage of the NDAA: We're approving President Biden's US, UK, and Australia nuclear submarine agreement …' [tweet], 14 December 2023.
5 Australian Parliament, Foreign Affairs, Defence and Trade Legislation Committee: Estimates—Defence Portfolio, 15 February 2023.
6 Matthew Knott, 'US nuclear-armed bomber visits allowed under Australian treaty obligations', *Sydney Morning Herald*, 15 February 2023.
7 Malcolm Turnbull, interview with author, Sydney, January 2023.
8 Nic Fildes and Demetri Sevastopulo, 'Australia's defence dilemmas: Projecting force or provoking China?', *Financial Times*, 7 November 2022.
9 Samantha Maiden, 'Former home affairs secretary Michael Pezzullo sacked after bombshell texts leaked, *news.com.au*, 27 November 2023.
10 Australian Public Service Commission, 'Media statement on the inquiry into possible breaches of the APS Code of Conduct by Mr Michael Pezzullo AO', Australian Government, 27 November 2023.

NOTES

11 Kim Gillis, interview with author, Canberra, March 2023. Other quotes from Gillis in this section are also from this interview.
12 Statement to the author, March 2024.
13 Confidential source with detailed knowledge of the Australian submarine procurement process.
14 Turnbull interview. Other quotes from Turnbull in this section are also from this interview.
15 Clinton Fernandes, interview with author, Canberra, 2023.
16 For example, see Hugh White, *How to Defend Australia*, La Trobe University Press in conjunction with Black Inc., Carlton, Vic., 2019.
17 'Making Big Deals of Defence', *The Australian*, 7 November 2021.
18 Roggeveen, Sam, *The Echidna Strategy*, La Trobe University Press, 2023, pp. 195–6.

Further reading

Curran, James, *Unholy Fury: Whitlam and Nixon at War*, Melbourne University Press, Carlton, Vic., 2015.

—'Fighting with America: Facing up to the unpredictable', *The Interpreter*, 9 January 2017.

Fernandes, Clinton, *Subimperial Power: Australia and the International Arena*, Melbourne University Publishing, Carlton, Vic., 2022.

Gyngell, Allan, *Fear of Abandonment: Australia in the World since 1942*, La Trobe University Press in conjunction with Black Inc., Carlton, Vic., 2021.

Hellyer, Marcus, *Special Report: Understanding the Price of Military Equipment*, ASPI, Canberra, 2022.

Herman, Edward S and Noam Chomsky, *Manufacturing Consent: The Political Economy of the Mass Media*, Pantheon, New York, 1988.

Richelson, Jeffrey T and Des Ball, *The Ties that Bind: Intelligence Cooperation Between the UKUSA Countries—United Kingdom, the United States of America, Canada and New Zealand*, George Allen & Unwin, Sydney, 1985.

Roggeveen, Sam, *The Echidna Strategy: Australia's Search for Power and Peace*, La Trobe University Press in conjunction with Black Inc., Carlton, Vic., 2023.

Rudd, Kevin, *The Avoidable War: The Dangers of a Catastrophic Conflict Between the US and Xi Jinping's China*, Hachette Australia, Sydney, 2023.

Turnbull, Malcolm, *A Bigger Picture*, Hardie Grant, Richmond, Vic., 2021.

von Hippel, Frank N, 'The Australia-UK-US submarine deal: Mitigating proliferation concerns', *Arms Control Today*, 51(9), 2021.

White, Hugh, *How to Defend Australia*, La Trobe University Press in conjunction with Black Inc., Carlton, Vic., 2019.

Index

A2/AD (anti-access/aerial denial) systems 101, 139

Abbott, Tony
appoints Naval Shipbuilding Advisory Board 13
Howard and 52
on Japanese submarines 6, 11, 12, 13, 15, 31
on nuclear-powered submarines 22
pro-US attitude 4, 6, 7
replaced as PM 4, 6
UK trade adviser 75
visit to Japan 6
Abbott coalition government
national security adviser *see* Shearer, Andrew
public service changes 164
treaty on US import of material 142
Abe, Shinzo 11–12
Adelaide shipyard (Osborne) 57, 77–9, 81–2, 122
AFiniti (Australia–France Initiative) 27
aircraft
F-35 aircraft 52, 141
nuclear-capable bombers (British) proposed for Australia 146–7
nuclear-capable bombers (US) stationed in Australia 10, 127, 133, 140–1, 161–2
aircraft boarding priority 46
Albanese, Anthony
AUKUS latest phase announcement 121
learns of AUKUS 123–4
visit to France 40
Albanese Labor government
AUKUS deal and 10, 107, 121, 122, 156–8, 159, 168–9
compensation to Naval Group 40, 161
media briefings 95

national security issues (Morrison government legacy) 10, 161–2, 164
Alvarez, Luis 38
American Global Strategies (AGS) 167–8
Andrews, Kevin 13
Angleton, James Jesus 105
ANZUS agreement (1951) 52, 62; *see also* Australia–United States alliance
Armagno, Nina 131
Armitage, Richard 44–5
Arnhem Space Centre 132, 133
assassination target information 54–5; *see also* Pine Gap, Northern Territory
Astute-class submarines 155
Attack-class submarines 45, 76; *see also* French submarine deal
Attorney-General's Department 95
AUKUS deal 5
announcements 10, 108–9, 121, 124, 125–7
Australian Albanese government embrace of 10, 107, 121, 122, 156–8, 159, 168–9
Australian ALP Opposition not informed of plans 8, 10, 116–17, 123–4, 125
Australian ALP Opposition notified of pending announcement 10, 123–4
coalition partner not informed of plans 158
concern about non-nuclear states acquiring HEU 36, 115–16, 153–5
conflict of interest 73
cost 9, 117, 119, 121, 158
flawed process 108, 158–60, 165
IAEA inspection of submarine reactors 154–5

implementation report 139–40
initial planning 116–17
integration of US and Australian military 8, 127–8, 167
media coverage 9, 97–103
Morrison government secret discussions 7–10, 47–8, 108–10, 115–17, 127–8, 150
Morrison's idea 160
munitions ownership 141–2
no requirement identified 108, 159–60
Non-Proliferation Treaty (NPT) issues 37–8, 115–16, 117, 153–5
nuclear waste management 153–4
opposition to 9
related business opportunities 167–8
submarine base 133–4
submarine operations (proposed) 120–1
submarine supply issues 117–22, 124–5, 127, 155
submarines ownership questions 154
see also nuclear-powered submarines for Australia; United States bases in Australia
AUKUS Forum 167
Austin, Lloyd J 95, 100, 126–7
Australia–France relationship 3–4, 26–30, 40–1
Albanese visit to France 40
damage to 125
France invites Australia to G7 63–4
Macron visit to Australia 26–30
Strategic Partnership Agreement 42, 83, 85, 88
Australia–United States alliance 20, 42–5, 123–4, 168

INDEX

ANZUS agreement (1951) 52, 62
Australia as subimperial power of USA 5–6, 97
Australia's bipartisan commitment 103–7, 156
Australia's fear of abandonment 5, 97
Australia's security alignment shift to US 51, 52–8, 107
   Dutton on 97, 127–8
   integration of Australia into US military 8, 46–9, 51, 71, 107, 127–35, 138–43, 167
   Morrison government agenda 46–9, 51, 65–6, 71, 107
   NPT and 106–7
   public questioning of 92–3
   symbol of 90
   treaties on storage of weapons and military hardware in Australia 141–2, 162–3
   USSC support for 94–5
   and war over Taiwan 97–8, 119–20
   see also AUKUS deal; US bases in Australia
Australian Atomic Energy Commission (AAEC) 145–6, 155
   Lucas Heights nuclear reactor 147–50, 153
Australian Defence Force *see* Defence Department; Royal Australian Air Force (RAAF); Royal Australian Navy (RAN)
Australian Defence Force chiefs/vice chiefs *see* Campbell, Angus; Houston, Angus; Johnston, David (Vice Admiral); Mead, Jonathan
Australian governments *see* Abbott coalition government; Albanese Labor government; Hawke Labor government; Howard coalition government; Morrison coalition government; Turnbull coalition government; Whitlam Labor government
Australian industry capability 86
Australian Labor Party (ALP)
   alleged weakness on national security 53, 107, 116–17
   commitment to US alliance 103–7, 156–8; *see also* AUKUS deal
   policy on nuclear power in Australia 123–4, 148–9
Australian Labor Party (ALP) governments *see* Albanese Labor government; Hawke Labor government; Whitlam Labor government
Australian Labor Party (ALP) Opposition 125
   blindsided on AUKUS deal 8, 10, 116–17, 123–4, 125
   Morrison wedge politics against 10, 69, 104, 107, 116–17, 121
   notified of pending AUKUS announcement 123–4
   US belief that ALP had been informed on submarine deal 125
Australian National Audit Office (ANAO) 66–7
Australian Naval Infrastructure (ANI) 81
Australian Parliamentary Library report on satellite destruction 131–2
Australian Security Intelligence Organisation (ASIO) 31, 95, 105
Australian Senate
   hearings 41–2, 67–8, 108, 115, 159–60
   questions in 161–2
Australian sovereignty 3, 29, 30, 162–3, 168–9
   assertion of 53
   disregarded 51, 103
   Fernandes on 166
   threat to 9, 53–4, 107, 120–1, 123–4, 139
   Turnbull on 3, 9, 165–6
Australian Strategic Policy Institute (ASPI) 62, 74, 101, 138, 155
Australian Submarine Corporation (ASC) 12, 81–2

B-52 bombers 10, 127, 133, 140–1, 161–2
Ball, Des 54
Barngarla people opposition to nuclear waste dump 153
Barracuda-class submarines 21–2, 32, 39, 71, 155 *see also* French submarine deal
Barrow-in-Furness shipyards, UK 121–2
battlefield and target information 54–5; *see also* Pine Gap, Northern Territory
Baxter, Philip 145–6
Beazley, Kim 103–4, 116
Berne, Brendan 3–4, 7, 10, 26–30, 63–4
Bible, Geoff 93
Biden, Joe 8, 10, 110–11
   apology to Macron 49, 125
   AUKUS announcements 121, 125–6
   on French submarines 10, 110
Biden administration
   dropped plan to add nuclear warheads to submarine-based cruise missiles 138
   involvement in nuclear submarine project 47–8, 110, 115–17, 124; *see also* AUKUS deal
   misled about Australian Opposition being informed 125
   misled about the French being fully informed 49, 125
   opposition to Australia's French submarine deal 10, 110
   space military strategy 128–33
Billig, Jean-Michel 24, 83
Bisalloy 25
Bishop, Julie 164
Blinken, Antony 95, 100, 110, 126–7

INDEX

bombers *see* aircraft
Bondi Partners 168
Bonne, Emmanuel 64–5
Bowman, Frank 117
Briggs, Scott 164
Brown, Timothy 50
Burdeshaw Associates 58–9
Burg, Avraham 37
Bush (George W) administration 5–6, 44
Bush, George W 61
  on Howard and Australia's role 5
  meetings with Howard 92–3
Butcher, Andrew 93

Campbell, Angus 61–2, 68–9, 74, 155–6, 164
Campbell, Kurt 8, 44, 47–8, 99, 103, 115–17, 121, 124
Canada's use of nuclear power 151–2
HMAS *Canberra* 138
USS *Canberra* 137–8
Carter, Jimmy 106, 116
Center for Strategic and International Studies (CSIS) 31–2, 45, 94–5, 101–2
Central Intelligence Agency (CIA)
  black ops programs 54, 62, 156
  feared role in destabilising Whitlam government 105–6, 156
  former director *see* Pompeo, Mike
  and NASA 132–3
  at Pine Gap 53, 54
Centrus Energy 60
Chalmers, Jim 134
Chan, Michelle 112
Cherbourg 1, 21–3, 32
Chessell, James 101
China
  Australia's foreign interference law 31
  Macron on 29, 43
  nuclear weapons policy 135–6
  oil tanker targets 134–5
  perceived threat from 3, 5, 6, 9, 12, 14–15, 101–2

  potential war with 44–5, 97, 102, 117–20, 139, 161
  South China Sea operations 31
  support for NPT 136
  trade sanctions on Australia 55
  US and Australian actions against 14–15, 102, 166
  US concerns about 12, 31–2, 95, 134–5, 141
  see also Taiwan
Chomsky, Noam 9
Christopher, Warren 106
Clark, Pilita 148
climate change
  nuclear power option 150–1
Clinton, Bill 149–50
Collins-class submarine replacement selection process 5, 9, 13–15, 18, 45
  contender short-list 15–20, 22
  costing 67–8
  decision 18, 19, 20, 22; *see also* French submarine deal
  first submarine's name 45
  specifications 14–15
Collins-class submarines 12, 16, 17, 50, 59, 117, 135, 155
Columbia-class submarines 121, 135
conflict of interest, potential for 46, 57–60, 72–3
Congressional Research Service report on Virginia-class submarine procurement 119–21
Conroy, Pat 157
conventionally powered submarines 34, 47; *see also* Collins-class submarines
Costello, Peter 101
Costello, Sean 87
COVID-19 pandemic 41, 70, 75, 89, 111
Crean, Simon 53
Crosby, Lynton 66
Crosby Textor 65–6
CSIRO, on nuclear power 151
Curran, James 52

Darwin *see* Northern Territory
Davis, John 69, 87
DCNS (Directions des Constructions Navales Services) 22; *see also* Naval Group
Defence Committee 18
defence contracts, magnitude of 1, 9; *see also* AUKUS deal; French submarine deal
Defence Department
  defence capability enhancement review 68–9
  Future Submarine Program Office 66–7
  on German submarine 16–18
  interest in French submarine intellectual property 18–19, 25
  interest in nuclear weapons (1950s) 145–6
  nuclear submarine feasibility study 71–3
  officials/former officials *see* Gillis, Kim; Moriarty, Greg; Sammut, Greg
  praises Naval Group progress 49, 124
  relations with Naval Group 83
  role in AUKUS process 108, 159–60, 164–5
  satellite activities and NRO 128–9
  and secret plan to abandon French submarine deal 42, 49, 68–9, 74, 108
  submarine replacement project *see* Collins-class submarine replacement selection process
  US military personnel in 9, 15, 46, 49–50, 58–60, 61, 73, 108, 139
  see also national security issues; Royal Australian Air Force (RAAF); Royal Australian Navy (RAN)
Defence ministers *see* Dutton, Peter; Marles, Richard; Payne, Marise; Pyne, Christopher; Reynolds, Linda; Smith, Stephen
Defence Planning Guidance 42

INDEX

Defence Strategic Review
(Houston and Smith)
139–40, 158
Defence Strategic Update
(2020) 73–4
Defence White Papers 41–2,
44
Dien, Peter 8
diesel-electric submarines *see*
conventionally powered
submarines
Donald, Kirkland 59–60,
73, 108
Downer, Alexander 52
Dutton, Peter
appointees to Submarine
Advisory Committee 108
AUKUS press conference
127–8
Defence minister 69–70
Home Affairs minister 31
Howard and 52
leadership challenge 43
member of Naval
Shipbuilding Enterprise
Governance Committee
75–6
on nuclear power stations
151–2
political leanings 12
on war and US alliance 97,
127–8
DYNE Maritime 167

East Timor crisis (1999) 17
Ellerston Capital 167
Esper, Mark 62
Étienne, Philippe 26, 27, 64,
100, 114, 124
European Union free trade
agreements 64
EY consulting group 57–8,
167

F-35 aircraft 52, 141
Faulkner, John 66
Federation of American
Scientists 38
Fernandes, Clinton 5–6, 8,
166
Finkel, Alan 102
Finkelstein, Yaron 65

Foreign Affairs Department
funding for uranium
enrichment monitoring
program 149
foreign policy *see* national
security issues
Fox, Nicky 132
France
Albanese visit 40
Australian ambassadors 3–4;
see also Berne, Brendan
deceived by Morrison 110,
112–15
deceived by US 100,
110–11, 124, 125
defence and armaments sales
1, 21–2, 23, 28
defence contracts *see* French
submarine deal; Naval
Group
invites Australia to G7 63–4
nuclear deal with Iran 65
policy on China 29, 43
presence in Indo-Pacific 2,
21, 26, 28, 43, 100
recalls ambassadors 124
refusal to join Iraq War 50
relations with Australia
see Australia–France
relationship
relations with Morrison
government 6–7, 70,
72–3, 88–91
see also Étienne, Philippe;
French submarine deal;
French submarine deal
cancellation; French
submarines; Hollande,
François; Macron,
Emmanuel; Thébault,
Jean-Pierre
Fraser, Malcolm 9, 140
free trade agreements 21,
27, 64
French steel 25
French submarine deal
21–30, 40, 70, 74
advantages of 1–3, 8,
79–80, 155
announcement 1–2
Australian industry
capability 86
benefits for France 79–81
budget, cost and schedule
48, 49, 51, 66–8, 87,
114–15, 124

cancellation *see* French
submarine deal
cancellation
communication difficulties
6–7, 70
contract provisions 22,
32–3, 69, 78–9, 89–90,
124
conventional submarines
offered to fill Australian
capability gap 40
delivery options 39–41
first submarine's name
45
leaks to media 114, 115
local (Australian) content
22, 39, 69, 79,
84–9
Lockheed Martin weapons
system 80, 87
media coverage 66–7, 68,
79–81, 87
Morrison government
deception of the French 8,
110, 112–15, 124, 160
Morrison government
misleading of US 8, 9,
47–9, 125
Morrison in charge 75–6,
86, 89–91
Naval Shipbuilding Advisory
Board 13, 42, 51, 75
nuclear submarines offer
32–3, 155
nuclear technology sharing
offer 40
opposition to 2–3, 4, 9, 10,
42–3, 49–50, 51–2, 68–9,
81–2
risks 67
Strategic Partnership
Agreement (SPA) 42,
83–5, 88, 112
technology transfer 18–19,
22, 25, 40, 42, 79–80,
86
US attitude 10, 110
see also Naval Group
French submarine deal
cancellation
announcement 124
Australian Opposition
notified of pending
announcement 123–4
compensation payment 40,
161

INDEX

decision-making process for AUKUS nuclear submarines 159–60; *see also* AUKUS deal
  French government notified 124
  implications for Australia 40, 117–18, 121, 122, 155–6, 164
  Morrison government secret plan 65–9, 72–4, 108, 112–15
  Naval Group plans to rescue deal 40–1, 155
French submarines 6, 8, 18–20
  Barracuda-class 21–2, 32, 39, 71, 155
  Collins-class replacement option 18–20, 22
  features 19–20
  intellectual property 18–19, 25
  nuclear fuel system 33–5, 39–40, 155
  production line 39
  see also French submarine deal; Naval Group
frigates 76, 78, 81

German submarines 16–18, 19, 22
Gillard, Julia 103–4, 138
Gillis, Kim
  on Australian industry security clearances 86
  on French nuclear submarines offer 32–3, 41
  on French offers to rescue submarine deal 40–1
  on independent public service 164–5
  on local content issue 88–9
  on shipyard costs 81–2
  on US opposition to French submarine deal 49–50
  on visit of French admiral 115
Gorton, John 148
Gould, David 13–15, 18–19, 41, 50–1, 153–4
Graham, Euan 130
Green, Michael 93, 94–5

Grossi, Rafael 37–8, 117
Group of Seven industrialised nations (G7) 30
  meetings 63–5, 111, 113
Guillou, Hervé 32, 79–81
Gyngell, Allan 97

USS *Halibut* 137, 138
Hardy, Clarence 148–50
Hartcher, Peter 99, 100, 102, 103
Hawke Labor government
  closure of uranium enrichment plant 148
Hayden, Bill 53
Hennessey, Tom 167
Hertz, Leon 93
Hilarides, William 58–9, 75, 115
HMAS *Attack see* Attack-class submarines
HMAS *Canberra* 138
HMAS *Stirling* naval base 32, 38, 134–5, 139
Hockey, Joe 62, 101, 167
Hollande, François 1–2, 6, 26
Holt, Harold 56
Home Affairs Department 31, 95, 108, 164
Houston, Angus 139, 158
Howard, John 12, 61
  Bush's 'deputy sheriff' 5
  conservatism 52
  influence 52
  Iraq War commitment 5, 52, 92–3
  opposition to French submarine deal 4
  wedded to US 52, 141
  wedge politics 150
Howard coalition government
  advisers *see* Jennings, Peter; Shearer, Andrew
  and centre for US studies 92–5
  'children overboard' election win 66
  F-35 aircraft deal 52, 141
  offers Australian training facilities to US marines 52
  public service changes 164
  Silex Agreement 149–50

Howard Doctrine 5
Huawei (Chinese telecommunications company) ban 31, 55
Hughes, Jim 108
Hunter-class frigates *see* frigates
Huntington Ingalls Industries 59, 108
Hurst, Daniel 107

Indo-Pacific region 21, 28–30, 101–2
  French presence 2, 26, 28, 43, 100
  military modernisation in 69
  see also China
intellectual property 18–19, 25
intelligence agencies
  attitude to French submarine deal 2–3
  US *see* Central Intelligence Agency (CIA); National Security Agency (US NSA)
intelligence gathering *see* Pine Gap, Northern Territory
International Atomic Energy Agency (IAEA) 35, 37–8, 117, 149, 154–5, 161
International Court of Justice ruling on whaling 11
International Criminal Court (ICC) 54–5
International Traffic in Arms Regulations 80
Iran 37, 38, 65
  nuclear submarine program proposal 154–5
Iraq uranium purchase hoax 45
Iraq War 3, 5, 33, 45, 50, 52, 62, 92–3, 97
Israel 37

Jackman, Simon 94
Japan
  Abbott visit to 6
  South China Sea operations 14

INDEX

Japanese submarines 6,
  11–12, 13, 18
  Abbott's behaviour 6, 11,
    12
  Australia/US interoperability
    with 43
  Collins-class submarine
    replacement option
    15–16, 18, 22, 67
  features of 15–16, 22
  Shearer on 6, 7, 43
Jennings, Peter 101–2
Johnson, Boris 8, 10, 75,
  110, 111, 124
  AUKUS announcement
    125–6
Johnson, Stephen E 15, 46,
  58, 59
Johnston, David (politician)
  12, 13
Johnston, David (Vice
  Admiral) 108, 160
Joint Geological and
  Geophysical Research
  Station, Northern Territory
  142–3
Joyce, Barnaby 158

Kagan, Edgard 103,
  116–17
Keating, Paul 9, 101, 163–4
Kendall, Frank 131
Kennedy, Caroline 106
Kibble, Matthew 167
Kimba district, South
  Australia 153
Kissinger, Henry 53, 62
Kuperman, Alan J 38–40,
  151

Labor governments *see*
  Albanese Labor government;
  Hawke Labor government;
  Whitlam Labor government
Labor Opposition *see*
  Australian Labor Party
  (ALP) Opposition
Le Drian, Jean-Yves 2, 100
Lee, Lavinia 101–2
Levick, Ewen 71
Liberal Party

nuclear energy ambitions 5,
  51, 148, 150–2
right wing politics 6, 11,
  12–13, 31, 51
see also Abbott coalition
  government; Howard
  coalition government;
  Morrison coalition
  government; Turnbull
  coalition government
Lockheed Martin weapons
  system 80, 87
Lowy, Steven 93
Lucas Heights nuclear reactor
  147–50, 153

MacArthur, Douglas, on
  Australia as US military
  base 46
Macfarlane, Allison 152
Mackay, David 93
Macmillan, Harold 145
Macron, Emmanuel 6, 8, 21,
  88, 110
  Biden apology to 49
  on China 29, 43
  deceived by Morrison 68,
    112–14, 124
  meetings with Morrison
    63–4, 112–15
  notified of contract
    cancellation 124
  relationship with Turnbull
    63, 125
  visit to Australia 26–30
  see also France
Marchetti, Victor 105–6
Marles, Richard 95, 104, 120,
  123–4, 134, 161
McCormack, Donald F 108
McDonald, Hamish 44
Mead, Jonathan 68–9, 116,
  117
media briefings 95, 96–8, 100
media reporting
  AUKUS deal 9, 97–103
  on China 101–2
  French submarine deal
    66–7, 68, 79–81, 87
  leaks to media 10, 31, 96,
    114, 115
Melvin, Steve 131
Menadue, John 98

Menwith Hill, UK 54
Menzies, Robert 145–6
Mercer, Don 148
Michael West Media 98
ministerial code of conduct
  58
ministers' post-politics
  appointments 57–8, 167–8
Molan, Jim 98
Moore, George 35–6
Moriarty, Greg 18, 42, 49,
  68–9, 74, 83, 108, 159–60
Morrison, Jenny 64
Morrison, Scott
  advisers 65–6; *see also*
    Shearer, Andrew
  AUKUS announcement
    125–6; *see also* AUKUS
    deal
  becomes PM 6, 43
  characteristics 6, 46, 51, 64,
    70, 115
  covertly holds multiple
    ministries 48, 70, 108
  deceives the French 110,
    112–15
  directs submarine program
    75–6, 86, 89–91
  duplicitous behaviour 7–10,
    96
  excludes France from nuclear
    submarine feasibility study
    69, 72–3
  family graveyard trip 111
  Howard and 52
  leaks to media 96
  meeting with US Joint
    Chiefs of Staff 62–3
  meetings with Biden and
    Johnson 110, 111, 112
  meetings with IAEA 117
  meetings with Macron
    63–4, 112
  meetings with Trump 61,
    62–3
  orders secret nuclear
    submarine feasibility study
    50, 71–3, 90
  post-politics appointments
    167–8
  relationship with Trump
    administration 48–9, 51,
    61–3, 65, 167–8
  stance against Naval Group
    83–5, 88–91

wedge politics against Labor Opposition 10, 69, 104, 107, 116–17, 121
Morrison coalition government
anti-China rhetoric 62, 70, 74, 96–8
AUKUS *see* AUKUS deal
breach of due process 158–60, 165
closer military ties with US 8, 46–9, 51, 65–6, 71, 107, 127–35, 167
Defence Strategic Update (2020) 73–4
duplicitous behaviour 7–10, 41
French submarines and *see* French submarine deal; French submarine deal cancellation
legacy 10, 161–2, 164, 168
media briefings 95, 96–8, 100
ministers' post-politics appointments 57–8, 167–8
misleads US 8, 9, 10, 47–9, 125
Naval Shipbuilding Enterprise Governance Committee 75–6
nuclear submarine negotiations with US *see* AUKUS deal; nuclear-powered submarines for Australia
relations with French government 6–7, 9, 70, 72–3, 88–91
relations with Naval Group 81–91
relationship with Trump administration 48–9, 51, 75
secrecy 8, 10, 65, 70–4, 158
Submarine Advisory Committee 75, 108
US alliance *see* Australia–United States alliance
Murdoch, Lachlan 62, 98
Murdoch, Rupert 62, 93

National Aeronautics and Space Administration (NASA)
launches from Australia 132
radar 130–1
work with CIA 132–3
National Party not included in AUKUS planning 158
National Reconnaissance Office (NRO) 128–9, 133
National Security Agency (US NSA) 8, 53
bases *see* Pine Gap, Northern Territory
National Security Committee of Cabinet (Australia) 18, 107, 167
National Security Committee (US) 93
national security issues
ANZUS security agreement 52
Australia's security alignment shift to US 46, 51, 52–8, 168
Defence White Papers 41–2, 44
Morrison government legacy 10, 161–2, 164; *see also* AUKUS deal
see also Australia–United States alliance; China; Defence Department; Taiwan; United States bases in Australia
national security-related business opportunities 167–8
Nautilus Institute for Security and Sustainability 143
Naval Communications Station Harold E Holt *see* North West Cape, Western Australia
Naval Group
compensation for contract cancellation 40, 161
contract provisions 22, 32–3, 69, 78–9, 89–90, 124
cost for use of Osborne shipyard 81–2
cultural approach and work practices 23–6, 51

Guillou's boast about jobs 79–81
plans to rescue submarine deal 40–1, 155
praise from Australian Government 49, 124
relations with Australian Government 70, 81–91
relations with Defence Department 83
reported project on track 114–15
selected to build Collins-class replacement 18, 20
strengths 22–3
undermined in Australia 24, 51–2, 79–81, 113–15
see also French submarine deal; French submarines
Naval Group Australia 69, 83–4, 86–9
Naval Shipbuilding Advisory Board 13, 42, 51, 75
Naval Shipbuilding Enterprise Governance Committee 75–6
Naval Shipbuilding Expert Advisory Panel 58, 115
Netherlands Government allows USAF storage of nuclear weapons 142
Neuberger, Anne 8
New Caledonia 2
Newport News Shipbuilding 73, 108
News Corp 94
Nicholls, Vanessa 117
1941 Fund 167
Non-Proliferation Treaty (NPT) 36–7, 136, 142, 148–50
AUKUS issues 37–8, 115–16, 117, 153–5
Australia abstention in UN vote 106–7
signed, later ratified, by Australia 148
and Silex Agreement 149–50
Noonan, Michael 7, 71
Norman, Greg 62
North West Cape, Western Australia 105, 161
joint US–Australia facility 142

INDEX

radar installations 130–1
Space Surveillance Telescope 129–31
submarine communications 55–6
Northern Territory
 Arnhem Space Centre 132, 133
 Joint Geological and Geophysical Research Station 142–3
 Pine Gap *see* Pine Gap, Northern Territory
 RAAF Base Tindal 127, 133, 139–42, 161
 US marines rotation through Darwin 133, 138–9
nuclear energy
 ALP policy 123–4
 arms race 36
 Liberal Party ambitions 5, 51, 148, 150–2
 Lucas Heights nuclear reactor 147–50, 153
 nuclear waste 152–4
 small modular reactors (SMRs) 151–2
 see also uranium
nuclear power stations
 ban in Australia 151
 cost of nuclear power 151
 Dutton on 151–2
 in France 34–5
 not a solution for climate change 150–1
 planned for Australia 147–8, 150
 problems 35–6
nuclear waste 152–4
nuclear weapons 36, 37
 China's policy 135–6
 Dutton on US weapons in Australia 127–8
 Non-Proliferation Treaty (NPT) 36–7, 117, 136, 142, 148–50, 153–5
 planned for Australia 143–50
 public opinion 147, 162
 submarine communications 56; *see also* North West Cape, Western Australia
 transiting Australia 142, 162, 163

UK tests in Australia 146, 147, 153
US capability, in Australia 139–43
US policy on use 132, 135
US submarine armaments 136–8
nuclear-powered submarines
 crew requirements 50–1
 features 33–4, 41
 fuel systems 33–41
 industrial base necessary for support 50
 spent fuel reprocessing 153–4
 US, in Australia 32, 136–8
 see also Astute-class submarines; Barracuda-class submarines; Columbia-class submarines; Ohio-class submarines; Virginia-class submarines
nuclear-powered submarines for Australia 9–10
 Abbott on 22
 Defence Department process and accountability lacking 159–60
 fuel system (AUKUS deal) 38, 153–4
 fuel system (French deal) 39–40
 Morrison government secret discussions with US 7–10, 47–8, 71, 99–100, 103, 108–10
 Naval Group contract option 22, 32–3, 40–1, 155
 no proof of requirement 108, 159–60
 Non-Proliferation Treaty (NPT) issues 37–8, 115–16, 117, 153–5
 reasons advanced 14–15, 41, 117–18
 secret feasibility study ordered by Morrison 50, 71–3, 90
 US administration involvement 47–9, 110, 115–17, 124
 US purpose in providing submarines to Australia 103, 110, 161, 166
 see also AUKUS deal

Obama administration
 Pivot to Asia program 48, 138
 Yucca Mountain nuclear waste dump stopped 153
O'Brien, Robert 167
O'Connor, Brendan 123–4
Office of National Intelligence (ONI) 43, 65, 69, 99, 112, 139, 166
Ohio-class submarines 56, 135
Osborne shipyard, South Australia 57, 77–9, 81–2, 122

Parkinson, Martin 58
Parliamentary Joint Committee on Intelligence and Security 96
parliamentary process on defence requirements, ignored in AUKUS planning 159–60
Parly, Florence 100
Patrick, Rex 33–4, 41, 81, 121, 157–8
Payne, Marise 75–6, 77–8, 88, 90, 117, 126, 164
Pence, Mike 48, 51
Perth submarine base *see* Stirling naval base
Pezzullo, Michael 95–8, 164
Pine Gap, Northern Territory 8, 105–6, 133, 161
 'joint US–Australia facility' 142
 role 53–5, 143
Pivot to Asia program 31, 48, 138
Plame, Valerie 45
Pommellet, Pierre-Eric 69, 83–5, 88, 89–90
Pompeo, Mike 48, 51, 167
Pratt, Anthony 93–4
Price, Melissa 75–6, 90
Prime Minister's Office 7, 80, 88
Princeton University 36
propaganda lies 45, 62, 66, 92

INDEX

public service
 independence versus political compliance 163–5
push polling 66
Pyne, Christopher 18, 55–8, 78
 post-politics appointments 57–8, 167

Radakin, Tony 7
radar installations *see* North West Cape, Western Australia
Raymond, Jay 130
Reagan administration 44
renewable energy 151
Réunion island 2
Reynolds, Linda 74, 75–6, 86, 87, 90
Richardson, Dennis 14
Roggeveen, Sam 139–40, 163, 168
Royal Australian Air Force (RAAF)
 F-35 aircraft 52, 141
 RAAF Base Tindal 127, 133, 139–42, 161
Royal Australian Navy (RAN) 1, 28
 chiefs *see* Johnston, David (Vice Admiral); Mead, Jonathan; Noonan, Michael
 nuclear submarine operations (proposed) 120–1
 optimisation 139–40
 recapitalisation 78
 Stirling naval base 32, 38, 134–5, 139
 on US naval visits to Australia 136–8
 see also AUKUS deal; Collins-class submarine replacement selection process; French submarine deal; nuclear-powered submarines for Australia
Royal Navy
 industrial base necessary for support 50
 submarine fuel systems 34, 35; *see also* uranium

Rudd, Kevin 98, 103
Ryan, Mick 102

Saltzman, B Chance 131
Sammut, Greg 49, 68, 83, 85
satellite activities 128–33
Schumer, Chuck 161
Seebeck, Lesley 102
Senate hearings *see* Australian Senate
Shackley, Theodore 105
Shearer, Andrew
 Cabinet secretary 43–4, 65
 at CSIS 45
 dinner with Macron's advisers 112
 influence 4, 7, 31–2, 48–9, 51, 65, 94, 166–7
 on Japanese submarines 6, 12
 meetings with US officials 7–8, 47–8, 99–100
 at ONI 4, 32, 166–7
 opposition to French submarine deal 43, 48, 69
 pro-US attitude 7, 43–5, 69, 99, 156, 167
Shields, Bevan 113
shipbuilding 28, 75–9, 81–2; *see also* French submarine deal
Shortfin Barracuda submarines 32; *see also* Barracuda-class submarines
Silent Barker spy satellite 129
Silex enrichment process and Silex Agreement 149–50, 151
Sinodinos, Arthur 47–8, 167
Smith, Stephen 53–4, 55, 133, 139, 143, 158
Soryu submarines *see* Japanese submarines
South China Sea operations
 China 31
 Japan 14
 USA/Australia 14–15, 41, 166
South Pacific Nuclear Free Zone Treaty 142, 162
space military strategy 128–33

Space Surveillance Telescope (SST), North West Cape, Western Australia 129–31
stealth 17, 19–20
steel 25
Steele-John, Jordan 161–2
Stirling naval base 32, 38, 134–5, 139
Strategic Partnership Agreement (SPA) 42, 83–5, 88
Submarine Advisory Committee 75, 108
submarine communications 55–6; *see also* North West Cape, Western Australia
submarine deals
 with France *see* French submarine deal
 with US and UK *see* AUKUS deal
submarine noise 16–17, 19–20, 34
submarine roles 16–18, 45, 101, 103, 161, 166
submarines
 conventionally powered 34, 47; *see also* Collins-class submarines
 nuclear-powered *see* nuclear-powered submarines
 see also French submarines; German submarines; Japanese submarines; *and specific classes*: Attack-class submarines; Astute-class submarines; Collins-class submarines; Columbia-class submarines; Ohio-class submarines; Virginia-class submarines
Sullivan, Jake 44, 48, 99–100, 103, 124
Sullivan, Paul E 59
Sunak, Rishi
 AUKUS latest phase announcement 121
Switkowski, Ziggy 150
Switzer, Tom 94
Sydney University United States Studies Centre (USSC) 92–5, 101–2

INDEX

Taiwan 31, 44–5, 97, 102, 119–20, 139, 161
Tanter, Richard 140–1
technology transfer 18–19, 22, 25, 40, 42, 79–80, 86
telescopes *see* Space Surveillance Telescope (SST), North West Cape, Western Australia
Textor, Mark 66
Thales 2, 28
Thébault, Jean-Pierre 88, 112, 124
ThyssenKrupp Marine Systems 16, 22; *see also* German submarines
Timor-Leste 17
Tindal (RAAF Base) 127, 133, 139–42, 161
trade sanctions by China 55
Treaty on the Non-Proliferation of Nuclear Weapons *see* Non-Proliferation Treaty (NPT)
Trump, Donald
 associates 61–2
 meetings with Morrison 61, 62–3
 Pratt and 93
 on US Space Force 128
Trump administration
 attitude to China 28, 31–2
 AUKUS deal and 10
 launches US Space Force 128
 Morrison and 48–9, 51, 61–3, 65, 75, 167–8
 Nuclear Posture Review 135
 plan to add nuclear warheads to submarine-based cruise missiles 138
Turnbull, Lucy 94
Turnbull, Malcolm 1, 71
 advised French president of submarine contract award 1–3
 on Australian sovereignty 3, 9, 165–6
 characteristics 3, 12–13, 70
 criticism of AUKUS 9
 dealings with Japan 11–12
 on French submarine deal 20–2
 Macron's visit to Australia 28–30

on nuclear weapons in Australia 162–3
opposition within Liberal Party 12–13
relationship with Macron 63, 125
replaced Abbott as PM 4, 6
replaced by Morrison 6, 94
Turnbull coalition government
 defence allocation 57, 73
 foreign interference law 31
 French submarines *see* French submarine deal
 on potential for nuclear-powered submarines in Australia 32
 shipbuilding plans 77–9
 strategic outlook 28–30

United Kingdom
 Abbott as UK government trade adviser 75
 AUKUS *see* AUKUS deal
 nuclear tests in Australia 146, 147, 153
 nuclear weapons for Australia suggestion 143–7
 perceived natural ally of Australia 3
 submarine base in Australia 134–5
 submarine shipyards 121–2
 submarines 2, 155
 see also Johnson, Boris; Royal Navy
United Nations Security Council 30, 136
United States
 alliance with Australia *see* Australia–United States alliance
 AUKUS *see* AUKUS deal
 believes Australia informed France of nuclear submarine discussions 49, 125
 believes Australian ALP Opposition informed of nuclear submarine discussions 125

complicit in deceiving France 100, 110–11, 112, 124
concerns about China 12, 31–2, 95, 134–5, 141, 161
embassy in Australia 103–4, 106, 107
feared role in destabilising Whitlam government 105–6, 156
foreign policy 97, 102
global power 5, 42
interest in Australia as a military base *see* United States bases in Australia
misled by Morrison government 8, 9, 10, 47–9, 125
National Reconnaissance Office 128–9, 133
National Security Agency 8, 53
National Security Committee 93
Navy *see* United States Navy
nuclear submarines
 discussions with Australia *see* AUKUS deal; nuclear-powered submarines for Australia
 opposition to Australia's French submarine deal 10, 110
 perceived natural ally of Australia 3
Pivot to Asia program 31, 48, 138
policy on use of nuclear weapons 132, 135
potential war over Taiwan 44–5, 97, 101–2, 119–20, 139, 161
presidents *see* Biden, Joe; Bush, George W; Carter, Jimmy; Trump, Donald
push against China's borders 102, 166
Space and Missile Systems Office 130
Space Command 128, 129; *see also* United States Space Force (USSF)
see also Biden administration; Bush (George W) administration; Obama

administration; Trump administration
United States Air Force (USAF)
  Air Force Intelligence 143
  B-52 aircraft stationed in Australia 10, 127, 133, 140–1, 161–2
  nuclear weapons store in Netherlands 142
United States bases in Australia 127, 133–4
  Australian sovereignty and 53–5, 133, 143–4
  Joint Geological and Geophysical Research Station 142–3
  lack of transparency about operations 140–3
  MacArthur on 46
  North West Cape 55–6, 105, 129, 130, 132, 133, 142, 161
  Pine Gap 8, 53–5, 105–6, 133, 142, 161
  US marines offered training base by Howard 52
  US marines rotation through Darwin 133, 138–9
  see also Australia–United States alliance; *Stirling* naval base; Tindal (RAAF Base)
United States Navy
  capabilities 46–7
  former leaders advising Australia 9, 15, 46, 58–60, 73, 108
  nuclear fuel systems 34–6, 38–40
  patrols 16
  submarine armament 136–8
  submarine communications 55–6; see also North West Cape, Western Australia

submarine supply issues 117–22, 124–5
submarine visits to Australia 136–8
submarines deployed by allied force 103
see also Columbia-class submarines; Ohio-class submarines; Virginia-class submarines
United States Space Force (USSF) 128–9, 130, 131
United States Studies Centre (USSC) 92–5, 101–2
uranium 33–40, 60, 154–5
  enrichment in Australia 148–50
  highly enriched (HEU) 34–40, 115–16, 153–5
  Iraq uranium purchase hoax 45
  low-enriched (LEU) 33, 34–6, 39–40, 155
  see also nuclear energy
Uranium Enrichment Team (UET) at Lucas Heights 148–9
Urenco 148
USS *Canberra* 137–8
USS *Halibut* 137–8

V bombers (Vulcan, Victor, Valiant) 147
Vietnam War 105, 141
Villers-Bretonneux, France 27
Virgin Airlines proposed aircraft boarding priority 46
Virginia-class submarines 124–5
  crew requirements 50–1
  maintenance requirements 40

manufacturer's board members advising Australia 59, 108
production issues 119–22, 124–5
proposed Australian purchase 103, 118, 119–21, 133, 155, 161, 166
refuelling and life of submarine (LOS) 35
spent fuel reprocessing 153–4
US purpose in providing submarines to Australia 110, 161, 166
von Hippel, Frank N 36, 154–5

war
  Campbell on 155
  Dutton on 97, 127–8
  Molan on 98
  Pezzullo on 96–7
  potential war over Taiwan 44–5, 97, 101–2, 119–20, 139, 161
  see also Iraq War; Vietnam War
wedge politics 10, 66, 69, 104, 107, 116–17, 121, 150
Western Australia see North West Cape, Western Australia; *Stirling* naval base
whaling 11–12
White, Hugh 44–5, 95
Whitlam Labor government 53, 105–6, 148, 156
Winter, Donald 13–15, 42, 58, 75, 88
Wong, Penny 95, 123–4, 159–60, 162